PETROC™

LEARNING TECHNOLOGI   RARY SERVICES

Please return this item on or before the last date shown below

3 0 SEP 2015

WITHDRAWN FROM STOCK

North Devon Campus: 01271 338170
Mid Devon Campus: 01884 235234
Email: library@petroc.ac.uk

ORDINARY HEROES

The Films of Danny Boyle

by

Edwin Page

eMPIRICUS
BOOKS

London, England

First published in Great Britain 2009
by Empiricus Books,
105–107 Gloucester Place,
London W1U 6BY

www.januspublishing.co.uk

British Library Cataloguing-in-Publication Data
A catalogue record for this book is available from the British Library

ISBN 978-1-902835-17-4

Cover Design: Edwin Page

Printed and bound in Great Britain

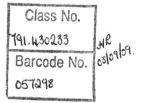

Dedicated to

my wife, Charlotte

for your faith in me

Jeannie

for your faith in my work

Danny Boyle

for your contribution to the British film industry

With special thanks to

Tim, Dan, Perry and Claire,

for your time and feedback

and

Leah and Andrew McDonald from DNA/Figment Films

for the use of stills from their films

Contents

Foreword

This book has been written for fans of Danny Boyle and includes chapters on all the feature-length films he has directed. It is an exploration of his themes, techniques and flair, showing how he has brought a recognisable style to each movie.

Each chapter, especially those relating to his better-known films, assumes prior knowledge of plot and storyline. In this way, the examination of each film is not simply a reading of the narrative, but a reading of Boyle's influence in bringing the tales to our screens. We find an interesting use of camera angles and symbolism, we discover certain trademark shots and themes and we also uncover the truth that Boyle is a great director able to turn his hand to any genre he chooses to work in.

There are no direct references to commentaries on the DVDs of these films. If you own these movies then the information given in these commentaries is available at any time and therefore it is not necessary to include it in this book. It is also important to note that not every example of Danny Boyle's filmic techniques is drawn attention to within the chapters. This was thought unnecessary due to the fact that those of note are discussed.

From *Shallow Grave* to *Slumdog Millionaire,* this book takes a journey through many narrative landscapes. Though each is different, all bear the hallmarks of one man's talent and ability, this man being Danny Boyle.

Danny Boyle: His Life and His Work

I want my films to be life-affirming ... I want people to leave the cinema feeling that something's been confirmed for them about life.

Danny Boyle[1]

The Man Himself

Enthusiastic, excited, brimming with thoughts and ideas, filled with energy – this is Danny Boyle when he's talking about his movies. In his private life, Boyle enjoys reading, watching films and supporting his local football club, Bury.

Owing to his working-class roots, Boyle finds the sums of money involved in making films to be quite obscene. Because of this, he tries to use as little money on his movies as is possible, something which allows more freedom in respect to control over a project, but less with regard to finances.

Boyle was surprised by the amount of money he earned when he started directing for television back in the 1980s and 1990s. He was being paid amounts much greater than his parents' wages and felt a little embarrassed by this. He also feels a kind of embarrassment when one of his films is a success and puts this down to his background. Because of this, he doesn't tend to revel in his achievements and remains down to earth.

Boyle creates his films in a very organic way. He usually has full control over the productions and influences the scripts. However, he is not a dictatorial director by any standards. He allows his cinematographers to have a positive effect on the film's direction and allows actors a say in the behaviour and development of their characters. He also often allows actors to play out a scene before the placement of cameras, letting them define the movement and action to a degree, this then acting as a guide when it comes to his decisions as to camera positioning and giving scenes a more fluid and natural feel.

Boyle always gives *Apocalypse Now* (1979) as the answer to questions about his favourite film, regarding this Francis Ford Coppola movie as one of the greatest. He also finds that there are occasions when he sees a film and wishes he'd made it. Two such films which he would love to have created are *Memento* (2000), Christopher Nolan's seminal film about a character with short-term memory loss featuring a superb performance by Guy Pierce, and *24 Hour Party People* (2002), directed by Michael Winterbottom. The screenplay for the latter film was written by Frank Cottrell Boyce, who wrote *Millions,* and it starred Shirley Henderson of *Trainspotting* alongside Steve Coogan. It is concerned with a subject which interests Boyle, this being the Manchester music scene. The film is a biopic about Tony Wilson, who co-founded Factory Records in Manchester during the mid 1970s.

> Both of my sisters have been teachers … They used to say you get asked between 300 and 600 questions every day which you have to answer. That's exactly what directing is.
>
> Danny Boyle[2]

His Life & Early Work

Born on 20 October 1956, Danny Boyle was the eldest of twin brothers. He also had two sisters and grew up in the town of Radcliffe in Lancashire, England. His father had been a labourer since an early age and his mother, who was from Ballinasloe in Galway, Ireland, worked as a dinner lady at the local school. His family were Irish Catholics and for a while Boyle embraced the religion of his parents and seemed to be heading for a life in the priesthood. He was an altar boy for many years and at the age of fourteen wanted to leave his grammar school to join the seminary.

A priest talked to him about his wish to join and warned him against the move. Then, as his teenage years wore on, he discarded religion, something which did not go down well with his mother. Music and film filled the gap his belief had once occupied in his life.

During his teens, Boyle and his friends would go to nearby Bolton in the hope of sneaking into the only cinema that showed pornographic films. On one of these occasions, the youths were stopped from getting in to see the X-rated film which was playing and so snuck into *A Clockwork Orange* (1971).

This Stanley Kubrick adaptation of Anthony Burgess' tale of gangs, violence, rape, murder and psychological brutality conducted by the establishment had quite an impact on Boyle. The film was withdrawn in the UK by Kubrick after only a limited time because it was blamed for a number of violent crimes. However, the striking style of the film stayed with Boyle, as did the surprising excitement at seeing scenes of realistic violence and its consequences.

As Boyle continued to attend Catholic grammar school he worked as an usher in the Octagon cinema in Bolton. Then he went on to study drama and English at the University of Wales in Bangor. There he enjoyed acting and found that he had some skill in directing. This did not immediately lead to his first directorial job, but rather to one as a truck driver for a London theatre company, where he began to work his way up the job ladder.

In 1982 he became the Artistic Director for the Royal Court Theatre, becoming Deputy Director in 1985. During his time there his productions included Edward Bond's *Saved*, which won a prestigious *Time Out* award. The Royal Shakespeare Company also utilised his talents and he directed five productions for them.

He married casting director Gail Stevens and they went on to have three children together. Despite separating, they remain friends and live on the same street in London, where Boyle, in his time off from the film industry, likes to spend time alone reading and watching movies, which is befitting a man who enjoys his privacy.

The 1980s also saw him become a drama producer for BBC Northern Ireland. He had apparently been the only applicant for the post from beyond the troubled region. Unlike many from mainland Britain, he didn't find the prospect of living in Belfast to be a frightening one, partly because of numerous visits there prior to applying for the job.

Upon his arrival, Boyle informed his new employers that he would direct as well as produce, but that he would do both jobs for a single fee. Amongst the work he produced was the controversial TV film *Elephant* (1989), written by Sandy Chanda and directed by Alan Clarke. It caused a stir because it was concerned with a series of brutal killings in Northern Ireland motivated by sectarianism. Its title came from the phrase "elephant in the room", which is used to refer to a problem that people fail to acknowledge despite its obvious presence.

In 2003, Gus Van Sant wrote and directed a film about a Columbine-style mass shooting at a US school. This film was entitled *Elephant* as a tribute to Clarke, Chanda and Boyle's film. It even aped the original in using unknown and non-professional actors, a minimalist style and tracking shots.

It wasn't too long before Boyle went on to greater things, directing a highly praised drama series called *Mr Wroe's Virgins* for the BBC in 1993. He also directed episodes of the Oxford based detective series *Inspector Morse*, starring the late John Thaw.

He then teamed up with writer John Hodge, producer Andrew MacDonald and rising star Ewan McGregor. This group of considerable talents went on to make a trilogy of movies together, starting with the acclaimed *Shallow Grave* in 1994. This delivered a welcome injection of interest in the British film industry and marked the beginning of a revival, one that would be given even more impetus by the team's follow-up, *Trainspotting*.

It wasn't all plain sailing for Boyle. The next two films – the Twentieth Century Fox backed *A Life Less Ordinary* and *The Beach* – were perceived as failures, not living up to expectations and being panned by many critics. It was after these experiences that the director returned to his roots to create two feature-length dramas for the BBC.

After this short hiatus, Boyle returned to the big screen with the hit horror flick *28 Days Later*. Since then he has remained a director of cinematic entertainment, bringing us three further films and changing genre with each. All his movies display his creative vision and it is one we cannot help but admire and enjoy.

> Whatever the film's about – easy to watch or not – I want them to be stimulating for my audience. It's not about appealing to the lowest common denominator. It's about working as hard as possible to get as big an audience as possible to see what's interesting to talk about.
>
> Danny Boyle[3]

His Collaborations

Danny Boyle has collaborated with a number of people on more than one occasion. These include both cast and crew members, and even pop groups. These collaborations have helped shape his career to an extent and it is interesting to note that a division is created by his two BBC dramas, *Vacuuming Completely Nude in Paradise* and *Strumpet*, which were both broadcast in 2001.

Prior to these two TV films there were notable collaborators who did not go on to work with the director again. During and after their production, Boyle met a new group of people with whom he has worked on more than one occasion. Therefore, these two dramas act as a demarcation point in his career, almost a watershed. He temporarily turned his back on the cinema and when he returned, he gathered a new team of people around him with whom he felt both comfortable and inspired.

Shallow Grave to *The Beach*

The collaborations that many people see as the most prominent even to this day are with writer John Hodge and producer Andrew MacDonald, who is one of only a few to make the crossing from the first half of Boyle's career to the second, having produced *28 Days Later* and *Sunshine*. It is also interesting to note that MacDonald is the grandson of Emeric Pressburger, who wrote, produced and directed numerous British films from the early 1930s until the early 1970s, winning a Best Writing, Original Story Oscar for *49th Parallel* (1941), which was directed by his long time collaborator Michael Powell.

MacDonald had founded his own film company called Figment in 1991, launching it with a film he directed called *Dr Reizer's Fragment*.

With only one public showing, MacDonald went on to be a locations manager for the Scottish crime drama series *Taggart*. It was during this time that he met John Hodge, who showed him the script for *Shallow Grave*. At that time, Hodge was working in Edinburgh's Eastern General Hospital and while he continued his employment there, the duo managed to arrange funding for the film.

MacDonald had decided that he preferred producing to directing and so they were on the lookout for a director. They met Danny Boyle and, unlike many prospective candidates, he didn't want to make any changes to the script. Little did they know that this would be the start of a working relationship that would last for the production of four films.

Boyle and Hodge teamed up on another occasion to create a short film called *Alien Love Triangle* (2002), which was about thirty minutes long. It was meant to be part of a larger production featuring three sci-fi shorts by different directors. However, this project fell apart when the other shorts were turned into feature films and released individually, these being *Mimic* (del Toro 1997) and *Impostor* (Fleder 2001).

A number of crew members were used on all or most of the first four films in the director's career, but would not be used again. Editor Masahiro Hirakubo worked on each film. Cinematographer Brian Tufano and production designer Kave Quinn worked on Boyle's first three outings and the former was upset when not used for *The Beach*. Costume designer Rachael Fleming worked on all but *Shallow Grave* and would go on to be part of the production team for *28 Days Later*.

Actor Ewan McGregor is commonly associated with Boyle and featured in the first three films Boyle directed. Though this is not even a third of the director's output, he is still commonly associated with Boyle. This is because it was the actor's roles in *Shallow Grave* and especially *Trainspotting* that effectively helped launch his career and led to Hollywood success.

Other actors who appeared in more than one film in the first half of Boyle's career were Robert Carlyle, Keith Allen and Peter Mullan, though only the former had a leading role on both occasions. Another actor actually made appearances in both halves of Boyle's career and is the only one to do so. This is Christopher Eccleston, who starred alongside McGregor in *Shallow Grave* and went on to appear in *Strumpet* and *28 Days Later*, thereby acting in as many Danny Boyle films as his Scottish counterpart.

There were a number of music acts which featured heavily in the first half of Boyle's career. Leftfield supplied music for three films, including the title music for *Shallow Grave*. Underworld was used on the soundtracks of *Trainspotting*, *A Life Less Ordinary* and *The Beach*, and would go on to be used in the creation of *Sunshine*. Brian Eno's work featured in *Trainspotting* and *The Beach* and would be heard again in *28 Days Later*. Other artists who were used on more than one occasion include Blur/Damon Albarn, Faithless, Elastica, New Order and Orbital.

28 Days Later to Slumdog Millionaire

Cinematographer Anthony Dod Mantle was one of Boyle's most important collaborators in the second half of his career. The two of them first worked together on the production of *Vacuuming Completely Nude in Paradise* and would work together very effectively a further five times, only parting company for the filming of *Sunshine*. Their relationship is very much one of mutual inspiration and the sharing of ideas, working almost as a team, rather than a director/cinematographer hierarchy.

Also teaming up with Boyle on '*Vacuuming*' and going on to work with him on every other film bar *Slumdog Millionaire* was editor Chris Gill. It was that BBC drama which saw the creation of yet another ongoing partnership, this time with original music composed by John Murphy, who has worked on all the same films as Gill.

Other crew members who have worked with Boyle on at least three occasions since '*Vacuuming*' are production designer Mark Tildesley, set decorator Michelle Day and art director Mark Digby. One special person of note is Gail Stevens, mother to Boyle's children and casting director. She teamed up with the director on all of his four latter films, but had also done the casting for *Trainspotting* and *The Beach*.

We also find that Boyle worked with writer Alex Garland on two occasions. Though *The Beach* was based on his debut novel, the screenplay had been written by John Hodge. However, in this later period of film-making, Boyle worked with Garland on *28 Days Later* and *Sunshine*.

As far as cast member collaborations are concerned, there was the already mentioned Christopher Eccleston. The only other actor to appear in more than one of the films in the second half of Boyle's career to date was Cillian Murphy, who took leading roles in *28 Days Later* and *Sunshine*. However, it is of note that Rose Byrne, who stars alongside Murphy in *Sunshine*, also makes an appearance in *28 Weeks Later* (Fresnadillo 2007), which was produced by Boyle.

> At the end of the day … it's the director that makes the decisions. You're not going to make Danny Boyle do something he doesn't want to do in a film and you shouldn't be able to.
>
> Dr Brian Cox, scientific adviser on *Sunshine* [4]

His Themes & Techniques

Danny Boyle has incorporated a number of common themes and techniques into his work. These identify his films with an individual fingerprint which is undoubtedly Boyle. They become recognisable as a result of his influence, which stretches beyond film directing.

He has an influence over the scripts being produced, discussing points with the writers, conducting read-throughs and making suggestions. Boyle tries to make sure that each screenplay is as close to what will eventually be filmed as possible before the production begins. This is because of usually limited budgets and his desire not to waste money. Each rewrite during the filming process can lead to new shots being necessary or old shots having to be re-filmed, all of which creates additional drains on a film's finances. By extensively working on a script before filming commences, Boyle ensures there is as little wasted money, time and effort as possible. Though he doesn't participate in the writing, he has a considerable effect on the final screenplay. *Millions* serves as a particularly good example, for by the time he and Frank Cottrell Boyce had finished working on the script together there was only one scene remaining that had been in the original version prior to Boyle's influence.

This said, it is actually the case that the directing itself is not simply down to Boyle. It is a synergy of talents, the director combining with the cinematographer to create the films. This is especially the case with Anthony Dod Mantle and shows that Boyle's movies are partly a collaborative effort, though he has the final say. It is partially for this reason that Boyle tends not to use storyboards very often.

In light of this information, we can draw out certain aspects that are common to most or all of his films and we can identify Boyle as being either wholly or partially responsible for their presence. In most cases it is the former, for the director has not consistently worked with the same writer or cinematographer throughout his career. Therefore, elements that are apparent in films with differing crew members must be down to Boyle, who carries his box of tricks and tropes to each location he films at. This box is his mind, one which has given birth to some striking cinematic visions that will be discussed in this book.

The following themes and techniques are not exclusive to Boyle. However, the frequency of use and combining of these elements is attributable to his direction, making it unique and identifiable as the work of an auteur.

1. Ordinary Heroes

All ten of Danny Boyle's films display an ordinary hero or anti-hero. Here, there is a distinction between ordinary and normal. It is clear that Strayman is not normal in *Strumpet*, and neither is Damian in *Millions*, but both are ordinary in the sense that they come from ordinary backgrounds and live in ordinary houses in ordinary locations. We can also see that though Capa is placed in an extreme location in *Sunshine*, he himself is intelligent and well-educated, but ordinary.

None of Boyle's leading characters display the usual traits of Hollywood heroes. They are not muscular or macho. The camera does not linger on them in heroic poses or make them out to be anything other than ordinary. They rarely conduct themselves in a heroic manner. The closest any come to heroic deeds is when Jim rescues the women from the soldiers in *28 Days Later*. However, any perception of true heroism is undermined by Boyle making it clear that he is under the influence of his own rage, simply a version of the infected, which have caused so much death and destruction.

2. Friendship

All of the director's films portray friendship and the importance of connecting with others. In his debut, *Shallow Grave*, we see three friendships torn apart by the introduction of money. In *Strumpet* the lead characters make a deep connection, which is of vital importance to the narrative and to their lives.

11

This friendship also applies to family members, as seen with brothers Damian and Anthony in *Millions*, while the idea of connecting also includes love. This latter form of deep connection between two individuals is especially apparent in *A Life Less Ordinary* and *Slumdog Millionaire*.

3. Abnormal Psychology

Examples of this theme can be seen in nine of Danny Boyle's ten films. The most extreme is undoubtedly in *28 Days Later*, where the infected display a distinct version of this theme. We can also see abnormal psychology in David's ascent into the attic of the flat in *Shallow Grave*, in the fanatical character of Captain Pinbacker in *Sunshine* and in Richard's jungle existence in *The Beach*. The use of heroin in *Trainspotting* creates moments of abnormal psychology rather than a continuous portrayal in regards to any of the characters, giving us a different take on this thematic.

4. Dreams & Visions

As with the theme of abnormal psychology, examples of dreams and visions are apparent in nine of the films discussed in this book. They are sometimes related to the former theme, such as Renton's hallucinations in *Trainspotting* or Richard's visions of Daffy in *The Beach*.

The film with the largest concentration of dreams and visions is *Millions*, during which we see six visions of saintly figures from Catholicism. The smallest example arises in *Slumdog Millionaire*, when Jamal has a vision of plunging from a tower block with his brother.

The only film not to clearly use this theme is *Strumpet*. However, at one point in the film, we do see flashbacks in relation to the character of *Strumpet*. These are presented like memories and could be regarded as a form of vision or possibly a daydream.

5. Religion

References to religion appear in all of Boyle's feature-length films and in *Strumpet*, where they are symbolic rather than direct. A couple of his films have a very strong religious thematic which is specifically Christian. In *A Life Less Ordinary* we see scenes from heaven, two characters who are angels and an underlying theme linked to the biblical story of Adam and Eve. In *Millions* the Christian theme is tied to Catholicism, Damian seeing visions of saints, as mentioned.

6. Moral Dilemmas

The most obvious of these arises in *Shallow Grave* in relation to the bag of money and its accompanying dead body. We also see such dilemmas in another seven of Boyle's movies, including the choice of taking the fatally wounded Christo into the jungle in *The Beach* and whether or not to kill Trey in order that the mission should succeed in *Sunshine*.

7. Large Amounts of Money

This links into theme number six in that dilemmas relating to bags of money arise in *Shallow Grave*, *Trainspotting* and *Millions*. The use of large sums of money is apparent in five of the ten films Boyle has directed and they are always connected with greed or a lack of such. In *Slumdog Millionaire*, for instance, we see that Jamal is on *Who Wants to be a Millionaire* not for the winnings, but for love, whereas his brother has amassed a lot of money out of greed.

8. Subcultures

These feature in the narratives of seven of Boyle's films, from the subculture of heroin addicts in *Trainspotting*, to that of rage virus survivors in *28 Days Later*. Even the three friends in *Shallow Grave* are essentially a subculture, as are the eight astronauts existing in the fragile confines of Icarus II in *Sunshine*. We can also see that the community living in the brooding paradise of *The Beach* are subcultural, deciding to live in a different way to the rest of the world in an attempt at creating an idyll, one which becomes bloodstained and finally shattered by screams.

9. Open Narratives

Many of the feature films discussed in this book present the audience with open narratives; that is, narratives which are clearly part of a wider and ongoing story. This means that the films are somewhat open-ended, giving us the impression that the story continues after the end credits roll.

Shallow Grave is a prime example as the film opens with the interviewing of prospective flatmates. We are not informed of why the main characters need an additional tenant or if they had one previously. This creates a sense of arriving within a story, rather than at its beginning. At the end of the film, we are shown Alex lying injured above the floorboards that conceal the money. However, we are not shown if he faces a jail sentence or even if he survives the injury.

Trainspotting is also a clear example of an open narrative. We enter the story as Renton is trying to quit heroin, never discovering how his addiction started in the first instance. We leave the story just when Begbie is about to be confronted by police and when Renton is about to lead a normal life. Thus, the narrative is clearly only part of a wider story.

10. Realistic Portrayal of Torture & Violence

This is both a theme and a technique for it involves suitable camera angles and shots by which to create a sense of realism and of consequence. This can be seen when Begbie smashes a glass into a man's face in *Trainspotting*, as Boyle does not linger on the effects of the violence or use close-ups. Unlike some other films, there is also no evidence of humour when violence or torture is shown in all ten of the director's films.

We see this theme/technique quite plainly throughout much of *28 Days Later* and at the start of *Slumdog Millionaire*, when Jamal is tortured in the police station. In *Strumpet* the evidence of its inclusion is far more subtle, only to be seen in the lingering bruises upon the title character.

We also see it in evidence in relation to mutilation, which is a form of this theme. In *The Beach* the three newcomers to the community have to mutilate each other with burns that mark their admittance into the small society. In *Slumdog Millionaire* Arvind, one of the street children, is purposefully blinded so as to be a more affective beggar.

11. Subverting Usual Cinematic Elements

This involves both thematic elements and the techniques Boyle employs in his films. We see the subversion of audience expectations in the majority of his films and in a number of different ways. One of the most obvious is through the portrayal of angels and saints in *A Life Less Ordinary* and *Millions*. Neither adheres to commonly held views of these holy figures, Boyle using swearing, smoking and even sexuality to subvert usual depictions.

In *28 Days Later* Boyle actually manages to subvert our expectations when it comes to the zombie horror genre itself, creating a new depiction of the infected by having them move rapidly, which is opposite to the portrayal of usual zombie types. In *The Beach* he includes a sequence that is drawn from computer games, something which is not normally witnessed in the movies and comes as quite a surprise.

12. Underwater Shots

Such shots appear in eight of Boyle's films and are the first example of a cinematic technique that he uses regularly. They add a distinct texture to shots, with ripples and currents passing before the camera's gaze, whilst also changing the appearance of elements either within or beyond the water. It is also the case that water often diffuses light, creating a softening effect. We see the highest concentration of these shots in *The Beach*, which is clearly due to the location and narrative content.

13. Shots Through Glass

These are not all necessarily through glass, but may also be through perspex or similar transparent materials. Boyle uses them in a similar way to the underwater shots in that they are most often seen to add texture to the shot. This is due to the purposeful inclusion of reflections and smears to interrupt the transparency. In such shots the glass acts like an additional filter placed over the camera lens. The inclusion of reflections and smears can also aid in the construction of realistic settings.

14. Mirrors

Like the shots through glass, Boyle often uses mirrors that are smeared or stained and in *Millions* we see the use of one that is cracked to distort images and thereby reflect the distortion of emotion, which is apparent in the relevant scene. In *Vacuuming Completely Nude in Paradise* a mirror is very effectively used to allow the audience to see another side to the character of Tommy.

Mirrors are also used simply to give us an additional angle of perspective within a scene, as in *28 Days Later* with the full-length mirror into which one of the infected stares, allowing us to see his face whilst the camera's gaze is concentrated on his back.

15. Screens

The use of television or computer screens in all bar one of Boyle's films links to his use of mirrors. Many of the mirror shots are to give us an alternative perspective of the scene in question and the director takes this a step further with the use of screens within the frame. They allow us a view into another scene beyond that which is being shown by the camera. We are essentially being shown a primary scene and a secondary one within it.

This is especially the case when the images on the screen are moving ones, such as the game show featuring Dale Winton in *Trainspotting* and the images of fear and horror being shown to the chimpanzee at the start of *28 Days Later*. The audience is thereby presented with a multi-layered scene, Boyle creating an extra dimension within the one framed by the camera.

16. Circularity

All eight of the director's cinema released films display circularity. This is when the beginning and end of a movie are brought together by common elements. The degree of circularity is often quite small, but nonetheless present. An example is *Millions*, which both starts and ends with a voice-over by the central character and with a specific title shot.

17. Voice-over

This cinematic technique is used extensively in two of Boyle's films and to a lesser degree in another four. The two where it is plainly apparent are *Trainspotting* and *The Beach*, both of which feature its use throughout the narratives. It is most often used to identify the main character and to set the foundation for narrative themes or plot lines.

18. High & Low Camera Angles

These can be seen in all of Danny Boyle's films other than *Shallow Grave*, though that film does include overhead shots of the flat. High and low angles are often juxtaposed with each other, as is the case in *A Life Less Ordinary* when Robert goes to see his ex-boss, the audience presented with a shot close to the floor followed by an overhead shot inside an elevator. Many of the high shots resemble those seen in CCTV footage or programmes such as *Big Brother* and there are numerous examples of these in *Strumpet*. The use of such angles is especially notable when the narratives are taking place in urban environments.

19. The Scottish Connection

Finally, we have the common inclusion of a Scottish reference. This occurs in six films within this book and has led to some believing that Boyle himself is Scottish; a belief supported by the fact that his first two films were shot in Glasgow and Edinburgh.

In *Shallow Grave* and *Trainspotting*, the Scottish connection is obvious. Ewan McGregor went on to create this connection in *A Life Less Ordinary* and one of his co-stars from *Trainspotting*, Robert Carlyle, did so in *The Beach*. Even in his most recent release *Slumdog Millionaire*, we find a reference when a Scottish woman rings Jamal while he is working in a call centre.

The amount of films that reference Scotland is greater than that which reference Danny Boyle's place of origin, this being Greater Manchester in England. Three of his films were shot in this location and Manchester itself is shown burning on the horizon in *28 Days Later*.

> I don't want people to just deliver the goods. I want them to feel like they belong to the film and that we work the film out together, and I treat them all as little mini-directors.
>
> Danny Boyle[5]

Final Words

Now that the director, his life, early work, collaborations and common themes and techniques have been discussed, it is time to move on to full discussions of each of his films in turn. The background presented in this chapter will help build a greater appreciation of Boyle's work and allow you to enjoy the fantastic journeys he takes you on all the more.

So read on and discover the depth and scope of Danny Boyle's films.

[1] Unknown. *Danny Boyle*
(http://www.imdb.com/name/nm0000965/)

[2] Unknown. *The Danny Boyle Interview: You feel guilty about money …*
(http://www.theherald.co.uk/features/features/display.var.2481973.0.The_Danny_Boyle_int
erview_You_feel_guilty_about_money.php)

[3] Overstreet, J. *Movies with Morals*
(http://www.christianitytoday.com/movies/interviews/2005/dannyboyle.html)

[4] Rea, D. *Dr Brian Cox* (http://www.sci-fi-online.com/2006_Interviews/07-08-27_brian-cox.htm)

[5] Murray, R. *Director Danny Boyle Discusses the Sci-Fi Thriller: Sunshine*
(http://movies.about.com/od/sunshine/a/sunshine070407.htm)

Shallow Grave

Shallow Grave came out of the milieu of the time. Margaret Thatcher was out of power, but her legacy was still there. So, it was very much like the film *Wall Street* and Gordon Gekko's "Greed is Good" speech. *Shallow Grave* was very much informed by that cynical self-interest.

Danny Boyle[1]

Shallow Grave was Danny Boyle's feature-film debut as a director. Released in 1994, it was also the movie debut for writer John Hodge and producer Andrew MacDonald. The film also saw Scottish actor Ewan McGregor in only his second role on the big screen, his debut having been in Bill Forsyth's *Being Human* (1993). He met Boyle while making *Scarlet & Black* for the BBC and thanks to this meeting was offered a part. Little did McGregor know at the time that he would go on to star in two more films by the director and that Boyle would be instrumental in launching his movie career.

It wasn't just McGregor who would go on to work with Boyle on other projects. Hodge would find himself writing three more feature-length screenplays for him, the last being an adaptation of Alex Garland's best-selling novel *The Beach*. MacDonald would also work with the director again, producing five other movies.

Deviating from films such as *Highlander* (Mulcahy 1986) and *Braveheart* (Gibson 1995), which used the often idyllic backdrop of rural Scotland, *Shallow Grave* was predominantly shot in an urban environment. Some scenes were filmed in woodland and by a small lake in a quarry, but this was entirely necessary in the context of the narrative and was not done in such a way as to glory in the wilds of Scotland.

Set in Edinburgh, *Shallow Grave* was predominantly shot in Glasgow. This was at least partly due to a £150,000 grant from the Glasgow Film Fund. FilmFour provided the main financial backing, the movie costing a relatively trifling £1.5 million, certainly in comparison with those produced in Hollywood. Also involved in the production was Figment Films. This was a company that had been founded by MacDonald in 1991, as discussed in the first chapter.

The film was distributed by PolyGram Filmed Entertainment, who managed to generate a good deal of publicity. When the film was shown at the Cannes Film Festival, the demand to see it was so high that three additional screenings had to be arranged. This popularity arose partly because the film challenges audiences in a number of ways. These include the lack of a clearly identifiable hero and narrative closure.

The relatively low budget helps to give this film a concentrated essence, making the characters and their interactions more prominent than the scenery or very limited effects. Both of these latter elements are at a minimum and allow the plot room to breathe. The script and story allow for such simplicity, and it is this simplicity which concentrates our attention on the characters and the effects of their greed.

One of Boyle's other films stands out as being the most obviously linked to *Shallow Grave*. This is *Millions*, in which a large sum of money arrives by accident and is central to the narrative. Both films reflect the times in which they were made, *Shallow Grave* the greed-driven mentality seeping into the 1990s from the yuppie 1980s and *Millions* the more altruistic approach of a generation aware of global issues relating to poverty and environmental concerns.

20

There are a number of links between *Shallow Grave* and Boyle's next film, *Trainspotting*, one being that of friendship. Other prominent links include the Scottish setting and the use of Ewan McGregor in a lead role. There are also two other actors who appear in both films. In *Shallow Grave*, Keith Allen plays Hugo and reappears as a London drug dealer in *Trainspotting*. Peter Mullan is one of two criminals hunting for Hugo and went on to play Swanney, the affable slum drug dealer (and can also be seen fighting alongside Mel Gibson in *Braveheart*).

A couple of other *Shallow Grave* cast members are also worth a special mention. The first is John Hodge, who not only wrote the screenplay, but also appears as DC Mitchell. The second is Ewan McGregor's mother, Carol, who, though uncredited, appears as one of the prospective room-mates that the friends interview at the beginning of the film.

Basic Premise & Main Characters

The film revolves around three friends played by Christopher Eccleston, Ewan McGregor and Kerry Fox. Their names are David, Alex and Juliet, and they are looking for a new flatmate. After interviewing a number of prospective new tenants, they finally opt for Hugo, a quiet and composed man who claims to be a writer.

Hugo's dead body is found naked upon his bed and Alex discovers a suitcase full of money tucked beneath. The flatmates then have to decide whether to ring the police and inform them of the body and money, or keep the money and dispose of the body. It doesn't take them too long to opt for the latter.

The mutilation of the body so it cannot be identified and its burial have a profound effect on the friendships and on David's mental state. The atmosphere in the flat changes dramatically, the tension rising, distrust and paranoia beginning to tear the friends apart.

After David begins dwelling in the loft and has dispatched two criminals who have come looking for the cash, the police discover the graves. Tracing Hugo's movements to the flat, the police then conduct interviews with the three friends and this brings the narrative to a finale fuelled by greed and distrust as each flatmate acts in their own self-interest in order to keep the money.

Narrative Themes

Boyle and Hodge create an important dynamic from the film's outset. The three flatmates are introduced straightaway and we see them interviewing prospective new tenants. During this process they are sarcastic and downright rude to these people. They are shown sitting together, revelling in the nastiness in such a way that implies their familiarity with each other and a shared sense of wickedly dark humour. We can see they are a tight unit and have an arrogance born of their upwardly mobile lifestyles and careers. They are, essentially, all yuppies who look down on many of the people they interview. Because of this they have specific standards as to whom they will accept into their little, three-person community. This then puts the candidates in the position of "outsiders", reinforcing the close-knit relationships between the main characters.

This view of outsiders helps greatly in making it believable that the three friends do not tell anyone else about the death that occurs in their flat or the money that they find in a suitcase beneath the dead man's bed. It is vital in creating the suspension of disbelief. The friends have their own subculture, one which anyone else would find it hard to gain entrance to. Theirs is a closed unit and therefore we do not expect them to have other friends. They are self-contained and therefore none of them have anyone else to whom they can relate the events which unfold. Without this factor the basic premise of the film cannot operate within a believable sphere.

This self-containment is aided by Boyle's limited use of shots beyond the flat. The narrative is centred at that location and we only see a few glimpses of life beyond. Their lives clearly revolve around their home life and friendships. David works studiously as a chartered accountant, but seems entirely unfulfilled by his job. Juliet clearly doesn't care about her colleagues at the hospital where she works, allowing both Alex and David to make fun of and abuse them verbally. Alex is a reporter who only cares about getting good human interest stories, something which is shown when the body of Hugo is discovered. Alex is unfazed by the discovery and starts looking through the dead man's personal effects. When Juliet questions him about his callous actions he replies, 'It's not every day I find a story in my own flat,' to which she replies, 'It's not a story, Alex. It's a corpse.'

Greed soon becomes a motivational force after their discovery of the money beneath the bed and a moral dilemma relating to this find is central to the narrative. The plot of *Shallow Grave* hinges on the moral dilemma of whether or not to keep the money and dispose of their new tenant's body. The audience is complicit in this as each viewer chooses which course of action they would take. We then get to watch the result of the choice to keep the money, the precise amount of which is never revealed. What is witnessed is the steady deterioration of the friendship between the three room-mates and the collapse of the bonds of trust they once shared.

> It's a great trick, in any movie, because a bag of money changes everything. It is like throwing a grenade into a room.

> Danny Boyle[2]

When the moral dilemma first becomes apparent in the narrative, when the grenade is thrown into the room and the friends have the suitcase of money resting on the table between them, we find that David and Juliet are against the idea of keeping the money, at least initially. Alex is clearly in favour, is the one proposing to keep it in the first instance, apparently having no moral problem with doing so. In fact, when referring to a comment Hugo made to Juliet earlier in the film concerning the "search of the self", Alex doesn't comprehend such an existential comment, flippantly saying to look behind the fridge. This implies his character is not introspective and this, coupled with his desire to keep the money, shows a man with little or no moral compass.

David is like the positive to Alex's negative, clearly being affected by the unfolding events. He is quieter and more studious than Alex, more self-contained and with a thoughtful, introspective nature, dwelling in brooding silence on the choices the room-mates eventually make. Thus, David's characterisation causes him to be more susceptible to feelings of guilt, something that can be seen as a human weakness in the context of this film.

The personalities of Alex and David create a balance, but also present us with a dichotomous response to the choices the friends make. The former remains unaffected, remains lively, humorous and cocky, his life continuing as normal. The latter suffers greatly from guilt and trauma.

Alex's personality also has the effect of acting as a kind of pressure valve as the darkness of the film builds towards its crescendo. His humour and energy counterbalance the growing gloom, just as his character is the counterbalance to that of David.

We witness the deterioration of David's sanity. He is the one burdened with the task of mutilating the corpse in order that it cannot be identified and this duty understandably plays on his mind. The character of David is such that he is the least capable of carrying such a burden of guilt and horror. The burden becomes so great that his mind is unbalanced. He becomes a loft-dwelling wraith of his former self, haunting the eaves and guarding the suitcase of money he has hidden in the water tank. Such severe behavioural changes are a sure sign of mental disturbance and strain, something not lost on Alex and Juliet, who not only worry about David and his actions, but also, underneath their facade of continued friendship, worry about their ability to retrieve the money.

The camera lingers on David, allowing us to see his turmoil and descent into inner darkness.

Here it is important to note the commentary on human nature which is apparent in the film. The idea of what it is to be human is actually introduced during a segment of speech near the start of the narrative. When Juliet is interviewing Hugo the phone rings and she asks him to answer it. He gives the caller, Brian, the brush-off on her behalf. Brian tries to ring back immediately and while the phone rings, Juliet comments, '... he needs treatment.' Hugo replies, 'For what?' Her response is to say, 'A certain weakness,' and he responds, 'The human condition.' This suggests that humans have certain weaknesses and we are introduced to such during the course of the film. Greed is one such weakness and we also see that guilt and betrayal rear their ugly heads as the narrative unfolds.

The civilised, contemporary existence of the characters is slowly corrupted by the fact they gave in to the weakness of greed. Their relationships descend from those we recognise in our own lives to ones touched by a more primitive nature behind the everyday facade we each have.

Not only do we see them succumb to weakness, but, partially because of this, we find there is no hero present in any form that we recognise from previous viewing experiences. All of the friends are ordinary people with traits common to those we come into contact with during our everyday lives.

What we find is that the character of Alex is essentially a kind of anti-hero. This image of him is cemented by such things as his slightly unkempt appearance, his cocky and loud nature, his wish to keep the money and bury the body (both of which make him pivotal to the plot) and his job as a reporter; a job that we commonly associate with a lack of scruples thanks to the reputation of tabloid journalists. This job is a defining element of his character. We find that he opens and reads his friends' mail and that when Hugo's body is discovered he sees it as a potential story and exhibits no sign of being overly shocked or horrified by the discovery, David being the most obviously shaken by the macabre sight.

Alex's character, his lack of an ethical or moral compass, is highlighted very clearly when the three friends attend a banquet to raise funds for the children's unit of the hospital where Juliet works as a doctor. When he discovers the reason behind the fund-raising he states, 'I hate children. I'd raise money to have the little fuckers put down.' This is a cold-hearted response and one opposite to most people's in relation to children, who are commonly seen as precious, partially due to their innocence and vulnerability, both traits being evident in the two Danny Boyle films featuring children in starring roles: *Millions* and *Slumdog Millionaire*.

It is also of note that when the friends are finally motivated to deal with the body in the fourth bedroom it is Alex who breezily talks of what to do with it, of how to mutilate it beyond recognition. Alex also states to David while buying the tools necessary for his plan of action, 'We're all gonna do it, each of us. You, me and Juliet will do his or her bit.' This, however, does not turn out to be the case. Faced with the possibility of having to do all the mutilation on his own, Alex makes them draw straws and David pulls the short one, something that leads to an increasing darkness in the narrative and his behaviour. Alex's course of action here is a hint at the underlying self-interest which will slowly come to the fore.

During the burial of Hugo's corpse, David asks Alex, 'Is that going to be deep enough?' This implies the grave is too shallow, and it is this shallow grave that gives the film its title and is ineffective in keeping the body hidden, therefore causing the final destruction of the friendships as the fear of police discovery increases.

It isn't until after Hugo's burial that David feels the need to hide the money in the attic of the flat. It is at this point that the situation gains a more tangible reality of risk and consequence. There is no going back. The body has been mutilated and concealed, the friends can no longer call the police and the money is the only evidence remaining of the crime. Prior to the burial no crime had been committed. Yes, the friends had kept a corpse lingering in the flat, but they had not made any attempt at concealing the money or the body.

The friendships become strained when David retreats into the darkness both literally and metaphorically. Not only does he make the gloom of the attic his home, only descending when the others are out, but he also retreats into his own mental darkness, one that increases as time wears on and the bonds of trust between the friends twist and then snap with the pressure. David's introspective nature creates an inner turmoil as he struggles with the moral implications of what he has done and the horror of mutilating Hugo's body, something completely opposed to who he thinks he is.

The burglary of the flat beneath theirs further unsettles David. Thoughts of the money continually linger in the back of his mind. As mentioned, the attic is symbolic of his mental state. The fact that the money is placed there symbolises that it is also central in his mind, as are the implications of its presence, for it is the only evidence of what has happened. It is his constant reminder of his actions to make the corpse unidentifiable. David cannot separate money and corpse and this is why when the body is buried the money must also be buried, hidden out of sight in the darkness of the attic.

I'd worked with Danny Boyle before and he's so enthusiastic about film and making films, it was a wonderful thing to do.

Kerry Fox[3]

Alex and Juliet start to become seriously worried when David begins to spend increasingly longer periods dwelling in the attic. This worry is elevated to fear for their own safety when they see the results of David dispatching two criminals who come looking for Hugo and the money. They are killed in a cold-blooded manner when they go into the attic and this reflects David's mental state, one still displaying his control, but lacking morality. The moral compass he once had no longer points north.

A common element seen in many of Boyle's films is a religious reference and this occurs when Alex is watching the original version of *The Wicker Man* (Hardy 1973). In the small segment we see on the TV screen the policeman, played by Edward Woodward, is being dragged towards the wicker man while calling out to Christ. The use of this scene and the segment from *Lose A Million* seen earlier adds popular culture references with which we can identify. Their use increases the depiction of the characters as ordinary people leading ordinary lives. This is especially the case considering that Woodward's character in the classic British film was that of an ordinary policeman.

When the police call in *Shallow Grave* the tension is elevated further. Each of the friends is asked if they recognise any of three men they are shown photographs of by Inspector McCall (Ken Stott). After the visit both David and Juliet are convinced the police know they are responsible for the bodies found buried in woodland graves. Alex states that whether or not they know is of no consequence because there is no evidence to link them to the bodies. However, David points out that the money connects them. This additional pressure caused by the police investigation is the final straw that causes him to act in his own self-interest, attempting to leave during the night, an attempt that brings about the final confrontation between the flatmates.

Alex, despite being the one who was vocal in his opinion that they should keep the money, despite being the one who said the body's hands, feet and teeth should be disposed of, is the one who attempts to ring Inspector McCall in order to inform him of what has happened. This adds to his persona in that he is prepared to inform on his friends despite being the one who instigated their problems. It also shows just how fearful for his life he really is, for he is choosing the possibility of a prison sentence over the possibility of what might happen in the flat.

By the time we reach the final throes of life in the flat the friendships are dead. Rather than being a tight unit, the three occupants are isolated individuals all trying to get the money for themselves, guided by self-interest and distrust. The jovial closeness at the film's outset has rotted like Hugo's corpse until what remains is unidentifiable in contrast.

This clarifies one of the themes of the narrative. This is that greed is destructive and creates a self-interest which leaves no room for lasting relationships with other people. In this sense *Shallow Grave* is a comment on materialistic society, one that has seen the corrosion of the family unit and social networks thanks, in part, to an encouragement towards material success and selfishness.

At the end we find that a strand of the narrative is left open through the character of Alex. This open-ended element is apparent in a number of Boyle's films, including *Trainspotting, 28 Days Later* and *Millions*. In *Shallow Grave* it relates to Alex having hidden the money without the knowledge of David or Juliet. He alone knows its whereabouts and owing to his survival at the film's close, we can presume that he will eventually manage to keep all the money for himself.

Not only are we given a somewhat open ending, but we are also given the impression that the story has been taking place prior to the film's narrative. This is achieved through the three friends conducting the interviews at the start if the film. We are not informed of what happened to the previous tenant or even if there was one. Neither are we party to the reasons for finding a fourth member of the household. This gives us a past that, though unknown, hints at the film's narrative being part of a wider story. What we are witnessing are the final throes of the friendships due to the moral dilemma. We do not know how these friendships formed and the characters' families are never mentioned. In this way the narrative is pared down to the importance of their friendship and the impact the money has upon them.

The ending of the film creates circularity. Both the beginning and the end feature David's lifeless face in close-up and both have a voice-over by the character. This voice-over is virtually the same in both instances, but in this final shot his words, 'Take trust, for instance, or friendship. These are the important things in life. These are the things that matter, that help you on your way. If you can't trust your friends, well what then? What then?' take on much more significance now that the narrative has come to an end. His greed-motivated journey into the depths of guilt, trauma and distrust has come to a fatal end and his words from beyond the grave underline the message of his character; friendship and trust are more important than money.

Some might say that the film acts as a critique of greed, whilst also leaving us in no doubt that the moral choice that was made by the flatmates was the wrong one. If the three friends had simply contacted the police and declared the existence of the money then their lives would most likely have continued on as normal. Instead, they were motivated by greed and this motivation is shown to lead to dire consequences.

However, this idea may hold up to mild scrutiny, but take a closer look. Who is the one who clearly wanted to keep the money at the outset? Alex. Which friend seems to have ended up with the money at the close of the film? Alex. Can it truly be said that this moral tale is anti-greed, or could it be argued that it is showing us how a lack of a moral compass can allow a greater freedom of thought and action, one which bears rewards? It seems that Alex carries with him a message: those who are guided by greed lack a conscience or moral compass and though they may attain wealth, they will have no true friends and no bonds of trust.

Considering the time when the film was made, it seems clear that we are being shown a choice: friendship and trust or greed and suspicion. It would appear that money is a poison to friendship, especially in large doses.

You could also say that its ultimate message is that money does not bring happiness, at least for most people. For Alex, this does not necessarily hold true. Though he has suffered, ending the film with a knife protruding from his chest, the money is in his possession and he has a wry grin on his face.

We have already seen how Alex can be defined as an anti-hero, but this is also the case with David. He is the character seen in close-up both at the beginning and the end of the film. It is also David over whom the camera lingers, allowing us to see his inner turmoil. He is the last to agree to their course of action and he does not shirk his agreed responsibility in mutilating Hugo's corpse. Furthermore, he defended the money and possibly their lives when the two criminals gained entry to the flat.

So in the final analysis it is David, not Alex, who is the crux of the narrative. He is the conscience of the small group of friends and whether we like to admit it or not, it is he and not Alex who the majority of us most closely resemble. Therefore it is his mental collapse with which we most closely identify, understanding his anguish, for we would have felt the same way. And, yes, most of us would have chosen to keep the money as well. In this light David is not only the conscience of the friends, he is the conscience of the majority of viewers. He is a reflection of the audience and, like Alex, his character carries a message; for those with a moral compass and conscience, greed is a destructive force, friendship and trust being far more important than wealth. In his descent into mental imbalance, we are given a stern warning as to the dangers of being motivated by money and greed.

Cinematic Techniques

David, Alex and Juliet are very effectively introduced by Boyle at the start of the film when we see them interviewing prospective room-mates. We cannot fail to note how well they interact together and their shared sense of humour. We also see their full names when the first of these interviewees, Cameron, rings the door buzzer, a plaque next to it stating: "Alex Law, David Stevens, Juliet Miller". The interviews and the plaque are an interesting and effective way not only to give us their names, but to allow us a glimpse of their friendship and how they treat those beyond their tight circle.

Boyle introduces us to the three main characters in a very simple, but effective way.

The simple *mise en scène* of the flat helps us not only to concentrate on the narrative and the characters, but also accentuates the presence of the apartment itself because there is very little clutter. The size of the apartment is considerable, with large rooms and high ceilings. This gives it an almost hollow feel when coupled with the sparse scattering of furnishings and decorative items. There is also a slight echoing quality which reflects the hollowness not only of the characters' choice to take the money and dispose of the body, but also the space that opens between them as they are torn apart by the circumstances they have brought upon themselves. This echoing, specious quality also adds to the suspense as the narrative tension rises.

> On *Shallow Grave* we all lived in a flat together for a week in Glasgow, and lived and breathed it to create the relationships between the three of us.
>
> Ewan McGregor[4]

The stripped-down simplicity of Boyle's film echoes that of Quentin Tarantino's directorial debut, *Reservoir Dogs*, which was released two years prior to *Shallow Grave*. This simplicity was in both cases caused, in part, by financial constraints, but the films differ greatly when it comes to the characters involved. Boyle chose to portray a group of ordinary people, as is his habit, whilst Tarantino opted for a gritty gangster style. It is also pertinent to note that the narratives of both films revolve around a large sum of money.

The first shot through glass apparent in any of Boyle's films can be seen near the start of *Shallow Grave* when the main characters are at a squash court. We see Juliet watching Alex and David as they finish their game. The reflection in the glass allows the audience to see the men playing even though the camera's gaze is focussed on Juliet. As with the common use of mirrors and screen-within-screen shots, Boyle presents us with two images, though in this case one overlays the other.

Another noteworthy shot through glass occurs when the two criminals are torturing a man by holding him captive in a chest freezer with a glass lid. We are presented with the victim's point of view both as the criminals look down at him and as he witnesses heavy bags being placed upon the glass. This increases audience feelings of entrapment and also our horror in relation to his impending death.

We see a large mirror used in the lounge of the flat. It is utilised by Boyle when Hugo gives Brian the aforementioned brush-off. The shot is of Hugo on the phone, but at the same time the mirror allows us to see the edge of Juliet as she reclines on the settee. The mirror thereby acts as a device by which to present us with both characters on screen. In this way it is linked to the shot through glass at the squash court, which allows us views of both Juliet waiting to play and the men playing their game.

The burial of Hugo's body is one of the scenes where Boyle's directing excels. The director presents the audience with a juxtaposition of humour and horror which unsettles the audience. Taking into account David's quite dull and straight-laced character, the scenes of him sawing off Hugo's extremities and then taking a hammer to the corpse's face are curiously engaging in both a humorous and disturbing manner. It is mildly amusing to see a man of his nature performing such terrible premeditated acts and it is also disturbing that even he, when pushed, can plunge to such depths.

The director's use of backlighting for the second burial scene adds to its impact, making David almost a silhouette, reflecting the shadowy nature of his actions and symbolising his slip into mental darkness. In both this and the first burial scene Boyle allows the audience's imaginations to create images of what David is doing. He achieves this by not actually graphically showing the character's actions, only allowing us to see the hammer falling and not its impact, for example. Our minds fill in the blanks with the help of the sound effects, in this case the crunch of a jaw being smashed to pieces. We conjure horrific images, which are often more terrible than anything that could have been portrayed on screen and the scene is more powerful because of this.

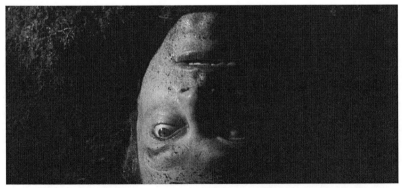

Boyle provides us with a brief shot of Hugo's lifeless face just before David takes a hammer to it, the image increasing the impact of the scene as we conjure macabre sights within our imaginations.

A shot echoing those of David's lifeless face at the beginning and end of the film is cleverly used by Boyle after the burial of Hugo's body. It is symbolic of David dying internally. The act of decapitation has killed who he was and, like a corpse, he is now emotionally dead and cold inside.

Interestingly, after burying Hugo, we see an unaffected Alex sitting watching TV. The show he is watching is *Lose A Million* hosted by Chris Tarrant. This was a forerunner of *Who Wants to be a Millionaire* and both programmes share the same presenter in the UK, and thus a notable connection is created with *Slumdog Millionaire*, which would come some fourteen years after the release of *Shallow Grave*.

There is only one occasion in the film when any of the money is spent. Though we do not actually witness the purchases, we see that Alex and Juliet have been to the shops and bought a number of items, the most prominent being a £500 camcorder. We then see these two friends watching a film they have made. Boyle keeps the camera low so that we almost feel as though we are seated on the floor of the room watching them. He also presents us with a screen within a screen, as he does in the majority of his other films, as discussed in the first chapter.

Alex talks directly to the camera in this home-movie footage and therefore it feels as though he is addressing the audience. This means that his words have greater impact because he is talking directly to us. His short monologue ends with the words, 'And now at last, at long last, nothing will ever be the same again.' Though said in a positive light, implying that the money will make their lives easier, the audience understands its negative connotations. We see the double meaning and our expectancy is increased as to the consequences of the friends' course of action. This simple sentence acts as an announcement of the trouble just around the proverbial corner and we witness an angry outburst from David just moments later when he discovers that his friends have spent some of the money.

The clip from *The Wicker Man* used by Boyle is a clever way in which to mislead the audience and also adds to the sense of impending doom. In the classic British film, the policeman is burnt alive in the wicker man, which is a terrible fate. The audience, or at least those who know the plot of the 1973 film, assumes there is a terrible fate lying in wait for the friends. More specifically, we can link this dark destiny to the character of Alex as he is the one watching the film. However, this turns out to be a clever example of misleading the audience. The clue we are given is a red herring, one which helps to make the end of the movie more unexpected. Coupled to this is the fact that in most Hollywood films the heartless, callous character with few scruples would ultimately be punished, but in Boyle's film he is the one who potentially ends up with the money.

The scene of Alex watching TV is also one of three screen-in-screen shots presented in the film. The other examples are the viewing of *Lose A Million* and of the home movie made by Alex and Juliet. The use of screens within shots would become one of Boyle's trademarks and presents the audience with two views. First, there is the primary view, which is framed by the camera's gaze. Then there is the secondary view, framed by the TV or computer screen, the latter evident at the end of *The Beach*. The director thereby uses such shots to give an additional dimension to the scene and to introduce other narrative elements, this being the imminent destruction of the friendships in the case of Alex viewing *The Wicker Man*.

David's descent into mental instability is captured perfectly by Boyle. Using lingering camera shots, he allows us to see the character's brooding, dark expression. Thanks to Eccleston's acting, we can almost feel the turmoil within him as he struggles to come to terms with what he's done. Such lingering shots also help us identify with him and his inner torment, for the audience cannot help but think about how we would be affected if in his position.

Adding to the camerawork is the location where David spends most of his time; the loft. Boyle makes it purposefully dark, even to the extent of using a short in the electrics so that the light no longer works. This darkness reflects David's mentality perfectly. It also reflects the oppressive nature of his thoughts concerning what has happened, ones which continually press on his mind. This feeling of oppression is aided by the contrast of the loft's low ceiling with the high ceilings of the flat below, the difference in space being very noticeable.

When David drills holes into the floor of the loft and lets light pierce the gloom from the flat below we see a fantastic and striking use of light and dark. The shafts of brightness rising into the space are like torch beams from his former life searching for the man who has become lost in his own mental gulag. They also reflect the beginnings of a change, this being his thoughts on taking the money and starting a new life. In this way they can also be seen as rays of hope for a return to a normal existence.

The holes are drilled in order to allow David to spy on his friends and thereby inform the audience of his growing paranoia, for he needs to know Alex and Juliet's location at all times. Boyle uses point-of-view shots from these holes, giving us David's perspective. These overhead shots of the flat are a forerunner to the director's use of high and low camera angles that would be seen in his other films.

David's descent into a more primitive and paranoid mentality, along with the descent of the character's relationships, is symbolised in a seemingly insignificant aspect of the *mise en scène*. Seated on a chair in the large entrance hall, off which all the other rooms are located, is a full-size figure of an ape. This is only seen in the background until the last throes of the narrative. As the final threads of friendship tear apart, David assaulting Juliet and the three of them fighting in order to take ownership of the money, the tussling David and Alex fall into the ape and knock it from its seat. Its symbolism becomes clear; it is a statement of how humans are still, in essence, only apes wearing clothes, wearing a facade of civilisation over our primitive and somewhat barbaric nature.

The final song of the film is *Happy Heart*, something which is initially playing as Juliet discovers that the suitcase she has managed to escape with is no longer packed with money. This song then continues to overlay the final scenes of Alex with a knife in his chest lying on the kitchen floor, followed by the face of David's corpse as his voice speaks from beyond the grave about friendship and trust.

Happy Heart is one of only four songs used on the soundtrack of this film, the music for the opening titles having been created by Leftfield. There is only one example of diegetic music and this occurs when the friends are attending the fund-raising banquet. The relatively sparse use of music, coupled with the simplicity of the *mise en scène*, helps the audience to concentrate on the narrative, though the reason behind such limited use is most likely to have been due to budget constraints.

Another element that increases concentration is Boyle's interplay of frenetic action and brooding calm. The juxtaposition of these two very different types of scene heightens each and holds our interest. This strategy effectively jolts the audience with the sudden electricity of on-screen action.

Examples of often violent and always frenetic scenes include those of the criminals torturing people as they follow the trail Hugo has left in order to discover his whereabouts. These cutaway scenes are used to unsettle the audience, unexpectedly interrupting the scenes relating to the friends with shocking suddenness. These short episodes of violence and torture have the effect of making us more alert and their images linger once the narrative has returned to the more sedate build-up of tension within the flat.

A torture scene arising as a result of the two criminals searching for Hugo's whereabouts is reminiscent of one witnessed in *Slumdog Millionaire*. A man's head is thrust into water which is tainted red with blood. This is seen from beneath the water, looking up at the victim's face, just as it is when Jamal is being tortured at the police station at the start of *Slumdog Millionaire*, both providing the films with Boyle's trademark shot of a character through the medium of water.

We see other shots through water in relation to the suitcase filled with money. The audience are provided with upward shots of David and Alex at different points in the narrative, and these are from within the water. These shots create a slightly distorted image which is befitting the distortion of their thoughts and friendships after the discovery of the money.

> It was effortless and it was beautiful to work with Danny. I don't think I've ever been happier working with another director.
>
> Ewan McGregor[5]

At one point in the film Boyle uses a doll of a baby which could be said to symbolise the fall of innocence. We see it crawling along the floor and then falling down the stairs, tumbling out of frame. The characters had been normal, law-abiding citizens, until the discovery of the money. Until that point they were innocent of crime or misdeed. Then, thanks to the motivation of greed, they stooped low and committed theft, concealing Hugo's body after mutilating it.

The doll is also seen in a short but disturbing dream sequence experienced by Alex. This is very apt considering Ewan McGregor's character in *Trainspotting* also has a vision of a baby, one fearfully crawling along a ceiling while he is suffering from withdrawal symptoms relating to his heroin addiction.

There are two other links with *Trainspotting* that arise through filmic techniques. The first is introductory images of city streets to give us a sense of place. In *Shallow Grave* we are shown streets in Edinburgh at the start of the film and at high speed. In *Trainspotting* the sights of London are shown in a similar way when the main character moves there, though the shots are not speeded up. The second is voice-over, which is used at the beginning and end of the film and is spoken by the character of David. In *Trainspotting* it is used far more extensively because the character of Renton acts as the film's narrator.

Boyle uses voice-over at the start of a number of other films he has directed and this is usually in order to help identify the main character. *Shallow Grave* is no different in this sense and the voice-over helps position us so we see that what happens to David is of primary importance. This is then reinforced by the use of voice-over at the end, the narrative beginning and ending on this character's words and the image of his face.

Criticism

Though Juliet is one of only three main characters, she dwindles when set against the counterbalancing characters of David and Alex. She moves from Alex's company to that of David and back again, her behaviour and mood echoing that of whomever she is spending time with as if she is merely an extension of them. When she is with Alex she is lively and playful, when with David she is more subdued and thoughtful. In this sense she is akin to an empty vessel, only filled by the more powerful characters of the male flatmates. Her role in the narrative is relatively minor and could have been given greater weight, though this is only a minor criticism of the script.

Awards

The omen of extra screenings at Cannes turned out to be a very good one. Though the film was not entered into any categories at that film festival, it ended up receiving critical acclaim and went on to garner fourteen awards at other events. Included amongst them were Empire Awards for Danny Boyle, Ewan McGregor and in the category of Best British Film. Showing just how highly regarded his directing ability was, Danny Boyle was given Best Newcomer of the Year at the London Critics Circle Film Awards. Most noteworthy of all the awards heaped upon the film was a BAFTA. This was presented to Boyle and MacDonald and was the Alexander Korda Award for Best British Film.

Final Words

Though based on a simple premise, *Shallow Grave* is an interesting and observational film about the splintering of friendships thanks to the unexpected arrival of a large sum of money. The combination of film noir, thriller and horror that is evident blends seamlessly to create a dark tale of greed and conscience, which is highly atmospheric thanks to Boyle's direction.

This is an impressive piece of cinema, especially when considering it was the director's first big screen outing. It hints strongly at what was to come and launched his career thanks to critical acclaim. Shots and themes that would become his trademarks were seen for the first time, but it wouldn't be long until they made each of his films recognisable as being undoubtedly the work of Danny Boyle.

[1] MacDevette, B. *Danny Boyle*
(http://www.independentfilmquarterly.com/ifq/interviews/dannyboyle.htm)

[2] MacDevette, B. *Danny Boyle*
(http://www.independentfilmquarterly.com/ifq/interviews/dannyboyle.htm)

[3] Djurica, R. *Probe: Kerry Fox* (http://www.wildviolet.net/birthday_blue/fox2.html)

[4] Wootton, A. *Ewan McGregor* (http://www.guardian.co.uk/film/2002/oct/23/features)

[5] Wootton, A. *Ewan McGregor* (http://www.guardian.co.uk/film/2002/oct/23/features)

Trainspotting

The truth is that I'm a bad person, but that's going to change, I'm going to change. This is the last of that sort of thing. Now I'm cleaning up and I'm moving on, going straight and choosing life. I'm looking forward to it already. I'm going to be just like you.

Renton

Trainspotting was the second film made by the team of Danny Boyle, Andrew MacDonald and John Hodge, along with Ewan McGregor on screen. It was also the finest of the three they made together, one which, at the time, was the second highest grossing film ever at the UK box office after *Four Weddings and a Funeral* (Curtis 1994).

Costing considerably more than *Shallow Grave* at $2.5 million, it was a co-production by Channel Four Films and Figment. The latter was Boyle, MacDonald and Hodge's own company and it has been compared to Tarantino's A Band Apart in the US because of its impact upon contemporary cinema. It was part of a British film industry revival that was led by the very different directing talents of Danny Boyle and Richard Curtis.

Set in Edinburgh, most of the film was shot in Glasgow, as was the case with *Shallow Grave*. It was released in 1996 and is packed with energy, gritty and hard-hitting situations, humour and heroin addiction. To help in his portrayal of such addicts, McGregor met a few upon his arrival in Glasgow prior to filming. This gave him the grounding for his character and the acting of all the cast is excellent, the film featuring stellar performances by a group of young, talented and, at that time, largely unknown Scottish actors.

The film is postmodern, this label earned due to a number of elements apparent in both its style and content. The first is the blend of different genres. The use of light and shadow and the gritty nature of the film are akin to film noir. The drug use can be equated with such films as *Drugstore Cowboy* (Van Sant 1989) and *Fear and Loathing in Las Vegas* (Gilliam 1998), which can be said to be of subcultural appeal. There are also touches of horror, specifically relating to Renton's hallucinations when he is coming off heroin. The playful use of camera angles and self-reflexivity, specifically seen when people wave at the camera during the introductory shots of London, are common to postmodern films. This blend is added to by British realism, which is here watered down by humour and surreal elements, such as Renton's dive into the toilet. The realism is therefore tempered, restrained by the surreal and the use of humour, so that what we are presented with is an amalgamation that transcends all these elements individually.

It could be said that this combination of both realistic and surreal elements is a clever use of the camera's gaze due to its reflection of the human mind. Our own consciousness is an amalgam of the real and unreal. Therefore *Trainspotting* reflects this aspect of what it is to be human. This could also be why Boyle finds the use of dreams and visions to be so important in his work, as they are part of our everyday experience, counterbalancing the reality of the world around us.

Basic Premise & Main Characters

The film revolves around a group of five friends. The central character is a young man called Mark Renton, who is a heroin addict. His life is cyclical due to his addiction. He finds himself quitting the drug only to return to its comfort, each new hit demanding finance which is often secured through theft.

Ewan McGregor plays Renton, who displays a ready wit and never-say-die attitude. He really shone for the first time in this role thanks, in part, to Boyle's direction and skill with actors. His charismatic performance led to Hollywood demand and success, the most notable being his role as Obi-Wan Kenobi in the *Star Wars* prequels.

Robert Carlyle turns out a suitably threatening and manic performance as the psychotic Begbie, lover of alcohol and the feeling of power extreme violence gives him. Jonny Lee Miller is also convincing as Sick Boy, an addict with a mind full of useless knowledge about the career of Sean Connery. Ewan Bremner plays the hapless but dependable Spud, whose amphetamine-fuelled job interview is one of the most memorably funny scenes of the film. Completing the line-up of five friends is Tommy, who turns to heroin after his life takes a turn for the worse, and who is played by Kevin McKidd. We also see producer Andrew MacDonald make an appearance as the potential purchaser of a house in London and we see writer John Hodge as a plain-clothes security officer.

In the latter stages of the film Tommy has passed away and the four remaining friends have the opportunity to make a one-off drugs sale for a substantial amount of money. Travelling to London in order to meet a dealer played by Keith Allen, they sell the drugs and the film closes with Renton making off with the bag of money.

Narrative Themes

The sense of gritty reality portrayed in the movie is helped greatly by the use of dialogue, both diegetic and non-diegetic. Not only does it contain a realistic degree of swearing, but it is also littered with both UK and Scottish slang. Though the Irvine Welsh novel from which *Trainspotting* is adapted had a much stronger dialect, the film still retains the use of vernacular speech. This gives the movie a more down-to-earth feel, adding a greater realism to the scenarios and characters.

The narration by Renton also helps to identify him as the main character. It begins with what is almost a rant. He speaks about the choices in life, talking with a scornful tone about the ordinary, everyday choices we are all encouraged to make by social pressure and ideology. This is underlined by his final comments in regards normal lives. 'Choose rotting away at the end of it all, pishing your last in a miserable home, nothing more than an embarrassment to the selfish, fucked-up brats you have spawned to replace yourself.' This is a damning indictment of the reward for living a "normal" life. It makes the everyday population seem nothing more than lifeless zombies who only exist to work, consume and then pass away after a period of social exclusion in old age.

The first ten minutes or so of the film are mainly concerned with Renton. This acts as an effective introduction to his character. He is our anti-hero for, as with *Shallow Grave*, there are no traditional heroes present in this story. He is also ordinary, the main difference between him and the majority of the audience being his heroin addiction.

The infamous toilet scene when Renton climbs into the disgusting, sewage-smeared loo of a betting shop is seen early in the film. It was the forerunner to a similar scene in *Slumdog Millionaire*. In that film, the character's reasons for entering the toilet were positive and this was reinforced with the use of colour and daylight. In this scene from *Trainspotting* there is no daylight, only the hollow glow of a bulb illuminating "the worst toilet in Scotland"; a dank, mucky and claustrophobic toilet which looks as though it has never been cleaned.

The claustrophobia of the infamous toilet scene.

It is here that we see the first of what can be described as drug-related visions. Renton, rather than simply fishing around in the sickening remnants of other people's bowel movements, actually vanishes into the loo in a quest to retrieve the suppositories he has inadvertently expelled from his body. What follows, accompanied by calm music featuring the calls of whales, is a vision of him swimming through clear ocean waters and finding his drugs on the ocean bed.

This scene can be viewed as symbolising the character's use of drugs. He takes them to escape from the reality of his life, which he views as a shite-filled toilet in a metaphorical sense. This escape is symbolised by the clear water, accompanied by calming music. However, this drug-induced escape is temporary and he must return to reality after a while, must go back to the tight confines of his stinking, shitty life. In comparison with this reality the drug high, the clear blue ocean, is an idyll, and we can understand why he wishes to escape into it, how the addiction to heroin can be so strong.

> Although I quite enjoy watching realist films, I can't write that way myself. I'm always looking for a way out of a realist situation. So when I came to write the scene in the toilet, the idea of seeing that in a totally realistic way was totally off-putting to me. So I just went with the flow.
>
> John Hodge[1]

Another drug-related vision occurs when Renton visits the affable drug dealer called Swanney after appearing in court. It is in Swanney's flat that scenes of heroin use are most commonly seen in the film. After taking the drug, Renton sinks into the floor, the audience seeing his point of view. Visually, this looks similar to a grave, though lined with red carpet. He has overdosed and this sunken view is that of someone close to death.

We soon witness Renton being put into a cab and taken to hospital. The non-diegetic music playing during these scenes is Lou Reed's *Perfect Day*. There are two lines of the lyrics that are particularly striking during this sequence and are made all the more pronounced by the lack of diegetic speech. The first is, "You just keep me hanging on", which is repeated as he is dropped outside the hospital, implying that he will be saved. Soon after that we hear the repetition of "You're going to reap just what you sow", implying that Renton is suffering as a result of his own actions.

In traditional filmic structures Renton would also suffer for transgressions conducted during the narrative. The fact that he does not end up paying for his misdeeds subverts audience expectations. Thanks to the majority of films, we expect an almost karmic reward and punishment system to be enacted within the movie. Those who are deemed "good" will find reward, while those who are seen as "bad" will be punished. Boyle subverts this expectation and allows the "bad" anti-hero to escape with the cash. It is also the case that Tommy, the friend who is initially living the most "normal" life and who is last to fall to heroin addiction other than Begbie, is the only one to die. This is another subversion of usual cinematic reward and punishment themes. Such subverting of audience expectation is common to his work and helps to make his films more gripping in that they tend to deviate from normal cinematic and narrative formulations.

Can Renton's relatively unscathed escape from the life he has known be said to carry any message? It certainly isn't a portrayal of addiction being good, for Renton ends the film reformed, having ended his need for heroin. Instead, this need is replaced by the needs of normal society; to 'Choose a job. Choose a career. Choose a family. Choose a fucking big television. Choose washing machines, cars, compact disc players and electric tin openers...' He has made the decision to choose life, which is the positive to heroin addiction's negative. In Renton's case, this concept of what normal life should entail is a replacement for his addiction. Instead of needing a hit he now needs a new TV or a new car.

In this light we are all addicts in a materialistic system. The heroin addiction promises Renton escape and therefore happiness through the high. Materialism promises happiness through the consumption of products, the equivalent of drugs, but socially accepted, almost demanded. The pushers of these drugs for the masses are the manufacturers who try to persuade people they need their products. In both cases, that of heroin addiction and that of materialism, we can argue that there is no real happiness, only temporary highs that do not solve the underlying problem, do not end the search for contentment, but fuel it in order for us to continue using or buying.

Does the film provide us with a viable alternative to either of these options? No. Though there is clearly a theme of friendship, as there was in *Shallow Grave*, Renton abandons his friends in the final scenes. It is not shown as a solution and the idea of love – which is central to Boyle's following film *A Life Less Ordinary* and to *Slumdog Millionaire* – barely raises its head other than in relation to Renton's parents loving their son. Thus, love is virtually absent in the narrative of *Trainspotting*. It is his parents' motivation for getting Renton off heroin, but their attempt is unsuccessful.

We actually find that the urban environment depicted is highly symbolic in the case of both the life of a heroin addict and someone who chooses a normal existence. Boyle has intentionally made it claustrophobic, to the point of most interior scenes taking place in small and pokey rooms. This serves to create a feeling of entrapment which is equally applicable to both lifestyles. The user cannot easily escape their addiction and the consumer cannot easily escape the domination of consumerism. Both have their own claustrophobia within the enclosed streets and small interiors, as we can see when Renton is off heroin and living in a cramped flat in London after having chosen to lead a more normal life.

Making the flat more cramped is the arrival of Begbie. An important point of note in relation to Begbie's violence is that it is not glorified in any way. Boyle presents it without the use of close-ups or lingering shots. This "real life" portrayal adds to the film's gritty feel and gives the violence more impact. This is because it is such a contrast to usual filmic violence, which is either glorified, humorous or glossed over. The effects of the usual depictions are to desensitise the audience to the effects of violent acts. This is partly due to the fact that much of this violence is committed against the "bad guys", for whom we do not care. You only have to watch *Indiana Jones* films to see examples of this type of violence. In comparison, *Trainspotting* shares common ground with films such as Stanley Kubrick's *A Clockwork Orange*, which Boyle saw as a youth, the on-screen violence depicted in the 1971 classic having quite an impact on him because of its realism. Boyle clearly likes to take the gloss off normal movie violence and give it a more real feel, creating a true depiction of consequences and a greater degree of shock and horror for audience members. This is also seen in a number of his other films.

> If you're going to be angry be fucking angry. If you're going to be insane, be fucking insane, be honestly insane. Don't be afraid of being ugly.
>
> Robert Carlyle[2]

The heroin addicts are a subculture. They are a lower stratum of society beyond the commonplace normalities of everyday life. For them, everything revolves around heroin, if not actually being high, then trying to arrange the next hit, whether that be through theft in order to fund their habit or through spending their Social Security benefits when they visit Swanney, played by Peter Mullan, who was one of the criminals hunting for Hugo in *Shallow Grave.*

This subculture existence isn't simply because they take drugs. It is because they take a socially demonised drug. Renton says early in his narration, '... my mother, who is, in her own domestic and socially acceptable way, also a drug addict.' This comment is in reference to a bottle of Valium, which he has stolen from her. During the course of the film we also see Begbie using and abusing alcohol, another drug that is not only common within society, but which is actually seen as the norm, those who do not indulge being seen as unusual.

Therefore, we see that Renton and his addict friends are partially victims of an enforced castration from mainstream society through its ideology and laws. They are forced to the fringes of society, their kind of existence having been marked out as "wrong" by the establishment and social stigma, whereas Valium, alcohol and other legal drugs are "right" or at least socially accepted to a large degree.

The humour of this film is vital. Without wit this movie would have been a bleak vision of drug culture and would have been hard to bear. The humour is entirely necessary as a way to disrupt the gloom whilst also adding depth to the characters who, despite being confronted with lives they clearly wish to escape, still manage to employ humour as a strategy by which to deal with some of the adversity they are faced with. One good example of humour in the face of undesired circumstances occurs early in the film when Renton is attempting to come off heroin on his own. He needs a last hit and visits a drug dealer called Mikey, played by Irvine Welsh, the author of the novel from which the film was adapted, who supplies Renton with opium suppositories. Unhappy with this "score", Renton places them up his anus while stating, 'For all the good they've done me I might as well have stuck them up my arse.'

One of the most memorable examples of humour arises through the character of Spud. He goes to a job interview high on some speed Renton has given him. He doesn't really want the job and must tread the fine line between obviously failing at the interview, thereby risking the withdrawal of his benefits, and actually getting the position. We see him seated before three interviewers and chuckle as he can't stop talking, stating such things as, 'I'm a bit of a perfectionist, actually. Yes, I am. See, for me it's got to be the best or it's nothing at all. Like, if things get a bit dodgy, I just cannot be bothered.'

Another memorable example of humour combines it with disgust. This is when Spud wakes to find that his bowels have emptied during his drunken stupor. He then goes into the kitchen where his girlfriend, Gail (Shirley Henderson), and her parents are having breakfast. After a tussle with Gail's mother over who is going to put the bed sheets in the washing machine, the family blissfully unaware of what is smeared on them, the contents are flung across the room, spattering the walls, the breakfast table and, most disgustingly of all, the family themselves. With grimaces on our faces, the audience can't help but laugh at the scene as the characters gag and the new speckling on the walls begins to dribble down towards the floor. The juxtaposition of the grotesque with the comical has the effect of accentuating both, making this a truly unforgettable scene.

Further notable humour arises from Sick Boy's philosophy of life, which is linked to Sean Connery's film career and is related to Renton while the two of them are coming off heroin and spending time in a park. This also ties into the theme of friendship which is apparent within the narrative.

A point of interest arises in relation to Jonny Lee Miller, who plays Sick Boy and was the only non-Scottish member of the main cast. Considering his character's interest in Sean Connery and James Bond it seems very apt that his father was the actor Bernard Lee, who used to play "M" in the Bond movies.

> What could be better than doing something that's challenging and break a few taboos? You don't get a chance to do that very often and it gives an actor a real kick to get people arguing and discussing the film.
>
> Jonny Lee Miller[3]

Before Renton temporarily moves to London we are shown friendships that share the common ground of drug taking, even to the extent of Begbie and alcohol. This is the bond that ties the friendships together. They drink together, take heroin together, try to quit together and rob and steal to fund their habit together. However, the friendships are ultimately seen to be ineffectual when it comes to quitting heroin. It is something only the individual can do. This is shown at the start of the film when Renton intends to stay barricaded in his flat while kicking the habit. Though his parents try to help him, this is an example of parental love rather than friendship.

The view of friendship is a negative one in the context of the film. Underlining this are Renton's words when he is sitting with friends and family after appearing in court and promising to give up heroin. He states, 'Here I was, surrounded by my family and my so-called mates and I've never felt so alone.' This is clearly not a positive view of his friendships and is one that gives us an insight into Renton's opinions as regards Sick Boy, Spud, Tommy and Begbie. He does not see the friendships as "real", as substantial and vital. This is further highlighted by his words after the big drug deal at the end of the film. 'And just for a moment it felt really great. Like we were all in it together, like friends, like it meant something.' The word of note here is "like". He obviously doesn't believe they are really friends, only the semblance of such. Maybe he realises that the friendships are predominantly based on drugs and what can be gained for each individual, Begbie and Sick Boy having used and abused his hospitality in London.

It can actually be stated that it is the friendships with Sick Boy, Spud and Swanney to a lesser degree that keep Renton addicted. Mixing with other addicts only leads to encouragement to continue, each one's addiction reinforcing the others'. This is also seen with quitting, as Renton and Sick Boy both do so at the same time.

We can see that the friendships lead to continuing addiction in the contrast that Renton's move to London provides in comparison with his life in Edinburgh. When he is removed from the circle of drug-taking friends, he manages to stay off heroin and hold down a "normal" job while also renting a flat. At this friendless time Renton states, 'For the first time in my adult life I was almost content.' Not only does this reflect on the shallowness of the drug-related friendships evident in the narrative, but it also reflects on the job he has taken.

This job is as an estate agent, something Renton clearly enjoys. Society's view of estate agents is generally a negative one, seeing them as driven by profit and willing to stretch the truth, sometimes so far it snaps. This degree of money-driven ruthlessness and amorality is almost a substitute for that of heroin addiction, where greed for profit is the equivalent of greed for the drug. The persona of a stereotypical estate agent is made clear in regards to Renton when he describes one of the houses for rent as, 'Ideally located in a quiet road near to the local shops and transport … In excellent decorative order.' This house is situated on an extremely busy road and he later calls it, 'The worst place in the world,' when he allows Begbie and Sick Boy to live in it so he can be free of them.

My writing acknowledges that drugs are now unremarkable ... As British society changed under the Thatcher 80s, drugs and drink became less recreational and more a way of life because people had fuck all else to do.

Irvine Welsh[4]

One of Boyle's common themes, referencing religion, may seem absent from *Trainspotting* at first glance. However, Tommy's funeral is clearly religious and the drug dealer named Swanney has the nickname "Mother Superior" due to the length of his heroin habit. The latter reference could be seen to relate to the need to escape everyday reality. The addicts portrayed in the film have replaced religion with heroin, the spirit of God with the rush of the high. It is heroin rather than God that gives them a crutch to lean on. However, Christianity is a means by which to cope with loneliness, hardship, adversity and the harsher aspects of life, whereas heroin is a means by which to escape, although temporarily, from all these things. As with socially accepted drugs, religion is the socially accepted way by which some find comfort and support to help them through life. Renton and his addicts have chosen a different route, one where the ability to cope is overshadowed by a wish to escape completely.

When Renton and Spud are caught stealing and appear in court we find a second religious reference. During a close-up shot, one emphasising the insincerity of Renton's words, he states, 'With God's help, I'll conquer this terrible affliction.' We know he doesn't view his addiction as a "terrible affliction" and we have not heard him talk about God or belief at any other point, so can presume he has no such belief and we also know he probably won't kick the habit.

It is also worth mentioning that Karl Marx said, 'Religion is the opiate of the masses.' This clearly underlines the idea that religion is used for similar reasons as drugs such as heroin; as a way to alleviate hardship, but also to subdue people. This latter point is important, for both religion and drugs such as heroin can, from a certain point of view, be seen as a way of making members of society docile in the face of injustice, whether real or perceived. Thus, the addicts and the believers share a docility. This lack of action is partially a result of the fact that both groups expect their "heavenly" reward to make up for wrongs done to them and social injustice, the addicts through the high and the believers through life after death.

There are two instances in the film when motherhood becomes an important theme. The first is through Renton's mother, from whom he steals both Valium and money, but who, with his father, tries to help her son despite his misdeeds. The second is Allison (Susan Vidler), whose baby is the focus of the most hard-hitting scene of the film.

Renton, Spud, Sick Boy and Swanney have their heroin-induced stupor interrupted by Allison's wailing. As they go through to an adjacent room to find out what has distressed her, the camera performs an intentionally slow reveal, one that ends in a haunting close-up of baby Dawn's lifeless face as she lies motionless in her cot. Heroin has not only drained the life from the addicts, it can also be seen to drain the lives of those around them and society at large. This is by far the most gruesome and hard image which supports such a point of view and, at the same time, shatters any opinion that the film glorifies heroin abuse.

The image is also used to haunt both us and Renton later in the film during one of Boyle's three trademark dream/vision sequences seen in the film, the others already having been mentioned. Renton is being forced to give up heroin by his parents and, locked in his claustrophobic bedroom, he crawls with images symbolising his conscience. We see baby Dawn reanimated and crawling along the ceiling. We see Tommy looking like the undead thanks to the addiction that Renton introduced him to. Begbie and Spud also appear in the parade of images that fill his fevered mind, the latter chained and dressed in prison uniform.

As with *Shallow Grave*, *Strumpet* and *28 Days Later*, this movie is somewhat open-ended. The largest narrative strand is left undone. We do not get to find out what life Renton leads after stealing the money or if he has managed to break the hold of his addiction for good. We are also left with only the suggestion that Begbie will be arrested and face a spell in prison, though, thanks to his violent nature, we cannot rule out an escape from the two police constables who arrive at the hotel room he is last seen smashing up. This not only leaves the audience with the impression of the story continuing after the end of the film, which befits the documentary style employed to a degree in this film, but it also allows us to imagine what happens next. By not neatly tying up all loose ends we are left to use our own imaginations or simply to wonder at what might happen to the characters.

The narrative also begins in such a way that we are immediately aware that the story has been occurring prior to the arrival of cameras.

The film starts as Renton is trying to end his heroin addiction and we are not shown how he first became addicted. Thus, the story stretches both beyond the opening and closing titles, as it does in *Shallow Grave*.

Cinematic Techniques

The film plays to a voyeurism evident in society, just as *Strumpet* would do later in Boyle's career thanks to the camerawork employed, which utilises angles similar to those seen in CCTV footage, such as from the upper corners of a room. This voyeurism goes beyond that of normal film releases and can be seen in the growth of reality television. We love to see other people's lives and the way people react when placed in an unusual situation. To the audience heroin addiction is exactly that; an unusual situation. The movie therefore connects with this fascination, something aided by the use of camera angles similar to the kind found in programmes such as *Big Brother*. However, *Trainspotting* was created prior to *Big Brother* and was a kind of fictional forerunner to much of the reality TV we can watch today. The fact that the movie is fictional reflects the "fictional" surroundings that contestants of such shows as *Big Brother* and *I'm a Celebrity ... Get Me Out of Here* find themselves in. They are not reality in truth, but are constructed, as is a movie.

The idea of *Trainspotting* connecting with social voyeurism is also highlighted by Renton's narration, which helps to add a certain documentary quality to the film, something that is aided by the shots of London when he moves there, the audience seeing such people as a Pearly King and Queen waving directly at the camera. This is unusual to feature films and is more commonly found in such things as documentaries and the home movies of tourists.

When Renton explains what he needs in order to attempt to kick his heroin habit it is said in such a way as to appear like an informative documentary on the life of an addict. Even his language is different from that which he uses in everyday speech. It becomes more officious and sterile, like a presenter of a serious television programme. He even introduces this segment of his narration by stating that this is, 'Stage one: Preparation.' His pattern of speech is more formal, an example being, 'Tomato soup, ten tins of. Mushroom soup, eight tins of.' All the above qualities give the impression of an autobiographical documentary. We are being afforded a glimpse into the life of an addict

51

and watching his behaviour, along with that of his friends. This is intriguing to an audience familiar with the idea of heroin use, but totally unfamiliar with the lifestyle of such "junkies".

As with *Shallow Grave*, Boyle uses a device by which to introduce the audience to the main characters at the start of the movie. In *Shallow Grave* it was a shot of a plaque bearing the characters' names next to the doorbell and the following snippets of interviews the three friends conduct in order to find a new housemate. In *Trainspotting* it is a still of each character, the action halted for a moment while each character's name is displayed non-diegetically beside them on screen. Renton is shown to be the primary character partially through his name being the first to be seen on screen. Additionally, the audience see him named in a different piece of footage from the others, one that we actually witness as part of the narrative forty minutes into the film. This singles him out further and we can easily identify him as the character whose life the narrative will follow. The other main characters – Sick Boy, Begbie, Spud and Tommy – are all shown and named during a five-a-side football match, again using still shots amidst the action. This is an effective way by which to introduce the characters because it identifies them and shows they are friends.

The *mise en scène* of the flat where we predominantly see Renton and the other addicts taking heroin is intentionally dismal. Some might say this is comparable with the slums seen in *Slumdog Millionaire*, but this is not the case. The slums of Mumbai are shown to be filled with life and vitality. In contrast, this flat is a place where the addicts go to escape life. There is little vitality, only drug-induced stupors. Paper hangs from the ceiling, the limited furniture is worn and weary and the only colour is provided by the walls and carpet. It is this colour, specifically in the main room where they take heroin, which is important. The colour of that room is red, something commonly associated with both temptation and danger. Both elements can be seen in relation to the users. There is the temptation, the addiction which keeps them wanting more of the drug's escapism. And there is the danger, not only of overdosing, but of catching diseases from the use of needles, the worst of which is AIDS.

It is also worth noting that Boyle introduces us to this flat with one of the first examples of a low camera angle to be seen in his films. The camera tracks along the floor and we see the diegetic writing on the wall stating "Welcome to Mother Superior's". This writing is only a short distance from the ground and so we can assume that it has been written for our sake as it is well below the eye level of any of the characters. Therefore it is a purposeful and informative inclusion for the benefit of the audience.

There is also another flat which is of importance in the film, and this is Tommy's. Boyle uses it as a vehicle by which to contrast normal life with that of an addict. When Tommy has a job, a girlfriend called Lizzy (Pauline Lynch), money and no addiction, his flat is colourful, bright and filled with material possessions. After his girlfriend has left him, thanks in part to Renton taking a home-made sex tape of Tommy and Lizzy without asking, he takes up the heroin habit, which is also due to Renton. The next time we see his flat the word "plague" has been painted upon the front door and the interior has been completely transformed by his addiction. The *mise en scène* reflects that of the flat in which Renton et al. tend to get high, but the degeneration is more apparent because of the contrast with the appearance of his flat earlier in the film, which is now grey and lifeless. Tommy has sold his possessions, presumably to fund his habit, and is left with only a mattress on the floor and a football, the latter reminding us of the fact Tommy is part of the group of friends that we saw playing five-a-side at the start of the film. His appearance, once healthy and well groomed, is now drawn, dishevelled and sickly.

The visual change between Tommy and his flat before and after he takes up heroin is a striking juxtaposition. It is a brutal contrast which highlights the life-sucking nature of the drug. It has drained the flat of possessions and colour. It has also drained Tommy himself. This visual depiction of heroin's effect on someone's life has a strong impact on viewers and further undermines any argument concerning glamorisation.

> The film is about a group of guys who don't want to belong to anything – nothing heroic or normal or faithful, because they've been disillusioned so many times.
>
> Danny Boyle[5]

Tommy is a useful tool by which we can see that the addicts probably suffered disappointment prior to the opening of the narrative. We see that it is a series of misfortunes which turn Tommy to heroin, that it is a means by which to escape. We can therefore assume that the other addicts have experienced their own misfortunes, ones which initially caused them to take up the syringe. This character therefore acts as an example of the reasons behind using heroin.

The use of heroin to escape even physical pain is shown at Tommy's funeral when Gav tells Renton about Tommy's demise. After saying his death was caused by toxoplasmosis, he goes on to state, 'He starts getting these headaches, so he just uses more smack, you know, for the pain.'

When Renton is told how Tommy died we see a number of shots of the kitten he'd bought for Lizzy in the hope of rekindling their relationship. She rejected the gift and the kitten is seen wandering round Tommy's degenerated flat. The last of these scenes has the most impact. Boyle chooses a low angle, the shot hovering just above the bare, dirty floor as the camera slowly pulls back from the kitten. It sits alone in the grey vacancy of the flat, looking small and helpless in the expanse that is revealed by the growing distance of the shot. Also revealed, as the camera comes to a halt, are Tommy's legs, the rest of his body lying beyond the camera's gaze. Thanks to the *mise en scène* and placement of the camera, kitten and body, this is a very effective piece of filming. It is a shot that symbolises loneliness and helplessness, reflecting the last throes of Tommy's life.

The kitten is used as a symbol of loneliness and vulnerability in the desolation of Tommy's flat.

Other especially noteworthy shots are used during Renton's withdrawal hallucinations. Boyle, increasing not only the impact of Renton's visions, but also his suffering, takes the camera in close, creating an increased sense of the walls closing in. This is added to by points-of-view shots, where the room seems to be stretching away, warping with the character's mind. We also see shots beneath the sheets which are almost suffocating because of the closeness and feeling of entrapment. All these combine to create a very effective scene that disturbs the audience, thereby echoing Renton's on-screen disturbance.

Equally effective is a shot used near the end of the film. Just after witnessing the most shocking violence in the film when Begbie rams a pint glass into a man's face, Boyle presents us with a close-up of Renton's expression with continuing activity at the bar only vaguely in the background and out of focus. In that single shot we see Renton's internal struggle as he sits deep in thought. We understand he is internally debating whether or not to take the money and run, to leave behind his old life and those he has, at least occasionally, seen as friends. It is a great piece of acting by McGregor, coupled with great directing on Boyle's part.

The soundtrack of *Trainspotting* keeps pace with the energy of the script and the directing. It adds to the overall pulse of the film and alludes to its style and content. Tunes such as Blondie's *Atomic* clearly reference the narrative content. In this case the word "atomic" brings forth ideas of power, of nuclear explosion, of immense energy condensed in an atom being let loose upon the world, which is a very apt way to view this celluloid explosion of music, camerawork, humour, life and death.

Another noteworthy tune is *Temptation* by Heaven 17. This song contains the lyrics "Lead us not into temptation". As well as its religious connotations, this can be seen to reflect the character's desire for sex, for this song plays in the first nightclub scenes of the film, a time when Renton is simply seeking a night of physical gratification. It is also the case that it is an under-age girl called Diane (Kelly MacDonald) whom he ends up going home with, the idea of being led into temptation here being linked to the girl leading the man, for Diane is the one who instigates not only the journey to her home, but also the ensuing sex. This is of special note as Boyle's next film *A Life Less Ordinary* would feature the idea of a woman leading a man astray as part of its plot line.

Of special note in relation to Heaven 17 and the club where we hear their hit song playing is their homage to another movie featuring a subcultural group of youths. The name of the band was taken from *A Clockwork Orange*, which mentions a fictional group called "The Heaven Seventeen". During the duration of their song in *Trainspotting*, we see Spud and Tommy talking in the seating area of the club and four phrases written on the walls in large, glowing blue letters. The phrases, such as "Voloko Damo" and "Voloko Geconal", were inspired by scenes of the Milk Bar in Kubrick's adaptation of Anthony Burgess' novel, which also had large phrases upon the walls, though these began with the work "Moloko".'

The music accompanying the narrative takes us from the 1980s into the 1990s, helping to give the audience a sense of progression and the time span involved. This is done non-diegetically and diegetically, the latter clear in the two visits to nightclubs that we see take place.

During the first, we hear the aforementioned eighties tunes of *Atomic* and *Temptation* and later we hear the emergence of dance music and Britpop through such artists as Leftfield, Elastica and Underworld. In fact, Blur's Damon Albarn wrote a song called *Closet Romantic* especially for *Trainspotting*. In relation to music, it is also interesting to note that Boyle creates a homage to the cover of The Beatles' album *Abbey Road* when Renton, Begbie, Sick Boy and Spud go to meet the London drug dealer.

> My pitch for *Trainspotting* was through films like *Alfie*, *A Clockwork Orange*, *Goodfellas* and the Beatles' films – that it was going to have a lot of energy and that would express both sides, the lows and highs of the story.
>
> Andrew MacDonald[6]

Boyle's use of a panning shot to reveal the body of baby Dawn is a clever way by which to increase audience tension and complements the poignancy of the event. The same kind of shot is also used after Tommy's funeral when Spud is singing *Two Little Boys* in the pub, again adding to the sense of sadness through the slow movement of the camera, something which echoes the slowed pace of the narrative.

Viewing the film in its entirety allows us to see that it echoes the life of an addict through its highs and lows, its sudden bursts of energy followed by moments of calm. The narrative pace complements its content and makes the viewing experience one which is related to the addicts' lives, giving the audience an insight into the existence of Renton et al. and thereby allowing greater identification with the characters.

Shots beneath the covers are used to increase the sense of claustrophobia as Renton suffers withdrawal symptoms.

From Book to Film

Irvine Welsh's novel gained cult status after it was first published and its popularity grew mainly through word of mouth in the Scottish illegal party scene. It was written partly as a reaction to the effect Margaret Thatcher's leadership had on Scotland. During her time as Prime Minister the country's unemployment rate rose dramatically, as did drug abuse. At one point the latter was so prevalent that Edinburgh was thought of as the AIDS capital of Europe. Because of these points the book was partly a comment on the state of Scotland thanks to the Conservative government that had caused so much strife.

The book was eventually produced as a play which was originally performed in Scotland, but went on to be staged in London's West End. The play also enjoyed a successful run in San Francisco, proving to be so popular that this had to be extended twice.

Out of Boyle, Hodge and MacDonald, it was the latter who read the book first. Seeing its potential, he then showed it to the director and writer while they were finishing *Shallow Grave*. Boyle thought the book was fantastic and was only too happy to direct.

The original novel did not consist of a single plotline and a clearly identifiable lead character, something which the play echoed. Instead, it was a series of short stories. Because of this, the creators of the film had to choose a character to use as central to the film's narrative and they felt that Renton had the strongest identification. Once he had been chosen, the film could then be constructed around his character, drawing on the book in order to create a story suitable for cinematic interpretation. What was of utmost importance was capturing the tone of the book, though the content was tamed to a degree.

The novel had been written in vernacular speech, something that is clear from the opening sentence, which reads, "The sweat wis lashing oafay Sick Boy; he wis trembling." It was immediately apparent that many audience members beyond Scotland would not be able to comprehend at least some of the dialogue if this were not watered down for the sake of a broader audience appeal.

Welsh had used surreal fantasies in his book and this idea transferred well onto the screen, producing one of the most memorable scenes of Renton vanishing into the toilet. The novel had also been written with a clear energy which was then transposed onto film with the help of an often high tempo, contemporary soundtrack featuring such artists as Pulp, Iggy Pop and Leftfield.

In keeping with the book's critique of the state of Scotland during and immediately after Thatcher's rule was the location of much of the filming. This was an old cigarette factory, one of many industrial sites which were crumbling and decaying all over the north of England and in Scotland at the time. The factory was located in Glasgow and was the perfect location for the production.

> Welsh has said that the film is like a remix of a record – it's just one interpretation. All the stuff we've left out – there's another five films in there.
>
> Andrew MacDonald[7]

Criticism

Some claim that the movie glamorises heroin use. This is clearly not the case when we consider the most stark example portrayed in the film; Tommy's descent from a "normal" life into addiction, AIDS infection, destitution and death. This, coupled with the result of Allison and Sick Boy's addiction and the death of their baby girl, makes it clear that there is no glamorisation of heroin in the film.

The *mise en scène* of Swanney's flat, along with the neighbourhood in which it is situated and the toilet where we see Renton desperately searching for his expelled suppositories, greatly aids in undermining any argument put forward that this film glamorises heroin or its use. These are clearly disgusting locations where life is sucked from the addicts, where heroin has brought about a ruinous existence. There is no glamour here.

The opinion of glamorisation is often mistakenly underpinned by Boyle's use of a contemporary and upbeat soundtrack. This soundtrack, rather than making heroin use seem trendy, contrasts with the drug-induced stupors we see the addicts in when high. At those times the music is considerably softer and this highlights the lethargy and lifelessness of heroin abuse.

Other commentators claim that the film glorifies heroin users themselves, making them seem cool. This, on closer inspection, can really only be said for the anti-hero, Renton, whose ready wit, intelligence and final escape with a large sum of money puts him in the position of being the only main character to remain unscathed by the traumas depicted in the film. Sick Boy and Allison lose their child, as mentioned. Spud, though left with a bundle of cash, has been to jail and at one point is seen lying in the gutter barely able to speak because of his intoxication (though by which drug is unclear). And Tommy dies alone in his flat.

Any perceived glamorisation of addicts lies solely with Renton. He, unlike the others, does not get punished for his transgressions other than in the scenes when he is being forced to quit his heroin habit. He also finds no redemption through his actions. Renton is like McGregor's character in *Shallow Grave*, Alex, in that both escape with the money at the end of the film. Renton escapes most of the consequences of his life as an addict and ends up with most of the money from the final drug deal at the film's end.

The representation of women is extremely limited in the movie, just as it is in *Shallow Grave*, though this changes with *A Life Less Ordinary* due to the introduction of a pivotal female lead. In *Shallow Grave*, though one of the three central characters is female, she is actually the most minor and least defined. In *Trainspotting* the women simply exist within the narrative for reasons of sex or motherhood. The former of these is clearly seen when Renton and his friends go to the nightclub called Volcano, which is a very apt name considering the explosion of sex and lust which is about to occur. At the club the conversation and motivation is all related to sex. All the scenes that follow immediately afterwards are also related to sex. Even the relationship between Tommy and Lizzy is predominantly based on sex, as stated by Lizzy while in the club.

In regards to the representation of women, it is also important to draw attention to the opening sequence of the film. As stated, this introduces us to the main characters very effectively, but all of them are male. No women are named and therefore we presume no women are important within the overall context of the narrative, which turns out to be the case.

Awards

Despite the criticism, the film won eighteen awards and John Hodge was even nominated for an Academy Award in the category of Best Writing, Screenplay Based on Material from Another Medium. Even though Hodge didn't win the Oscar, he did win the corresponding BAFTA for Best Screenplay – Adapted.

At the BAFTA Awards, Scotland, Ewan McGregor won Best Actor – Film and Boyle, Hodge and MacDonald received the Best Feature Film award. There was also a Brit Award for Best Soundtrack and four Empire Awards; these being for Ewan McGregor in the Best British Actor category, Ewan Bremner for Best Newcomer, Best British Film and one also went to Danny Boyle for Best British Director.

These awards not only increased the reputation of the creators of the film, but clearly acknowledged the great performance given by Ewan McGregor. The Brit also confirmed Boyle as an expert when it came to creating the soundtracks to his films, something he sees as being of vital importance.

Final Words

Trainspotting grabs hold of the audience right from the outset and propels us through an energetic and edgy narrative with the help of an often pulsating soundtrack. Danny Boyle created an atmospheric movie with a great sense of humour, juxtaposed with scenes of poignant desolation. With a high standard of acting from the predominantly Scottish cast, the film gave us memorable scenes able to cause both smiles and nightmares.

A voyeuristic insight into heroin addiction, *Trainspotting* also reflects wider society. The viewer can identify with the addicts because they are extreme versions of us all. They seek the high of a hit, whereas we seek the high of a new consumer item. Both highs are fleeting and create a lull before enough money can be attained for the next hit. In light of the movie, we can see that we are all addicts, but our drugs of choice differ.

[1] Nelmes, J. ed. An Introduction to Film Studies, p.373 (Routledge, 1999, UK)

[2] MacGregor, F. *Robert Carlyle Interview: He's made a name for himself playing troubled characters. It might not be glamorous, but it's the type of role he enjoys best* (The Scotsman, 4 December 2008, UK)

[3] Unknown – *MMKF Trainspotting interview* (http://www.jonnyleemiller.co.uk/trainspotting/trainspotting.html)

[4] Burns, A. *Train Conductor* (http://zakka.dk/euroscreenwriters/interviews/danny_boyle_515.htm)

[5] Burns, A. *Train Conductor* (http://zakka.dk/euroscreenwriters/interviews/danny_boyle_515.htm)

[6] LJS. *The Sprocket Trainspotting Interview* (http://www.bradcolbourne.com/iwsprocket.txt)

[7] LJS. *The Sprocket Trainspotting Interview* (http://www.bradcolbourne.com/iwsprocket.txt)

A Life Less Ordinary

You're cleaning the floor of a diner, but she is an intelligent, passionate, beautiful, rich woman. The issue of whether or not she's your type is not one you're likely to have to resolve in this world or, indeed, the next, since she will be going to some heaven for glamorous pussy and you will be cleaning the floor of a diner in hell.

Al, owner of Al's Bar

Though created by the team of Boyle, MacDonald and Hodge, and including Ewan McGregor as one of the stars, this film marked a complete departure from their previous collaborations. It is the last of Boyle's films to feature McGregor and its difference from *Shallow Grave* and *Trainspotting* is immediately apparent.

A Life Less Ordinary is a romantic comedy with elements of thriller, animation and even a quickstep of musical. It delights in playing with audience expectations when it comes to the plot device of kidnapping. It has a strong Christian basis, one of the elements underscoring this being the use of angels as characters. Though most of Boyle's films reference religion, this film does so in a much more obvious way than all the others bar *Millions*.

The film is so different to the director's previous two movies that it's almost as if Boyle, Hodge and MacDonald intentionally tried to distance it and go in a completely different direction. Because of their previous films, expectations of both critics and audiences alike were very high. Therefore, it may be that the makers wanted to clearly differentiate this film so as to distance it from their other work and allow it to stand independently to a degree.

One of the most obvious differences this movie displays is with respect to location. For the first time the filming did not take place in Scotland and the narrative was not set in mainly urban environments. Boyle used the backdrop of rural America, revelling in its wide, open spaces after having purposefully used cityscapes in order to accentuate feelings of entrapment in *Shallow Grave* and *Trainspotting*.

Another departure comes in the form of ex-model Cameron Diaz as one of the main characters. This was Boyle's first use of a recognised film star, something which immediately raised the profile of this film, something aided by the presence of Ian "Bilbo Baggins" Holm in the cast.

Basic Premise & Main Characters

Two angels are sent to earth to make a mismatched couple fall in love. The female of this couple is Celine, played by Diaz. She is a rich woman, who lives a life of luxury. She is cold and calculating; a strong woman who is used to having every whim catered for. Her father, Naville (Holm), runs a large company which, at the start of the film, replaces its human cleaners with robots. One of these cleaners is Robert, played by McGregor. He is sensitive and vulnerable, and when he confronts his ex-boss about his redundancy he ends up conducting the unplanned kidnapping of Celine.

Through a number of misadventures and the interference of the angels, the couple develop a bond and begin to have feelings for one another. However, they eventually part and it seems as though their destiny is not to be shared. Frustrated at their lack of success, the angels kidnap Celine. She is rescued by Robert and then rescues him right back when her father and his right-hand man have him at gunpoint, their love finally acknowledged and its power made clear in the final scenes.

Narrative Themes

The opening sequence of the film includes scenes in heaven's police department, which is headed by the angel Gabriel. He sends the two angels O'Reilly and Jackson to Earth in order to make Robert and Celine fall in love. It is when these members of the heavenly host are on Earth that Boyle and Hodge subvert our expectations as to normal angel behaviour. Rather than the depiction of a traditional, kind angel, like that seen in Frank Capra's classic *It's A Wonderful Life* (1946), we find depictions that have more in common with the angels seen in contemporary films like *Dogma* (Smith 1999). We see O'Reilly and Jackson firing guns, swearing and spending time in a crummy motel. All of these elements are unusual because angels are holy and therefore not usually associated with such things. They are also not associated with sexuality and flirtatiousness, but both of these things are clearly displayed by O'Reilly, who we even see enjoying a saucy romance novel (supposedly written by Jennifer Hodge, which is actually the name of John Hodge's wife).

After the scene in heaven the opening sequence continues and features a voice-over. Though this is a cinematic technique, Boyle uses it to introduce one of the narrative themes. Usually, the director identifies the main character when using an opening voice-over, so this is strikingly different, like the film itself. A comedian is talking about the biblical Adam and Eve, thus introducing a second religious reference at the start of the narrative, after we have already seen heaven's police department.

He talks about Eve being told not to eat the apple in the Garden of Eden, but doing so nonetheless. This implies that a woman will be central to the narrative, unlike in the director's previous films. This is corroborated when we see shots of Celine in her swimming pool when the title of the film is displayed on screen.

In that biblical story it is Eve that changes everything and drags man along for the ride, something we see early in the film in regards the main characters of Celine and Robert. It is her interference that causes not only her father to be shot by Robert, but also her own kidnap to take place, though ineptly carried out by Robert. She kicks Robert's handgun back to him as he struggles with security guards and this allows both events to occur. She also says, 'Fire!' when he is pointing the gun at her father, the shock causing him to shoot.

Taking the opening voice-over as a cue, it seems as if the first half of the narrative is a reworking of the Adam and Eve story. If we take Celine's father as a God figure, one who has created her and employed Robert as a cleaner, we can see that when the two of them are brought together in his company it is Celine who tempts Robert. The loaded gun she kicks to him is akin to the loaded instruction by God to Adam and Eve: 'You must not eat from the tree of knowledge' (Genesis 2:17). This instruction is enough to arouse virtually anyone's curiosity as to the apples on the tree and Eve succumbs, then tempting Adam. God is hurt and angered, and due to their actions they are removed from the Garden of Eden. In the film Celine (Eve) initially hurts her father with bullet-like words that relate to his marriage, these being, 'Her biggest problem was marrying a man like you. A mistake I've taken great care to avoid.' She then tempts Robert (Adam) to also hurt him, which he does under her influence when shooting him in the leg. Their actions have the effect of expelling them from everyday life, which may have been Eden for Celine, but had become more of a cesspit for Robert. They are then alone in the wilderness, just as Adam and Eve were after being expelled from Eden. It is there that the basis of their love is formed.

> The situations are dramatic and serious, and the people involved in the situations are very serious about what's happening. For me, comedy is about honesty. People laugh the hardest when you're being most honest.
>
> Cameron Diaz[1]

In order to make the concept of a rich woman and a poor man falling in love work on screen, Boyle and Hodge had to use a device by which to remove them from their everyday lives. Normally, such people would rarely meet and even rarer still would be the creation of a relationship between them. So writer and director take them out of their everyday lives and place them out in the middle of nowhere, utilising the rural landscape to highlight their separation from the rest of the world. Only in this environment, free of the trappings of wealth and relative poverty, can they make a connection on a human level,

66

their personalities more important than their possessions or social status. It could also be said that the rural environment reflects the ideological distance between the characters.

To enable Robert and Celine to make a connection another device is necessary, and this is the kidnapping. Through this the main characters can develop a version of the Stockholm syndrome, which is when those who are kidnapped develop an empathy with the kidnapper. In this case there is more scorn than empathy in the initial stages, but this then develops into love.

Celine is clearly the dominant character. This creates an unusual slant on the normal relationship between the kidnapper and their victim as the power is commonly associated with the former role. Here the victim has the power, partially due to Robert being polite and well meaning. This subverts the usual expectations of a kidnapping, playing with audience expectations and creating an original take on this well-used plot device.

Another subversion of expectation occurs early in the kidnapping, when Celine is sexually aggressive to a degree. This is not expected of the victim and neither is it expected of a female. Elements of sexual aggression are also evident in other Boyle films, such as *Strumpet* and *28 Days Later*, but in a very different context.

In *A Life Less Ordinary* this aggression occurs when Robert ties Celine to a chair. After she is supposedly secured in place she asks, 'Are you going to try and have sex with me?' Robert, who is shocked by the question, replies in the negative, but Celine pursues this line of enquiry with questions like, 'Isn't that what you brought me up here for?' and, 'Do you have a problem with sex?' She appears to be trying to coax him into having sex. A victim would not normally bring up this subject, for fear the kidnapper would consider it and possibly carry out such an act. Celine not only raises the subject, but taunts Robert, which is one tactic by which to motivate him to prove that he has no problem with sex. This provides the audience with a role reversal, as does Celine taking charge of the kidnapping to the extent of deciding what amount will be demanded for the ransom and helping Robert in making a suitably threatening call to her father to make the demand.

Robert is seen as a bit of a fool and very much a bumbling idiot by Celine in the initial stages of the film. All through his apparent kidnapping it is Celine who has to metaphorically hold his hand and guide him, something that ties in with the idea of Eve tempting Adam to eat the apple. Cementing this is the fact that Celine brings attention to the importance of making a ransom demand. She tempts him with money after having tempted him to continue the confrontation in her father's office by kicking the gun back to him.

Her view of him alters as the film goes on and Celine eventually views him in a completely different light. She sees his childish innocence, his kindness and his gentle nature. Once these have been observed her opinion begins to change. Rather than viewing him as weak and her as strong, she sees that they create a balance and discovers that he reaches out to a part of her which yearns to be understood and treated not as a prize or trophy, but as a person. Therefore, the hard-nosed Eve is ultimately saved by the much more sensitive Adam.

Though the woman is ultimately guilty of tempting the man, it leads to the formation of love. This implies that love could not have existed in the Garden of Eden and this much is true. Adam and Eve were companions, not lovers (though they are often portrayed as such in visual depictions). They had an innocent existence where sex would have only been conducted in order to produce offspring. Love involves the addition of emotion, sensuality and physicality, none of which were part of Adam and Eve's innocence in Eden. It could be said that if it were not for Eve eating the apple there would be no concept of love in humanity, simply the mating urge to continue our species. Therefore, this film's Adam and Eve, Robert and Celine, must be removed from Eden in order to find the love that the angels have been sent to induce.

As mentioned earlier in this chapter, the film employs mainly rural landscapes as the backdrop for the action. In Boyle's previous film the urban cityscapes had a definite presence, acted as part of the prison the characters found themselves in thanks to addiction. Here, the wide-open spaces almost have a lack of presence, creating a feeling of emptiness. This reflects the emptiness of both of the main characters' lives when it comes to companionship and love. It could also be partially responsible for their bond, for in such isolation human company is vital for most people to feel secure.

As with four other films by Boyle, we see a large sum of money playing a part in the narrative. In *A Life Less Ordinary*, it is a minor element when compared to the relationship between Robert and

Celine, as the money being won on *Who Wants to be a Millionaire* in *Slumdog Millionaire* is secondary to Jamal and Latika's relationship.

This said, the ransom leads to evidence that Celine cares for Robert more than she wants to admit. We see his life apparently in danger as Jackson makes him dig his own grave. Celine, rather than choosing to go back to her pampered and easy life, chooses to possibly risk hers in order to save him. This incident helps both the audience and Celine to realise the depth of connection she has with Robert.

The film's theme of love being more important than money is highlighted by Celine's choice in this scene. This theme creates a common link with *Slumdog Millionaire* and further distances *A Life Less Ordinary* from either of Boyle's previous films. In the director's first two big-screen movies we saw that the characters chose money above friendship, reflecting the continuing influence of the selfishness and greed evident in the 1980s.

The point where Celine realises she cares for Robert, his life apparently at risk as Jackson points the gun at him and Celine risking hers to save him.

There is actually a second bag of money within the narrative that reinforces the themes of connecting with others and of love. This is a brown paper bag filled with the spoils of a robbery Celine commits at a bank, Robert essentially an onlooker. When the couple are in the parking lot after the robbery Robert has a vision, which is the second in the film, the first to be discussed in Cinematic Techniques. In this vision he sees Celine with a gunshot wound on the back seat of their stolen car. Because of this sight he moves in front of her when the bank's security guard opens fire on them and takes the bullet himself. This shows his protective and caring nature and the strength of the feelings he has for her. He is prepared to endure pain and possibly give up his own life for Celine in one of the only scenes in the film that displays real risk in relation to the characters.

During the scenes of the bank robbery there is a reinforcement of character definition. Celine is prepared to use a child in order to successfully rob the bank, pointing the gun at the daughter of a customer. Robert's reaction is one of shocked disgust and this highlights the differences in their characters. Celine will do whatever it takes to get what she wants, whereas Robert will take others into consideration over and above his own needs, something shown shortly afterwards when he takes the aforementioned bullet.

> What was always in the script was that he was always weak, while she was always strong. What happened as we started to shoot was that he became very feminine, while SHE became very masculine, and in the process he became very, very sensitive and would be deeply hurt by things she said. There was SO much for me to play there that I just fucking loved it.
>
> Ewan McGregor[2]

Tod Johnson, who lives just along the valley from the house that Robert and Celine use as a hideout, creates another of the many religious references within the movie. He states that he watches "mainly Biblical channels". This Christian background is reflected in his desire to know if they are good or evil. This black-and-white view of the world is common to many of religious faith because this dichotomy of good and evil is clearly presented in the Bible through such concepts as heaven and hell and God and the Devil. However, it is a view that ignores shades of grey and alternative perspectives. This is underlined by *Trainspotting*. The actions of the addicts can be seen as evil, but they are fuelled by drugs and addiction, so it is not an inherent evil on the part of the characters. It can also be seen in *Strumpet*, where two of the main characters commit theft, but we can see they are predominantly good people.

Tod and his friend Felix serve as examples of Boyle's use of abnormal psychology, most plainly seen in relation to those infected with the rage virus in *28 Days Later* and in the character of Pinbacker in

Sunshine. Both Tod (Maury Chaykin) and Felix (David Stifel) are veterans, the former a little slow and also unusual in appearance.

Tod's abnormality is highlighted by his angry tirade at the suggestion made by Robert that he'd talk to a dog. During this minor outburst Tod states, 'What do you think I am, some kind of crazy, backwoods lunatic with a barn full of human skulls and a sharpened scythe ready for Armageddon?' This sentence not only underlines his abnormality due to the strange imagery he conjures so readily from his mind, but it also creates additional religious referencing within the film.

Felix thinks he's a dog, barking and howling when Robert is introduced to the locals at the bar, before getting up to perform karaoke under the guise of pop sensation Ritchie Vanderlow, which is a persona Celine created as a cover for their presence in the rural house. The barking, unkempt Felix is like a premonition of Strayman, one of the main characters in *Strumpet*. Strayman has a pack of stray dogs and barks and growls at people on a number of occasions during the narrative of this BBC film.

In the local bar, we see Robert and Celine preparing to play a drinking game, Celine stating, 'Indulge me, Robert,' when he shows a reticence to join in. He replies, 'If that's what you want,' to which she responds, 'It's all I ever want.' This highlights her spoilt and selfish persona. All she wants is for her whims and desires to be indulged by those around her.

After the song-and-dance routine we witness in the local bar, we see a snippet of a dream Robert has been repeatedly having, one that features Celine. He says that the dream centres around a game show called *Perfect Love* and, 'The theme is universal,' clearly meaning the theme of love. This is evidently thematically relevant to the film. We also discover that in the dream Celine saves his life by piercing his heart with the arrow of her love and a version of this eventually occurs within the narrative.

The interference of the angels continues after the first kidnapping plotline has come to an end. Jackson writes a love letter to Celine which is supposedly from Robert, the two of them having parted company and the latter now a cleaner in a diner called Al's Bar (Al played by Tony Shalhoub). After Celine has visited and discovered to her distress that Robert didn't write the letter, she is kidnapped by the angels, who then hold her hostage at a warehouse.

Robert tracks her down and attempts a rescue. While he is doing so, Celine's father arrives with his right-hand man, Mayhew. Both of the angels are shot and then her father takes them both back to the shack in the country where they had been hiding because he wants the ransom money he paid to be returned.

Robert clearly doesn't know where it is. Celine is locked in the boot of her father's car. Mayhew is on the verge of killing Robert because his use has expired. Amidst this Earthly activity we see Gabriel make a call to God, asking Him to intervene in the situation, the Almighty eventually agreeing to do so. Though we never hear Him speak, we do hear Gabriel's responses and so understand what is being said.

Tod and Felix free Celine from the trunk and give her a gun, providing us with a Tarantino-esque shot from within the trunk from Celine's point of view. The two veterans can be seen as the tools of God. They are the way by which He interferes, though quite how they knew where she was or that she needed a gun is never clarified.

Celine goes into the shack and shoots Robert through the heart. The bullet passes straight through him instead of exploding and ends up wounding Mayhew, who is standing behind Robert. Robert's wound heals miraculously in bright light, which is representative of the light of love.

It is in these last scenes that we firstly see that Celine has a soft core, one which has yearned to be appreciated, but which has been neglected because of her wealth and the kinds of men this has attracted. We also see the angels adding to the subversion of their depiction by carrying out a kidnapping.

In the finale we find that love is all conquering. The love that Celine has for Robert heals his otherwise fatal wound, has become the elixir of life. This underlines the importance of love above all else, giving the film a message that is anti-greed and inclined towards a romantic and predestined view of true love.

Cinematic Techniques

Boyle uses an underwater shot at the start of the film, when we see Celine swimming in her pool. The medium of water adds an extra dimension to the shot as the sunlight catches on the ripples about her. This angle, coupled with the others used during this sequence and the *mise en scène*, effectively informs the audience of the kind of life Celine lives. The pool and its surroundings reek of money and Boyle makes sure the scene is bathed in golden sunlight to reflect this idea of wealth.

The use of a butler and her whim to shoot an apple from his head reinforces our impression of a rich woman who can indulge in any activities she wishes.

One activity in which Robert is engaged is that of writing a novel. Boyle introduces this characterisation very effectively in a scene set in a poky storeroom, one which contrasts with Naville's huge office seen a little later in the movie. The reaction of Robert's co-workers to the idea behind his novel is to describe it as both obvious and trashy. This ties in with the romance novel that we see Celine, Robert and O'Reilly reading further into the film. Both novels are for mass consumption and follow formulaic lines. The difference between the film we are viewing and the novels cannot escape notice. Boyle, with the inclusion of these novels, highlights how different *A Life Less Ordinary* is from run-of-the-mill romances. He seems to be saying that many mass-market plot lines are obvious and predictable, but this film is neither, so prepare yourselves for a wild ride.

The surprising song-and-dance routine which is one of the elements that makes this film stand out from run-of-the-mill romances.

We are given a prime example of Boyle's quick-fire use of varying angles and shot heights as Robert heads towards Naville's office. There is a shot of him walking along a road outside the high-rise which is taken at a sideways slant, and there is a low camera placement as he goes to the lifts which is followed by an overhead shot from the elevator's roof. All are intercut with shots of the interior of Naville's office and the effect is not only to hold our interest through the use of unusual angles, but also to heighten narrative tension, something aided by the increase in soundtrack pace. However, the use of such distinctive angle changes diminishes once the narrative moves into a rural location.

During and after this transition from urban to rural settings we are provided with numerous shots through car windscreens. One of these is of particular interest because it not only provides us with a shot through glass, but also a shot through water. This occurs soon after Robert has kidnapped Celine. They pull into a filling station and we watch their conversation through the windscreen, which is spattered with the remains of bugs, not only giving us slight distortion, but also a sense of realism. Then the station's attendant cleans the glass. He puts water on it and then we see the wiper move across the scene, both elements adding interest to the shot.

One of the most humorous scenes of the film is when Celine coaches Robert in the art of making a threatening ransom call to her father. Much of this scene is shot through the glass of the phone box that is being used to place the call, therefore providing the film with one of Boyle's trademark shots. The use of a phone box also gives the impression that Robert is trapped in the kidnapping scenario. The symbolism of Celine standing in the doorway and thereby blocking his exit is clear. It is Celine who is not allowing Robert to escape the situation he finds himself in, who is encouraging and coaxing him to continue.

During the first attempt at getting the ransom money, Robert opens the boot of a car to find a bomb inside. Here we are given a shot looking up at the character from inside the trunk, something which echoes one of Quentin Tarantino's trademark shots and may well be a nod to the American director. This is especially the case because Boyle was compared to the director of *Reservoir Dogs* (1992) and *Pulp Fiction* (1994) after his first two movies. This comparison was a favourable one, their creative visions and energy being highly praised.

At the local bar we find the longest dream/vision sequence that is evident in this film. Boyle creates a song and dance routine with Robert and Celine. We can also see the use of song and dance in *Vacuuming Completely Nude in Paradise* and *Strumpet*, though in both cases it is in much grittier and more realistic circumstances.

Like the use of dreams and visions in his other films, the director uses it to highlight or underscore a narrative theme. It cements the idea that the two characters are becoming closer, are developing a relationship.

We see the couple dancing while performing the karaoke version of *Beyond the Sea*. The fact that this is karaoke creates an additional link with *Strumpet*, which also features karaoke performances (and is also about two people finding a connection). A spotlight suddenly begins to shine on Robert and Celine, singling them out as they show an obvious rapport, Boyle drawing our attention to this so that their growing connection is not lost on the audience. The scene has a happy tone, implying they are happy together.

> I love dancing and I've always enjoyed singing, and here I do both with one of the best [Diaz]. To me, it kind of replaced the love scene in it, and was a refreshing thing to do in the middle of a shoot.
>
> Ewan McGregor[3]

Boyle uses a number of unusual shots in the film. These include one from inside Robert's mouth and another from inside a postbox. There is also one of his familiar shots through glass. This is quite striking because there are no other similar shots in the entire film. It occurs when Celine and Robert are at the rural house. We are presented with a shot of Robert, the camera's gaze peering in through a window. The inner frame of this window effectively divides the screen into four, giving it a multi-screen effect, each section displaying a portion of Robert's head.

An unusual shot used by Boyle, the camera appearing to peer out from Robert's mouth.

75

We also witness an unusual shot when the ransom exchange finally takes place. The audience see Robert dragging the bag of money along the road from a high camera angle that looks directly down on the scene, which is both unexpected and unusual. There soon follows a number of other overhead shots as Richard and Celine attempt to escape from the angels.

Soon after the shot of the money being dragged along the road we are treated to a scene that brings to mind scenes from both *Shallow Grave* and *Trainspotting*. Robert is being forced to dig his own grave by Jackson and this is reminiscent of the graves that had to be dug in Boyle's first film. However, there is a marked difference in that this grave is being dug in full daylight and under the direct duress of a loaded gun. Robert is then shown lying in this grave, which reminds us of Renton slipping into a grave-like hole while under the influence of heroin. In *A Life Less Ordinary* McGregor's character is facing downwards, whereas he was facing upwards in *Trainspotting*.

In this single scene it seems that Boyle is highlighting the fact that the tone of this film is the opposite of that seen in his previous two movies. When linking it with the similar scenes from his previous films we find that there is a clear use of opposites, that of darkness and daylight, looking upwards and looking downwards.

This film is clearly a stark contrast to *Shallow Grave* and *Trainspotting*. This is thanks to such things as the rural environment rather than urban, predominant brightness rather than gloom and the importance of friendship and love over that of money. All of these are also reflected in this simple grave-digging scene, which is rurally set, bright and involves Celine theoretically risking her life to save Robert despite the fact she could have left him to his fate and gone back to a life of wealth and luxury. In this one scene we are shown quite clearly that *A Life Less Ordinary* is a complete change of content and emphasis from Boyle's previous big-screen outings.

The theme of love had not been touched upon in Boyle's previous work other than in a brief mention by Spud near the end of *Trainspotting* and through the actions of Renton's parents. The director underlines this love theme with some clever shots during the narrative. The first relates to Celine shooting the apple that is balanced atop her butler's head at the film's start. The apple is purposefully red because it represents the human heart in a romantic sense. In this scene the bullet does not merely pass through, but to bring his point home, Boyle has the apple exploding in a sudden burst of fruity destruction. This simple shot underscores Celine's apparent heartlessness and the fact that she has no desire to find love, believing true love is a myth. She is cold and calculating, only using people for her own ends. It is also important to mention that this use of an apple ties neatly into the Adam and Eve theme.

The fact that this apple is symbolic of an exploding heart is confirmed shortly afterwards. Boyle uses a brief cutaway shot to show a heart exploding as it is hit by a bullet.

At the end of the film Boyle uses a technique only seen again in *Slumdog Millionaire*, further tying the two films together in a relationship of similar narrative themes. The director uses a montage of images from the film, highlighting some of the most memorable moments and giving the audience a sense of how the relationship between Robert and Celine grew.

Coupled with this montage, Boyle has the two characters sitting side by side and facing the audience despite the fact they are apparently talking to each other. The montage plays behind them as they speak about love, Robert depicted as the character in authority and Celine as the character who is seeking answers to questions about true love. This is an effective way of giving the film a spoken message at the end, one that reinforces the message of the narrative entire. By having the characters facing the audience Boyle makes their words have more impact upon us because we are being addressed directly.

After the couple have finished speaking they get up and we find they have been sitting in Al's Bar. Boyle then uses a knife spinning above the words "The End" and "The Beginning", its blade first stopping on the former and then on the latter. This not only brings a degree of closure to the narrative, but hints at the continuation of the story beyond this point.

This idea of the story continuing is then shown during the closing titles. We see Gabriel unzipping two body bags and O'Reilly and Jackson emerging (taking deep breaths despite the fact they are angels and therefore don't need to breathe air). What follows is a comedic stop-motion animation sequence showing Celine and Robert in an original VW Beetle after having got married. They go to Scotland and buy a castle, the other main characters of the movie seen in various guises along the way. The use of such animation cannot be seen in any other

Boyle film bar *Millions*, which features only tiny segments in relation to graphics showing the construction of Damian and Anthony's new home.

Criticism

Due to the overtly Christian basis of the storyline, which includes heaven, angels and the Adam and Eve story, this film could alienate those of different faiths or no faith at all. Though this is ultimately a piece of cinematic entertainment and not a sermon, it may be off-putting to some to be confronted with such a predominance of Christian references and themes.

This predominance could have easily been avoided, and in turn any chance of alienating or discouraging potential audience members. This could have been achieved by removing the narrative strand involving the angels O'Reilly and Jackson. Their plot line of being sent to Earth to make Robert and Celine fall in love is ultimately unnecessary. The events could have still been contrived to take place without their influence and this would not only have lessened the Christian theme to a great degree, but it would also have removed some of the complexity of the film's narrative.

Furthermore, the removal of this strand would have increased a sense of risk in relation to Robert and Celine, thereby raising narrative tension. By using angels, who the audience know will not kill either of the main characters, no risk and little tension is introduced. An example is the scene when Robert is digging his own grave. There is an element of humour involved in watching his fear while in full knowledge that Jackson will not shoot him, but there is no dramatic tension to make the audience really care about what is happening because we know Robert will survive. Simply by making O'Reilly and Jackson genuine bounty hunters the context of such scenes and the referencing of the Christian faith would have been greatly changed.

It is also the case that no real reason is given for the angels having to make this particular mismatched pair fall in love. By removing the angels, no reason is needed and so this narrative flaw is also removed.

There are also plot criticisms that arise towards the end of the film. The first is concerned with the second kidnapping plot line. No explanation is given for how Robert, and then Celine's father and Mayhew, manage to track the angels down to the warehouse. They simply turn up with no evidence of having searched or discovered evidence of O'Reilly and Jackson's hideout.

The end of the film, when the couple sit facing the camera and talk about true love, is akin to preaching the message of the film to the audience. As with the use of voice-over in *Trainspotting*, Boyle breaks the rule of "show don't tell". However, unlike in his previous film, maybe he should have taken note of this rule in regards *A Life Less Ordinary*. Most of the elements of this final segment of the dialogue have already been shown to us in the narrative and this speech is extraneous. Because of this, it also seems overly forceful when it comes to the film trying to get its message across. It is therefore likely that the narrative would have been better served by ending shortly after the miraculous healing, possibly simply with the couple embracing and declaring their love.

It is also the case that when the characters address the audience at the end of the movie their personalities seem to have changed. Throughout the film, Celine has been the strong one guided by a certainty of purpose, whereas Robert was the weak and uncertain character. This is turned on its head at the end. However, this may be because the emotional experience of love is far more familiar to Robert than it is to Celine. She is exploring it for the first time and so displays a degree of uncertainty.

Awards

The film was only nominated for three awards, none of which were for the film or its direction. The single honour actually won was an Empire Award, which went to Ewan McGregor for Best British Actor despite what many critics saw as a tepid performance.

Final Words

The film plays with thematic expectations as much as those regarding technique. We see the subversion of usual kidnapping scenarios and love stories. The gender roles are reversed, with the woman more hard-nosed and cynical and the man more sensitive and emotional. There is also the subversion of usual angelic depictions, something also seen in regards to Damian's visions in *Millions*.

In relation to techniques, we find a sudden song and dance routine interrupting our expectations, the scene coming out of the blue in a delightfully entertaining way. We see apples and hearts explode, along with Boyle's common underwater and window shots, and even a closing animation.

With an overview it is clear to see that this is a Danny Boyle film. It toys with the audience and displays many of the director's trademarks. Though not as gripping or as powerful as many of his movies, his fingerprint still makes *A Life Less Ordinary* a standout movie.

[1] Fischer, P. *Diaz, Cameron: A Life Less Ordinary*
(http://www.urbancinefile.com.au/home/view.asp?a=594&s=interviews)

[2] Fischer, P. *McGregor, Ewan: A Life Less Ordinary*
(http://www.urbancinefile.com.au/home/view.asp?a=593&s=Interviews)

[3] Fischer, P. *McGregor, Ewan: A Life Less Ordinary*
(http://www.urbancinefile.com.au/home/view.asp?a=593&s=Interviews)

The Beach

I think the first half is a pleasurable, sensual exploration of what
we all crave – paradise. The second half explores the moral
contradictions and complexities that surround it. So I hope
people will find the film both pleasurable and challenging.

Danny Boyle[1]

Following in the footprints left in the sand by *A Life Less Ordinary*, this
film was shot on location outside the UK. It predominantly featured a
rural environment in Thailand, the beach that gives the film its title
being located on an island called Ko Phi Phi Leh. Costing $50 million,
it was the biggest budget the director has ever had for one of his movies.

This finance was from Twentieth Century Fox, who had backed Boyle's
previous film and allowed him a great amount of directorial freedom. This
said, they did express concerns about elements of the movie, wanting the
narrative strand relating to the main character's love interest to continue
throughout the film and also voicing worries about the fact that he
watches while four people are shot without trying to help them. Their

largest concern was the fact that the main character lies on a number of occasions, purely in the name of self-interest. They didn't like this idea, especially when connected with the title character. All these concerns were argued against and Boyle got to make the film as he envisioned it.

As with his previous film, *The Beach* features a Hollywood star, one who was paid $20 million for the role. Leonardo DiCaprio had started out as a serious actor, starring in the films *What's Eating Gilbert Grape* (Hallstrom 1993) and *Romeo & Juliet* (Luhrmann 1996). He was then elevated to stardom by his leading role in the blockbuster movie *Titanic* (Cameron 1997). This role led to a view that he was a romance actor. A heart-throb pin-up for millions of teenage girls, he seemed like an odd choice for a movie with a masculine sensibility and psychological darkness. Unlike many commentators in the media, Boyle didn't allow DiCaprio's previous roles to affect his choice of casting, but actually saw it as an opportunity to toy with the actor's image, something which was also the case when Tim Burton first cast Johnny Depp as Edward Scissorhands (1990). As it turned out, DiCaprio revelled in the experience of working with the director, enjoying the chance to give input as to his character's dialogue and actions.

The casting of DiCaprio in the lead role had the effect of ending Boyle's working relationship with Ewan McGregor and the two of them would not work together again. Boyle had met with McGregor, who had expected to get the part, and told him that the main character was going to be American. This irked McGregor, who took the news as a rejection, though this wasn't truly the case. Since that time, Boyle has repeatedly praised the Scottish actor in the press, but McGregor still doesn't have contact with the director. Lesser known is the fact the cinematographer Brian Tufano was also upset by not being used on the film after having worked with Boyle on all three previous movies.

This would be the last feature-length production by the team of Boyle, Hodge and MacDonald. Though MacDonald would go on to produce two more Danny Boyle movies, Hodge only teamed up with the director again on the short film *Alien Love Triangle* (2002), as discussed in the first chapter.

The international cast was given a Scottish connection by the presence of Robert Carlyle, who played the deranged "Daffy", a founder member of *The Beach* community. This was quite a suitable role after having portrayed the psychotic Begbie in *Trainspotting*, starring alongside the aforementioned McGregor.

The cast spent time in Thailand prior to filming, this being Boyle's way of preparing them for their performances, giving the actors time to adjust to the situation their characters found themselves in. During this time a personal trainer was hired in order to give them the lean look required of people living in such an isolated community. Boyle and Hodge used a number of films as reference points for the feel of the film, especially the latter half. These were *Deliverance* (Boorman 1972), *Apocalypse Now* (Coppola 1979) and *Lord of the Flies,* all of which descend into an atmospheric darkness.

Some have said *The Beach* has echoes of *Lord of the Flies,* which was originally a novel by William Golding that was turned into a movie in 1963 by director Peter Brook. However, this isn't true. In Golding's novel the children arrive on a secluded island by accident, whereas in *The Beach* their presence is entirely purposeful. The children also descend into violence and barbarity with little social order, which is not seen in this film. The only similarity lies in the darkness that leeches into the story, allowing us to look into the human psyche.

The set on the island of Ko Phi Phi Leh was a closed one. However, the urban locations used numerous extras and this caused a number of problems which had to be clamped down on during the production. Excessive drinking and even theft occurred on set. At one point a group of real rave-scene travellers were brought over from Ko Pha-Ngan. Many were high on drugs and there were problems because they all wanted to dance close to the camera so they would be noticed in the scene.

Released in 2000, many people saw the film as a flop, but this actually wasn't the case. Not only did it take $39.8 million at the US box office – which is considerable compared with *Trainspotting*'s $16.5 million and *A Life Less Ordinary*'s relatively paltry $4.27 million – but it was the eighth highest grossing film in the UK in the year of its release, beating films such as *The Green Mile* (Darabont 1999) and *Scary Movie* (Wayans 2000), both of which were seen as successful.

Basic Premise and Main Characters

Richard is a "rough guide" type of traveller looking for something more beautiful, more exciting. The young twenty-something American arrives on Thailand's Khao San Road only to find it catering for the hordes of tourists and backpackers in evidence, altering the nature of the location simply by their presence.

Then he is given a map to a secluded and secret beach, one where a select community of travellers live and which is relatively unspoilt by tourism. Along with French couple Françoise and Etienne, he makes his way to the island, finding not only the beach community, but also cannabis growers upon the island.

Richard has foolishly given a map to a pair of fellow Americans and when they turn up on a nearby island intent on making the crossing in order to find the beach nothing good can come of it. A shark attack, mental imbalance, murder and the final disintegration of the community all turn the second half of the narrative into a journey into an *Apocalypse Now* styled *Heart of Darkness*.

Richard is played by the aforementioned Leonardo DiCaprio, whose mother Irmelin also makes an uncredited appearance as a woman in one of the bars. Playing Françoise and Etienne are Virginie Ledoyen and Guillaume Canet. The leader of the beach community is the dictatorial and cold Sal. Played by Tilda Swinton, her coldness would continue when she starred as the White Witch in *The Chronicles of Narnia: The Lion, the Witch and the Wardrobe* (Adamson 2005).

> Nothing was really that hard about *The Beach*. It was one of those really collaborative experiences with a director.
>
> Leonardo DiCaprio[2]

Narrative Themes

There are two examples of abnormal psychology evident in *The Beach*, this theme common to all but one of Boyle's movies, that being *Slumdog Millionaire*. The first example is seen early in the film and is concerned with the character of Daffy. His lack of mental stability is made very apparent by his bloody suicide. He forces his presence on Richard, who notes the Scotsman's mania with the amusing comment, 'No offence and all, but you're fucked in the head, right?'

The abnormal also arises later in the film in relation to Richard. He ends up living in the wilds of the island and during this time sees himself as taking part in a computer game, which provides us with a vision sequence. His mental state is affected by the guilt of giving out a map to the beach and by his loneliness in the jungle, where he shares some of his domain with the cannabis farmers who also inhabit the island.

Richard's abnormal psychology is directly connected with Daffy. He has dreams and visions of the Scotsman. In one sequence we see Daffy's bloodstained body. The character suddenly comes to life, Boyle using a sudden and loud sound to accompany the images and thus increase the shock value of the scene. The two of them fire guns out of the window of Daffy's room, shooting at the "parasites". This is Daffy's term for the throngs of young travellers perceived as desecrating the places to which they flock, indulging in such things as binge drinking, rave parties and general loutishness, exporting their brand of youth culture all around the world and having a detrimental effect.

Later in the film the dreams of Daffy become waking visions. Richard conjures these during his time spent alone in the jungle, Daffy becoming his companion during these hard times, one who encourages the insular, paranoid state which darkens Richard's mind.

The beach itself is essentially an escape from the reality of normal life, and in this sense bears a similarity with the heroin abuse witnessed in *Trainspotting*. Life at the beach and the injection of the drug are both forms of escapism indulged in by people on the fringe of society.

Like all communities, the one at the beach has it rituals. The most notable of these is the marking of the new arrivals. They have to burn three marks into each other's upper left arms using a hot blade. This is a mark of identification and, very importantly, of belonging. It is a small and exclusive community and each is a part of its valued seclusion from the rest of world. It is also of note that this marking is an act of mutilation, but one not occurring under duress, unlike the blinding of Arvind in *Slumdog Millionaire*.

The idyllic community before paradise is tainted.

We find three distinct religious references in *The Beach*, two of which are evident in relation to the shark attack plotline. The first is Sten's funeral, where Keaty states, 'May God take your soul.' The second is Christo's name coupled with his suffering. Christo is a derivative of Christ, who is said to have suffered for our sins and eventually gave His life. Christo also suffers due to the sins of the other community members, who do not let him go to the mainland to get proper medical care and try to ignore his suffering by placing him in the jungle, effectively allowing him to die an agonising death for the sake of their peace and the ability to sustain paradise, for paradise does not allow suffering or pain to intrude. Like the good samaritan who offered to carry Christ's cross, Etienne is disgusted by what the others do to Christo and makes it his duty to relieve some of the pain and care for him.

The first religious reference to appear in the film occurs when Richard's narration introduces us to Keaty (Paterson Joseph), a British member of the community, who has already been seen greeting the new arrivals. We see him standing on the white sands stating, 'We thank you, Lord, for the twin pillars of civilisation; Christianity and cricket.' Keaty's statement and his love of cricket lead to one of the elements of humour in the narrative. We see members of the community playing the game and Keaty asks, 'Is there anyone who does not understand?' in reference to the rules of the game. In response, all of those gathered on the beach raise their hands.

Further humour arises in relation to the chef, nicknamed Unhygenix due to his obsession with soap thanks to his skin being permeated with the smell of fish after cooking it every day. His name is humorous and links to the tales of Asterix. Also, his desperate wish to be rid of the fishy odour is amusing, something played upon when Richard buys him some large rubber gloves in order that he can protect himself from the stench.

Other notable elements of humour include the "Kentucky fried mouse" conversation Richard has with his fellow Americans Zeph and Sammy. The scene when members of the community are approaching Richard with their requests for items to be purchased when he visits the mainland with Sal is also humorous due to some of the requests made, such as Keaty asking for a copy of the UK daily newspaper, *The Telegraph*.

Gritty realism is not evident on the whole. This is because the beach is carefully removed from the reality of everyday life. A good example is the provision of toilet facilities. At no point is this mentioned or hinted at, though such a location would clearly need some sort of organised lavatory. This removal from normality is purposeful because this is supposed to be a version of paradise and when you think about paradise you don't think about the underlying reality of such a place, like the need to relieve yourself. This idea of paradise is seen in Tommy's dream in *Vacuuming Completely Nude in Paradise* when we see palm trees, white sand and gentle surf.

The Beach presents the audience with an idyll and this view is carefully constructed. This then makes the contrast with Ko Pha-Ngan far more brutal. It also means the shark attack becomes more shocking and begins to allow reality to seep into the camp, like blood from the bite marks. A complete departure from teen beach movies of the past, Boyle presents us with a film that doesn't pander to hedonism, but comments on it through the contrast between the beach and the mainland tourist environments.

Voice-over, abnormal psychology, underwater shots, dreams and visions – all are commonplace in Boyle's work, but there is one element of *The Beach* that is only seen in one other cinema-released film he has directed. This is sex, something which is also shown in *Trainspotting* when Renton and Diane first meet. In *The Beach*, Richard and Sal go the mainland on a "rice-run" and she discovers he has informed other young travellers about the beach, these being Zeph and Sammy, who have two female friends in tow. Sal strikes a deal with Richard; if he'll have sex with her, she won't tell the other members of the community about him giving out details of the beach. This sex is no more than a transaction and it is one treated with the coldness of prostitution, as is shown when Sal says, 'Now get some sleep. I may wish to have sex again before we have breakfast.' It is also used as a weapon later in the narrative when Sal, annoyed by the fact Zeph and Sammy et al. have arrived on the nearby island with the intention of trying to reach the beach, tells everyone about the sex. Richard and Françoise had been in a relationship, but this information brings it to a violent close when she goes to Richard at his camp in the jungle and slaps him round the face, not just once, but twice for good measure.

This use of sex not as a symbol of love, but as a tool for manipulation of the male involved is also the case in *Trainspotting*. Diane, who is underage, threatens to tell the police that Renton has slept with her, this threat made in order to try to persuade him to see her again. In this and the occasion in *The Beach*, we see women as "man-ipulative" and man as a relatively innocent victim.

It is of interest to note the contrast between the sex conducted by Richard and Sal and the romantic notion of physical contact portrayed when Richard and Françoise first begin their relationship. The two are poles apart, the former a simple depiction of two people having intercourse behind a mosquito net and the second an atmospheric scene utilising gentle music, darkness, the glow of plankton and gentle light upon water to heighten feelings of romance and genuine feelings of fondness and desire. Thus, Boyle clearly differentiates between the two occasions, even to the extent of ending the romantic scene before the couple actually engage in the final act of sex.

In both *The Beach* and *Trainspotting*, we see men trying to lure women, but the tables being turned. In the cases of Richard and Françoise and Renton and Diane, we see the males trying to use chat-up lines and the females seeing through such false and weak attempts at seduction. Both women draw attention to the fact they know the men are trying to seduce them. In this and the examples of sexual manipulation, we find the women in positions of power, which is an interesting reversal of usual gender roles. Sal is clearly quite a dominant female and Françoise displays a clear femininity and sensuality, which is an atypical love interest. However, Françoise is still in control of the situation right from the outset. It is Françoise who undermines Richard's "pretentious" attempt to chat her up. It is Françoise who chooses Richard over Etienne and invites him to go night swimming and it is she who ends the relationship.

> When I did *The Beach* I was very happy to do it, I really liked the movie. But I was living in France, and it wasn't like I was waiting to do an American movie – to forget about French movies. I received a wonderful proposition from Hollywood, and I liked the director they had hired.
>
> Virginie Ledoyen[3]

Sal's cold approach to sex as merely physical fulfilment in exchange for her supposed silence is a way of defining her character. It helps to make her final actions in the narrative believable, coupled with the fact she is a founding member of the community and clearly guards its existence like a very great treasure, to the extent of putting other lives at risk, as is the case when Christo needs medical treatment after the shark attack on the Swedes.

Sal's coldness relating to sex also implies a coldness concerning her relationship with Bugs, another founding member. She is clearly perfectly happy to engage in infidelity. These two elements hint at the chilling single-mindedness she displays in her final scene. She is given a choice by the head of the cannabis growers; either all of them must leave the island forever or she must fire a revolver at Richard in a Russian roulette gambit of five to one odds. She chooses the latter, pulling the trigger to reveal the chamber is empty. This event not only scares all the other community members, but also allows them to clearly see Sal's coldness. She is prepared to kill one of their own in order to stay on the island. A life is worth less than her dream. Sal would rather gamble with a life than return to the everyday world. This is shocking to the others, who "hide" at the beach to avoid the harshness of reality to a degree, only to find one of its ugliest faces in their midst, that of murder and death. Paradise is paradise no longer and the illusions of separateness and safety are shattered, this end having begun when the blood of the Swedes first stained the sands.

Therefore, we see both paradise gained and paradise lost in this film. We find that a large group of people is unable to sustain paradise. Reality creeps in and always lurks as a dark threat in the background, here in the form of clashing personalities (Richard and Bugs), relationship break-ups and the proximity of the cannabis growers. This presence suddenly elevates with the shark attack and reaches its apex when Sal pulls the revolver's trigger. With the loud click of the trigger, the vision of paradise is exploded like the apple that Celine shoots at the start of *A Life Less Ordinary*. This thematic is a statement more about humans than it is about paradise. We have no place there and only bring with us the things we wish to escape, which can be seen in a more severe way when Sal and Richard visit Ko Pha-Ngan.

However, Sal is not truly the one to blame for anything other than the shattering of the illusion of paradise. The blame actually lies squarely on Richard's shoulders. It is he who chose to make a copy of the map and leave it for Zeph and Sammy. This then instigated all the problems, other than the shark attack. Richard is therefore central to the plot and in essence finds the idyll he dreamt of finding, only to cause its downfall through his thoughtless actions.

Giving us additional forewarning of the finale of the film is an element of the narrative relating to an incident of toothache. One of the members of the community is suffering greatly from this symptom and requests to visit the mainland in order to see a dentist. Sal insists that he stays and has the problem dealt with there. After refusing his request, she says to Richard, 'Are you okay with this?' He responds by stating, 'Yeah, I mean, we have a secret here, right? Sometimes people need to take a little pain to keep it that way.' Sal is pleased with his response and, with a smile upon her face, says, 'Excellent attitude.' This short interchange puts us on notice of things to come. It is a hint that there will be more pain, but that keeping the beach a secret will take precedence.

When Richard and Sal are in the small boat returning to the island from Ko Pha-Ngan, we are given another hint as to what is to come. In a narrative sense, this excursion to the mainland acts as a turning point. The idyllic existence at the beach is broken both visually and literally by this visit and Richard returns changed. He has "paid for her [Sal's] silence" with regard to the map. As he states, 'I didn't even want to think about the real price.' This warns us of trouble to come. They are returning, but their secret deal is like a poison being administered into Richard's life at the beach. Things will never be the same again thanks to what has happened on the mainland and the rest of his stay on the island will be tainted by what he has done.

In this we can see that all the negative influences which come to bear in the narrative, finally causing the community to fragment, originate from beyond the beach. The arrival of Zeph, Sammy and their two companions is as a result of Richard leaving them a map while still on the mainland. The break up of his and Françoise's relationship is because of his and Sal's actions in Ko Pha-Ngan. The shark attack on the Swedes even occurs beyond the beach. In every major instance of disharmony and disruption of the paradise we can see that it is outside reality that ultimately causes it. Even Richard's unbalanced mental state arises beyond the beach when he is spending time lurking in the jungle.

Blood seeps into the sand after the shark attack and harsh realities seep into the beach community.

The shark attack mentioned creates a moral dilemma within the narrative. Sten does not survive the attack, but Christo is left alive, though badly injured. The sudden introduction of blood, gore, fear and horror is all the more powerful in the movie because of the relative calm which has preceded it. It is not only shocking for the community, but also for the audience.

The moral dilemma arises in relation to Christo and has already been touched upon. His moans and screams of pain disturb and upset the others, the community sharing a building in which they spend time relaxing or sleeping. They find his presence hard to cope with and the decision is eventually made to place Christo in a tent in the jungle so that he is removed from the community. As Richard states, 'Out of sight really was out of mind. Once he was gone we felt a whole lot better.' The only member who voiced protest against the immorality of this choice is Etienne, who, as previously mentioned, stays with Christo in order to tend his wounds.

What the community does to Christo can be seen as torture. The use of torture, along with unglorified violence, can be seen in the majority of Boyle's films. We see such violence when Zeph, Sammy and their two female friends arrive on the island. The cannabis growers, all armed with automatic weapons, shoot all four of them. There is no humour involved in this scene, no machismo or elongated fight scenes, and the camera does not linger on the bodies in a hawkish way. The shootings are presented simply and objectively and come as a sharp contrast to the happiness the four victims had been feeling upon their arrival and the discovery of the field of cannabis.

Shortly before the growers arrive at the community in the film's finale, we witness an act that shows this film not only subverts gender power relationships, it also subverts usual narrative expectations. Richard kills Christo by placing his hand over the Swede's mouth and pinching shut his nostrils. In many films this act, coupled with his act of giving out a copy of the map and thereby threatening the existence of the community, his betrayal of Françoise's trust and Etienne's friendship and the act of simply watching as the drug growers killed the four people who arrived due to his influence, would lead to Richard receiving punishment within the narrative. This would usually take a very obvious form and come near the film's climax. He does receive a minor punishment when Sal points the gun at his head, but in comparison with what he has caused – the ending of the community and five deaths – this seems very little.

However, he has also suffered mentally earlier in the film. His punishment could therefore be said to have come before his misdeeds came to full fruition, though the seeds had been sown. It is also the case that the killing of Christo is one conducted out of mercy rather than maliciousness. He is ending Christo's suffering as tears roll down his face. It is a necessity that is left to him and is punishment in itself, because he suffers as he kills the Swede and the memory, along with the guilt, will stay with him for the rest of his life.

> I like to work spontaneously, impulsively. [clicks his fingers] Bang. It's done. Don't worry about it. You've got to trust yourself. It's really important. It takes a long time, but you get there.
>
> Robert Carlyle[4]

What we can see by the end is that a different kind of society was being attempted at the beach. The founders had been trying to create a system that rejects most of Western ideology, including a class system. It is like the positive version of Colonel Walter E. Kurtz's society seen towards the end of Francis Ford Coppola's *Apocalypse Now* (1979). In that movie we were presented with a dystopia and in *The Beach* it begins as a utopian vision free of normal worries and problems. However, these leech into the bright atmosphere and slowly darken it, like the shadows of clouds drawing in across the ocean. Eventually a hard rain falls, bringing with it the realisation that humans take their problems wherever they go. We cannot escape ourselves and therefore can never attain paradise.

Some feel that the film delivers an anti-technology message due to the lack of such at the beach community. However, this is not the case. Technology is largely absent in part because the commonly held view of paradise is without it. The location of the community is meant to be a view of paradise, at least initially, and so this element could not be present on the whole.

It can also be argued that technology had to be removed in order to get a clearer view of the human psyche. It has been stripped away to reveal the truth about our nature, laying it bare on the screen so we can see that wherever we go we always take ourselves and therefore our desires, needs, hopes and wishes. Ultimately, the effect of depicting paradise in this movie is to reveal that we do not belong there.

Cinematic Techniques

The start of the film features a voice-over, as did all the other films so far in Boyle's feature-length directing career. This voice-over, like those in *Shallow Grave* and *Trainspotting*, is by the main character, Richard. As with those previous cases, it identifies him as the central character of the narrative. It also gives us an insight into his mentality and we are soon led to understand that he is a traveller seeking a place away from crowds of tourists, somewhere special and relatively unspoilt by hordes of foreign visitors.

The voice-over continues beyond the beginning of the film and, as in *Trainspotting*, is used frequently as a way to allow the audience to understand the thoughts and motivations of the lead character. Richard is effectively the narrator of "his" story.

This extensive use of voice-over goes against one of the often quoted rules of cinema, this being "show, don't tell". When Richard tells us – for he is addressing us directly through the use of this technique – what he thinks rather than showing us through action, it contradicts this general rule. Boyle's trick is to make it work in both this film and *Trainspotting*. He does so partly by getting the most from the actors so that their verbally related feelings are also shown in their expressions. Another reason it works is because we are fascinated by being able to hear the thoughts of the lead character, something which is quite rare, but can be seen being put to the same intriguing use in *Adaptation* (Jonze 2002), which stars Nicholas Cage as twin screenwriters and uses voice-over extensively. This fascination can only occur if we care about the characters in question. In *Trainspotting* it was Renton's humour which helped create this interest. In *The Beach*, it is Richard's dream of finding paradise, something that many of us also dream of from time to time.

It is apparent from the moment Richard sees Françoise that he is attracted to her. At that time, she is in a relationship with Etienne, but he still asks both of them to join him in attempting to reach the beach. During the journey Boyle gives us a small but effective forewarning as to what will occur between the three of them later in the narrative. This warning is a typically filmic one and is often used in the horror genre. It is simply the use of a thunderclap.

In *The Beach* this rumble of thunder occurs as the three characters are discussing getting to the island where the beach is located. Etienne says, 'It will be worth it. An adventure, and just the three of us,' and then he kisses Françoise, Richard turning his gaze downwards, with a dark look on his face, the thunder sounding as we see his expression.

We see the use of a number of high shots during the film, the camera looking down from quite some distance. One of these is particularly noteworthy because Boyle uses it to give us a sense of place. He provides the audience with a bird's-eye view from above as Richard, Françoise and Etienne swim towards the island, the camera moving upwards and away from the trio of travellers. It then ascends into and beyond the clouds in order that the audience can see the entirety of the island. We see its shape and its isolation, the director giving us a great sense of how far removed it is from the everyday world.

Another high shot is used when Richard and Françoise are embracing at night in the water just off the beach. To close the scene, Boyle gives us a distant view in which he identifies the characters' location with the use of glowing plankton. This is a wonderful trope by which to create a magical shot and illuminate Richard and Françoise in the night.

The effect of this plankton is reflected in an earlier scene when we see Richard from a shark-eye view. This occurs when the three characters are making their way to the island and the French couple pretend Françoise has been pulled under by a shark. We see a point-of-view shot as Françoise prepares to ascend and scare him. Richard is silhouetted and highlighted by the sun in the sky beyond, which Boyle positions behind the character to make him stand out, just as he did when Renton dived into the toilet in *Trainspotting*.

There is another high shot when the community swims away from the island. This creates a degree of circularity with the initial approach to the island, when Boyle used the first high shot mentioned.

A shark's-eye view of Richard, Boyle using the sun to highlight his position as Francoise swims up to him.

Due to the location of most of the narrative, it comes as no surprise that the film features the greatest use of shots through water, which are seen in many of Boyle's films. The first of these occurs when Richard, Françoise and Etienne swim to the island. We see both men from beneath the water, Boyle giving us a shark's-eye view towards the surface. Richard is not amused when the prank is revealed and it is important to note that the audience, like Richard, is ignorant of the joke until Françoise resurfaces. We are placed in Richard's position of ignorance, thereby highlighting the fact that we are being shown his story, being positioned to see the events in the narrative from his point of view.

We also see an underwater shot when these three characters jump into the pool of water shortly before arriving at the traveller settlement. Shortly after their arrival, there is an underwater shot of a jellyfish. Further examples of such shots are in evidence when Richard and Françoise first become intimate in the calm water of the beach.

Another shot beneath water is in evidence when Richard goes fishing alone in the rain. During this scene he is attacked by a young shark, which acts as a forewarning for what will happen later in the narrative. This shark and the reference to these creatures caused by Françoise and Etienne's practical joke as the travellers are swimming to the island carefully prep the audience so that when the fatal shark attack occurs the existence of the deadly fish in the location does not come as a surprise.

Underwater shots are clearly present, but so is Boyle's use of glass as a medium through which to film. We see this in evidence when Richard is temporarily in Ko Pha-Ngan with Sal. There, he makes a call to his parents and we watch the conversation through the glass of the phone box.

As with *Trainspotting*, there is an element of self-reflexivity in the film. This occurs when Richard discovers Daffy's body. He states, 'You hope and you dream, but you never believe that something's gonna happen to you, not like it does in the movies.' Though this is only minor – as was the example in *Trainspotting* with people waving at the camera when Renton moves to London – it shows that Boyle is confident enough in the acting, script and his own direction not to be concerned that such a reference will break the suspension of disbelief and cause the audience to think about the fact that they are only watching a constructed piece of entertainment. It may be the case that this is another way by which the director toys with audience expectations, creating an intense and surprising scene as the suicide is discovered, only to punctuate it with a self-reflexive voice-over comment.

Another small example of self-reflexivity arises when we are humorously introduced to the three Swedes: Christo, Sten and Karl. We see the trio standing facing the camera and talking directly to us as if appearing on a documentary. Sten says, 'We like fishing and in the winter we like skiing. Of course, in Thailand there is no skiing.' This is part of the humour of this brief scene.

During the humorous scene when community members request items from Richard before he leaves for the mainland we see the use of point-of-view shots. These are from Richard's perspective and act in the same way as the voice-over in that they position the audience so they are able to identify with him. Not only are we hearing his thoughts, but we are also seeing through his eyes.

When Richard and Sal go to Ko Pha-Ngan Boyle provides us with a stark contrast between locations. He juxtaposes the relative calm of the community scenes, including the use of relaxed, reggae-style music and natural light, with the thumping music, darkness, electric lights, cars and hustle and bustle of Ko Pha-Ngan. This urban environment is shown to be the antithesis of paradise.

After Richard and Sal have had sex, we see Boyle's great use of camera angle and shot distance. The two characters are lying in bed and Richard is initially silent and thoughtful. Keeping the shot at the same level as the character almost makes us a third party voyeur on the bed beside him. The close-up used also allows us to see that he is troubled, something that soon becomes apparent when he voices his concern about Bugs' reaction to what has happened. During the entire scene, the camera remains low and the shots continue to be in close-up. This aids in reinforcing the physical intimacy of the scene, making the audience part of it rather than distancing us from the closeness of the characters.

> I think doubtlessness is a problem. I really like testing that. The character in *The Beach* has that fanatical doubtlessness and becomes unstuck by it.
>
> Tilda Swinton[5]

During the time Richard spends dwelling in the jungle we see an element that is visually distinct from the rest of the film. Boyle employs the appearance of a computer game, including the use of non-diegetic elements, such as the points score which is shown on screen. We also see computer-generated creatures not, as is common in contemporary cinema, made to look like real animals, but rather to look like those from a relatively simplistic platform game. At the end we also see the non-diegetic words, "Game over. Try again?" The effect of the non-diegetic elements, the use of camera shots looking back at Richard as he passes through the jungle and the unusual and exaggerated way in which he moves, is to put the audience in the position of game player. Again, as with point-of-view shots, we are brought deeper into the psyche of the main character. We are also encouraged to feel as though we are part of the story, as if we are there, with Richard, watching events unfold.

This latter point is further highlighted when Richard is sitting at a camp fire in the jungle whilst talking to a vision of Daffy. The camera is placed at the same height as the character's head and the fact that Richard is looking off-screen to the left makes us feel as though we are sitting beside Daffy. This effect is continued when the shot is of Daffy, who is looking off-screen to the right, making us feel as though we've moved to sit beside Richard. These shots, along with everything mentioned earlier, draw us into the film and allow a deeper suspension of disbelief because of the depth to which we are pulled in through Boyle's direction.

In the final scene of the film we see Richard in an Internet cafe and are provided with one of Boyle's screen within screen shots when he opens his email and finds that Françoise has sent him a photo taken during the happiest time at the beach community. The director then uses a closing voice-over in which Richard states, 'I still believe in paradise, but now at least I know it's not some place you can look for.'

The soundtrack of this film is again loaded with contemporary music, creating a sense of youthful zeal which is a hallmark of many Boyle films. The artists whose tunes feature in *The Beach* include Faithless, Underworld and All Saints, who created the song *Pure Shores* especially for the film.

From Book to Film

This was the second of only three Boyle films to be adapted from an original novel, the others being *Trainspotting* and *Slumdog Millionaire*. Written by Alex Garland, *The Beach* was his debut novel and was released without much fanfare in 1996. Its popularity grew thanks, in part, to some rave reviews, but mainly as a result of word of mouth. At the height of its popularity travellers all around the world could be seen reading the book.

Written when Garland was only twenty-three, it drew on his experiences of travelling and it clearly hit a nerve with a generation who were searching for something more than ordinary tourist resorts, something beyond the package holidays and glossy brochures.

> Writing certainly wasn't something I thought I wanted to do as a kid. It was something I chanced upon. And, in a way, I don't think you could say I chose it as my profession. I gave it a try and it worked out, and I enjoy it and that's it.
>
> Alex Garland[6]

In the book Richard was a repressed Brit who didn't put voice to his feelings. Because of his quintessential Britishness and the fact that the character had quite a privileged background, Boyle et al. decided to change him into a more down-to-earth American. This allowed them to make the character more aggressive than was the case in the novel. It was this choice that led to the casting of DiCaprio rather than McGregor, as mentioned at the start of the chapter.

Richard isn't the only character to have undergone a change of nationality. In the book Sal is American, but she is English in the film. We also find small changes, such as the film showing Richard losing his beach hut key when in the book it is Zeph and Sammy, whose Bill and Ted's personas are only an act in Garland's novel. Further to this, the book also mentions and utilises the toilet facilities of the community during the narrative, unlike the film.

We also find that in the novel Richard does not have a relationship or sex with any female members of the community. Though he is attracted to Françoise, she and Etienne never split up, and this means Richard is more independent and aids in the creation of the other community members' perception of him as doing Sal's clandestine dirty work.

One of the biggest changes is the omission of the character called Jed. He plays an important role in the novel, being the community member who accompanies Richard on the "rice-run", the forerunner to Richard in patrolling the jungle and the character who nurses a stricken Swede after the shark attack.

Considering that Boyle would go on to make *28 Days Later*, it is also of note that the gory, *Apocalypse Now*-styled ending of the novel is altered considerably in the film. This is particularly interesting because, as mentioned, Francis Ford Coppola's film is Boyle's favourite movie. Because of this it is somewhat surprising that the director didn't stick to the book's tripped-out, blood-lust finale, though it seems likely that this could have been at least partly due to studio influence.

Criticism

Both during and after filming the movie drew criticism based on the environmental impact of the production. This was partly because the location of *The Beach*, the island of Ko Phi Phi Leh, was in a National Marine Park protected by law from tourist development.

While *The Beach* was being made it was incorrectly reported that local inhabitants were suing the makers when they were in fact suing the corrupt government, who had already allowed a host of hotels, restaurants, discos and other establishments associated with tourism to be built on other islands in the marine park, such as Phi Phi Don.

After filming was completed an investigation into its impact on the environment was carried out by EcoLert. This non-profit organisation checked to see if any lasting damage had been caused by the presence of the production, which had reshaped the beach and planted a number of coconut trees in order to aid in the impression of paradise. EcoLert found that no such damage had been done and the makers were exonerated.

Both the book and film can be criticised because of a strange paradox they create. There is a clear criticism of the impact tourism has on the world and yet *The Beach*, in both formats, has encouraged tourism and the search for an idyllic location. It can also be said that the movie, due to its manipulation of the beach environment and presentation of this idyll, panders to the tourist gaze because it doesn't portray a realistic tropical island, but a type of holiday-brochure depiction which is staged and false.

Criticism of the film's narrative arises as a result of there being little characterisation on the part of the community members other than Sal, Bugs and Keaty. The others, on the whole, remain indistinct and one-dimensional. This means that when the shark attack occurs the audience doesn't find themselves empathising with the Swedes or the other people dwelling there. Rather, we are simply shocked by events and intrigued to see how they will affect the community. Had the other members been given a greater role and definition there could have been more of a connection made and this would have helped the audience to care when the human presence in paradise begins to become darkened by events. As it is, we find it hard to care that the community has come to an end.

The reason for the lack of characterisation may be the relatively short duration of the film. If its running time had been greater there would have been more time in which to expand characterisation of the select inhabitants of the island idyll. Another reason could be that we are seeing events from Richard's perspective and, therefore, we only learn more about the people he interacts with, the others remaining on the periphery of the narrative. He is also away from the community for a long spell, removing any chance of the audience identifying with any other beach-dwellers.

Criticism also arose from people who had read the book prior to viewing the film. This related to the changes made and to the perception that the movie was not as good as the novel. This is a common claim when texts are adapted for the screen. However, it is impossible to depict everything contained in the narrative of a novel in the relatively short duration of a film. Therefore it is a rather unfair criticism, as all that can be distilled onto the screen is the essence of the book. It is also worth mentioning that Alex Garland himself clearly didn't have such qualms about the adaptation or he would not have worked with Boyle on two other occasions.

Awards

The film was nominated for seven awards and did not win any of them. One of these nominations was for Leonardo DiCaprio in the category of Worst Actor in the Razzie Awards, which is one accolade the actor and makers of the film would have been glad not to have picked up. This is the worst awards performance of any of Boyle's cinema-released films, even the panned *A Life Less Ordinary* managing to pick up an award.

Final Words

The Beach explores a vision of paradise and then bloodies it with the realities of human nature. It presents us with a vivid dream, only to turn it into a nightmare as the insecurities and impurities of humanity rise to the surface of the waters, bringing with them a storm of upheaval as our presence in paradise is ended.

With some good performances from the main actors, most notably Virginie Ledoyen and Tilda Swinton, we are carried on an initial tide of optimism and excitement. However, Daffy's mental imbalance is a stern warning of what is to come. In DiCaprio's finest moments, we see Richard lurking in the jungle as his past washes up on the beach below, replacing optimism with a sense of dread.

In the final analysis paradise is not ended, it is just left without the interference of humans and the darkness that balances the light in human nature. It is left to breathe with the pulse of the tide as the blood washes away, Boyle and his crew packing their equipment after giving us an interesting insight into our wish for Utopia, allowing us to discover the truth that it can only remain an idyll without our presence.

[1] Unknown – *Interview: Danny Boyle: Trainspotting's Visionary Goes to The Beach with Leo* (http://video.barnesandnoble.com/search/interview.asp?CTR=717275)

[2] Unknown – *The Beach made a man out of Leo* (http://www.guardian.co.uk/film/2000/jan/12/2)

[3] Chambers, B. *Virginie Speaks (sorta)* (http://www.filmfreakcentral.net/tiff/vledoyeninterview.htm)

[4] MacGregor, F. *Robert Carlyle Interview: He's made a name for himself playing troubled characters. It might not be glamorous, but it's the type of role he enjoys best* (http://news.scotsman.com/entertainment/Robert-Carlyle-interview–He39s.4759594.jp)

[5] Aames, E. *Interview: Tilda Swinton & Skandar Keynes on "The Chronicles of Narnia"* (http://www.cinecon.com/news.php?id=0512072)

[6] Rawlinson, N. *Alex Garland – The Beach: Backpacker Blues* (http://www.spikemagazine.com/0599alexgarland.php)

Vacuuming Completely Nude in Paradise

Ours is to sell or die. No one will do what I will do for a sale.

Tommy Rag

Aired in 2001, this was the first collaboration between Danny Boyle and screenwriter Jim Cartwright, who wrote the original play which was adapted into the movie *Little Voice* (Herman 1998). They had been in contact during the 1980s, when Boyle was still the director at the Royal Court Theatre in London. Cartwright had sent in segments of a play that impressed the director, who recognised a special talent. This play would become *Road*, but by the time the scripts were finished Boyle's career had moved on from the theatre.

Created for the BBC, *Vacuuming Completely Nude in Paradise* was one of two dramas that marked Danny Boyle's return from the rural landscapes of the US and Thailand to the urban cityscapes he employed in his first two films. The second of these films was *Strumpet*, which was also penned by Cartwright and is discussed in the following chapter. Both see a resumption of the gritty and realistic style seen in

Trainspotting. The use of vernacular speech also creates a link between this pairing of BBC productions and Boyle's second movie. In this film and *Strumpet* the dialect is that of Greater Manchester, where both are predominantly set.

Vacuuming Completely Nude in Paradise and *Strumpet* marked a new era in collaborative terms. They were the first occasions when Boyle worked with cinematographer Anthony Dod Mantle, music composer John Murphy and editor Chris Gill. All three would go on to work with the director on three further films beyond these two dramas, as stated in the first chapter.

Unlike in his preceding film, *The Beach*, the audience are not positioned into a single character's viewpoint. *Vacuuming Completely Nude in Paradise* presents us with a mainly omnipresent view which is common to many films. We watch the narrative unfold from a perspective beyond any of the characters, but are still able to identify and empathise with them.

Also unlike *The Beach*, Boyle was free from studio influence and therefore able to experiment. The BBC would not interfere with his decisions and so he had full control of the productions. Partially due to this freedom, Boyle chose to use digital video (DV) cameras for the filming of both dramas. Compared with the more usual 35mm cameras, DV footage is less detailed but more direct, adding to the realism and therefore complementing both BBC films. The smaller size of DV cameras created wider scope for angle choices, something the director demonstrates very clearly in this film with an intercutting rush of enthusiasm.

This initial burst of experimental camera placement is toned down in *Strumpet*, but Boyle and Dod Mantle clearly enjoyed the freedom DV cameras gave them when filming. The vehicle of these two small-screen, small-budget dramas was a perfect one through which Boyle could experiment with this relatively new technology and prepare himself to take DV use to a big-screen production, this being *28 Days Later.*

> I had the desire to do something that would open out the way I work, that would be more spontaneous.
>
> Danny Boyle[1]

Basic Premise & Main Characters

The dominant character of the movie is a vacuum cleaner salesman called Tommy Rag. He is loud, brash and speaks his mind, his personality reflected by his ownership of a gold-coloured car. Tommy is played by Timothy Spall, who is most commonly associated with the work of director Mike Leigh, having appeared in films such as *Secrets & Lies* (1996) and *Topsy-Turvy* (1999). His performance is high-octane and believably desperate as he tries to gain enough sales to win a two-week holiday and the Golden Vac for being the top salesman in the company he works for. His language is quick-fire and laced with profanity. He is to the point and prepared to do anything for a sale. These sales are of utmost importance, Tommy using fair means or foul to sell vacuum cleaners. The introduction of his new sales partner, the much more reserved and totally inexperienced Pete, ably played by Michael Begley, won't stop him. He is a one-man selling machine and his home-made motivational tape underlines this with the instruction, 'Sell, fuckin' sell, fuckin' sell. Sell, sell, fuckin' sell,' shouted with passion and a rabid determination over a backing track of heavy guitar.

Narrative Themes

Pete is a good example of Boyle's use of ordinary heroes. He is reserved and quiet, especially when compared to the character of Tommy. The contrast of the two heightens the characterisation of both through the obvious differences. Pete is more understated and introverted.

He, unlike Tommy, is also shown to have a conscience. It is Pete's first sale that gives rise to this distinction and also provides the film with a moral dilemma, something seen in other Boyle movies, like *Shallow Grave*. After making this sale to a single mother who's finding it hard to make ends meet, he finds that he cannot cope with the guilt he feels and so returns to the woman's home in the evening, rips up the purchase agreement, gives her the last of his money and takes the vacuum cleaner away. This act of redemption for his earlier actions is partially motivated by seeing the woman in tears after he has made the sale, her children gathering about her in order to give comfort.

However, Tommy reveals a soft underbelly in the scene when he arrives after Pete has discovered Leather Face's body lying on the floor of her flat. Amidst the piles of newspapers, he tells Pete of a dream he has had, Boyle again showing his use of dreams and visions, used here to tap into the depths of a character who wears a harsh mask. This dream enables Boyle to show us the man beneath, to reveal that Tommy is just an ordinary man, one who we later discover was shaped by his boyhood and a father who worked long hours for little money and abused his mother without his intervention, something he has always regretted.

During this scene his voice is lowered, a rarity in the narrative, and he is thoughtful and introspective. The humanity of his character is revealed as he talks about the dream of following the company's young and attractive new employee, Uki, into paradise through a computer screen. This vision of paradise is an echo of that seen in *The Beach*, with white sands, gentle surf and palm trees. Despite Tommy's driving force apparently being the sale of vacuum cleaners, we see that a part of him yearns for tranquillity and an escape from his current life. He has a faraway look in his eyes as Boyle's directing reflects the narrative calm and the shot lingers in close-up on his expression and we see tears upon his cheeks. This dream and the following shots of Tommy are vital to the narrative in order to show the audience the truth about his character and thereby create empathy.

His humanity is further highlighted when he invites "Spanish", a woman he has been flirting with, to attend the Golden Vac award ceremony. She also brings along her "slow" daughter, who is seen having sex with Pete on the sofa of her house earlier in the film. This invitation to accompany him implies that he cares for Spanish more than he is willing to admit. When she was previously mentioned by Tommy he gave the impression his visits to her home are simply in order to get a sale. However, by the time he travels to Blackpool for the ceremony she has bought the vacuum cleaner and he therefore doesn't need to take her so as to secure the sale. Tommy must be taking her because he wants her company, the ulterior motive removed to reveal his normal, human need for companionship.

Adding to this character's humanity is his reaction to failing to win the holiday and Golden Vac. Here Boyle successfully captures the moments after the result has been announced, a salesman nicknamed "Pockmark" having beaten Tommy. The shot zooms in steadily until we are presented with Tommy's shocked and indignant expression in close-up. Jim Cartwright's screenplay combines beautifully with Danny

Boyle's directing to create a poignant moment. It is obvious that sales are Tommy's driving force and, thanks to comments about his father made on the journey to Blackpool, we also understand that he never wants to fail. Here he is confronted with failure, with being second best at something he thought he excelled in.

> I've always been a great supporter of Jim's work because he's not like anyone else. So when I got sent the screenplay of Vacuuming I jumped at the chance to work with him.
>
> Danny Boyle[2]

At the end of the film we see a dream shattered and another come true. Tommy strips down to his underwear on Blackpool Beach and throws a vacuum cleaner into the sea. He is distraught at his failure to win the Golden Vac and the two-week holiday, Tommy's dream of a trip to paradise having slipped away. It is then that he suffers a heart attack, stating, 'You don't have to vac me heart up.' This is a scene of intense vulnerability, as Tommy lies virtually naked and alone on the sand in the darkness, only illuminated by the light of Blackpool seafront. Boyle accentuates this vulnerability by using a distant and high shot of Tommy, making him seem small and somewhat insignificant upon the beach.

The dream that has come true relates to Pete's wish to become a DJ. This is fulfilled at the award ceremony when he takes charge of the mixing decks and those attending chant his name.

In most of Danny Boyle's films we find examples of abnormal psychology, as is clearly the case in *Shallow Grave*, *Strumpet* and *28 Days Later*. In this film it is only in evidence on a very small scale in relation to Spanish's daughter. She is described as "slow" and her act of trying to entice Pete and then having sex with him on the settee is not normal behaviour, but is a darkly humorous scene.

The humour evident in *Vacuuming Completely Nude in Paradise* is sparsely scattered and always dark. An example arises when Tommy sees Leather Face's body and comments, 'At least she's dead. Could be worse. Ill people make me sick.' This last sentence clearly has a double, darkly humorous meaning. Shortly afterwards he makes an amusing reference to mobile phones, calling them "electrified Mars Bars". This is not only an element of humour, but also a popular culture reference.

The most memorable humour is evident at the award ceremony when a group of salesman do a dance routine to Sheena Easton's song *Morning Train (Nine to Five)*. This routine features men wearing suits and pushing vacuum cleaners around the stage. This is not only an amusing sight, but also subverts the usual stereotype of women using such household equipment.

Cinematic Techniques

Using DV cameras, Boyle adds a down-to-earth feeling to the film to such a degree you could almost be watching a home movie. He and Dod Mantle are playful and ingenious in the use of angles, one moment giving the audience a view from the bumper of a car, the next placing the camera in a glove compartment so we are presented with an unusual view of the vehicle's interior. We even see the use of a camera placed on a vacuum cleaner Pete is carrying at one point in the film. In this way the film keeps us entertained and alert purely through innovative placement of the camera's gaze and the energy of these changing shots perfectly matches that of Tommy Rag's character.

> The director of photography becomes the director to some extent, and vice versa. It blurs the edges and frees you up. DV is very liberating for actors as well: the cameras are so unobtrusive that they don't feel they're being watched so much.
>
> Danny Boyle[3]

Also seen in relation to camera angles and shot choices are Boyle's common use of shots angled down from ceilings and views through glass, usually windows. The first example of the latter is seen right at the start of the film when we see into the office where a retirement party is taking place. We also see the use of a view through glass when Pete witnesses the single mother crying in her kitchen after having made his first sale. Boyle uses the pane of glass in the door of the house as an additional lens and frame. There are drops of water on it that not only add scene distortion, but also echo the bitter tears the woman is crying, Boyle using a point-of-view shot so that the audience is effectively seeing what Pete is witnessing as he stares into the shadowy house.

The opening party has a feeling of gritty realism, helping to identify this as a drama. The quality of the picture is grainy as diegetic music plays on a portable stereo held by Pete. The camera movement is quick, as are the editing cuts from one angle to the next. This adds to the chaos of the scene, one created by the harassment the drunken salesmen gathered at the party give to the strippergram, who is actually Pete's girlfriend, Sheila (played by Katy Cavanagh). When the manager gives a motivational speech after the strip, the camera movement calms to a degree, reflecting the change of pace in the narrative.

The entire party sequence is presented as if those attending shot it. With some elements out of focus and the camera occasionally panning so quickly that the shot becomes blurred, we can imagine the drunken revellers trying to use camcorders to capture the celebrations as a salesman nicknamed "Throat" retires due to the fact he's only got a short time to live. This turns out to be a very short time indeed, as he is dead by the time the scene ends.

During the entire film the speed of the narrative is echoed by the speed of shot and angle changes. In scenes like that at the party and when Tommy is tailgating a lorry with his motivational rant roaring from the car stereo, the cuts are quick from one angle to the next. In calmer scenes, like the occasion when Tommy goes to the office and sees Uki, the woman who features in his dream, for the first time, the camera angles change less frequently. The frenetic nature of the one is juxtaposed against the relative calm of the other. The coupling of narrative pace with the cutting between different camera angles creates a contrast between the frenetic and calm scenes, one which accentuates both elements while also keeping audience members attentive.

Boyle uses CCTV images when Tommy and Pete stop at a petrol station so that the latter can visit the lavatory. While Pete is relieving himself Tommy actually manages to sell a vacuum cleaner to a family who have also pulled up, thus underlining the fact that his character never misses a chance to make a sale. The CCTV images are intercut with more usual camera angles and serve to add to the realism of the movie and the engrossing mix of shots.

High angles associated with CCTV are also very apparent in the directing of Boyle's next film, *Strumpet*. The use of such camera angles keys into something which is now very much in the consciousness of the Western world. CCTVs have become a familiar part of the urban landscape and images from them are often used in television programmes, not least the news.

Also familiar are the types of angles associated with programmes like *Big Brother*, which are closely related to those used with CCTV. The locations are similar to those Boyle employs, though it should be pointed out that he started directing and utilising such angles long before this particular show existed or CCTV became so widespread. By the inclusion of such shots in *Vacuuming Completely Nude in Paradise* the director links them with CCTV and observational images within the minds of viewers, thereby strengthening the impression that we are witnessing real life events.

Pete's flat is a good example of Danny Boyle's use of lighting. In one scene after Pete's first day as Tommy's sales partner, the yellow of the street lights shines through the window, the shadows of the window frame falling on the wall. This light gives the flat a jaundiced and sickly feel, hinting at the disharmony evident in his relationship with Sheila. Darkness is used extensively to increase the feeling of claustrophobic surroundings, the abode small and cramped, the *mise en scène* aiding this impression through a clutter of furniture and belongings.

Pete's flat also provides Boyle with a tool by which to present the audience with two angles of the same scene. This is the use of a mirror; something also seen in a number of other films by the director and put to the most obvious use in *Sunshine*. Here we find that when Sheila is thinking of leaving and when Pete wakes in the morning to find she is gone, a mirror within the *mise en scène* is effectively employed to create additional depth to the shots.

The impoverished woman to whom Pete makes his first regrettable sale lives in dismal surroundings, an element seen in *Trainspotting* in relation to Swanney's drug den and Tommy's flat after he has become addicted to heroin. The atmosphere that Boyle has created in the woman's house in *Vacuuming Completely Nude in Paradise* is depressing and lacking in natural light. The *mise en scène* is dated, reflecting the woman's lack of funds with which to afford new decor.

Also of importance is the appearance of her garden. This approach to her house speaks clearly of the kind of existence she has. Boyle presents us with a garden littered with discarded items, an abandoned washing machine dominant amongst them. This sight effectively prepares the audience for both the run-down nature of the interior of the house and the woman's poverty.

Such abodes are presented in a number of cases in this film. Tommy's flat is more like a tip and the woman who lives below Pete, who he calls "Leather Face", has filled her dark and dingy flat with piles of newspapers that she has collected over the years. In each case Boyle takes great care in presenting dishevelled living spaces, in part reflecting the dishevelled nature of the relevant people's lives. These oppressive environments are counterbalanced to a degree by Tommy's energy and that of Boyle's directing.

The use of piles of newspapers in Leather Face's flat has the same effect as the furniture and clutter in Pete's home in that it diminishes the amount of empty space and increases a sense of closeness, of confinement. Limited light and lots of shadow are key to the atmosphere, creating a sense of a lonely life hidden from the world and adding to the general dinginess of the flat. It is this location that also provides one of the clearest examples of Boyle's skill in conveying calm and energy in keeping with the narrative. As Pete explores the flat the camera movements are calm. Then a small fire breaks out and as he desperately tries to put it out the camera angles change rapidly. After the fire is out and when Tommy enters, the narrative and directorial pace again slow.

Soon after his entrance, Tommy talks about the dream mentioned earlier in this chapter. It is at this point that a mirror is again used by the director, but not to show an additional angle of shot. Here, its use is very different. The glare from Leather Face's window makes Tommy's face indistinguishable at points as he stares at himself in the mirror. The smears upon its surface also add distortion to the image, like the drops of water seen on the window of the poor woman's house. The mirror allows us to see the thoughtful sadness in Tommy's expression. In this simple directorial touch we are presented with Tommy's true face, one which reflects his loneliness.

He leans forwards and sombrely blows out some candles, themselves symbolic of life coming to an end, their trails of smoke like souls rising into the air. As they rise the emergency services answer his call and ask what service he requires, Tommy replying by repeating the word "emergency" like a strange mantra as we see him continuing to stare at himself in the mirror. This heightens the realisation that beneath his mask Tommy is unhappy and lonely, which is the underlying message of his dream. We can now see that Boyle's use of a mirror in this instance is an invitation to the viewer to look beyond the mask Tommy wears in everyday life.

> It's lovely to play characters that are surprising. I think it's great – particularly characters who, you know at certain points, audiences are going to make decisions about you and that you know also that they're going to be terribly wrong about what they thought at the end.
>
> Timothy Spall[4]

The use of music is minimal in *Vacuuming Completely Nude in Paradise*. This is no doubt at least partially due to budget constraints. Boyle predominantly uses non-diegetic music, but there are three examples of diegetic music. The first is at the retirement party at the start. Another can be seen in the song and dance routine witnessed at the awards ceremony and the last is also seen in this location and relates to the disco taking place after Pockmark has won.

Criticism

With Boyle's return to a more realistic style and content, along with his return to the use of an urban environment, we also find a return to women in only minor roles. They are of only minimal importance to the plot and none are given the same degree of characterisation that we see in relation to Tommy and Pete. The narrative revolves around their relationship and this leaves women as peripheral participants. The gaze of this film is again orientated towards the masculine, as is the case with all his previous films.

However, the male dominance in this film is counterbalanced by *Strumpet* and the use of a central female character and one who, unlike Celine in *A Life Less Ordinary*, isn't manipulative.

Awards

Vacuuming Completely Nude in Paradise only received one notable nomination for an award. This was for Timothy Spall in the category of Best Actor at the BAFTAs in 2002. Though he didn't win this accolade, the fact that he was nominated reflects favourably on his brilliant performance, one that captures the essence of Tommy and manages to surprise the audience by revealing the humanity beneath the bluster and bravado of the character.

Final Words

This film bears the hallmark of a director revelling in rediscovered creative freedom. It also clearly shows Boyle's playfulness in relation to the use of DV cameras, coupled with the interesting and always engaging results of his collaboration with Anthony Dod Mantle. We find an energetic directorial style coupled with a spellbinding performance from Timothy Spall, which is perfectly married to a suitably thoughtful and slightly browbeaten performance from Michael Begley.

The film is a contemporary reworking of Arthur Miller's *Death of a Salesman* with a sense of poignancy. It gives us both sad and happy endings in relation to the two main characters, Boyle's distant shots of the deceased Tommy adding greatly to the impact. Ultimately, Tommy's death is both real and symbolic, the latter arising due to the emergence of Internet marketing and sales, something which is gently touched upon in Jim Cartwright's excellent screenplay. Therefore, the traditional salesman is no longer needed, but films like this will be needed for a long time to come. It is both engaging and entertaining, the narrative and directorial pace keeping us hooked from beginning to end, an end in which Tommy possibly finds paradise, but only after taking a journey from which he'll never return.

[1] Smith, R. *Back from the beach* (*The Guardian*, 10 August 2001, UK)

[2] Smith, R. *Back from the beach* (*The Guardian*, 10 August 2001, UK)

[3] Smith, R. *Back from the beach* (*The Guardian*, 10 August 2001, UK)

[4] Grady, P. *All of Spall* (http://www.reel.com/reel.asp?node=features/interviews/S/spall/2)

Strumpet

When life gives me a line I never refuse it, I write it down.

Strayman

This film has a strong relationship with *Vacuuming Completely Nude in Paradise.* Not only were they both dramatic productions for the BBC in 2001, but they involved many of the same people behind the scenes, including writer Jim Cartwright and cinematographer Anthony Dod Mantle. They were also shot on DV, thus enabling numerous different angles to be used for shots, many of them not seen in the majority of film releases. There is a strong sense of realism to the films and the acting is of such high quality that this impression of watching real lives is reinforced by the performances. In *Strumpet* this realism is underscored by the use of nicknames and vernacular speech, the latter also heard in *Trainspotting* and *"Vacuuming"*.

Due to their lack of a cinema release, many reading this book will not have seen either of these films. Both are engrossing and clearly identifiable as being the result of Danny Boyle's direction. Any fan

115

should take a look at these movies as they add greatly to the pantheon of his work and marked a return to his roots, not only in the sense of being predominantly set in Lancashire where he grew up, but also in the energy expressed without studio control.

Basic Premise & Main Characters

Strumpet is about a spontaneous poet called Strayman. He is played by Christopher Eccleston, who produces a gripping performance, one which incorporates the touch of madness we saw in *Shallow Grave* and even the authority displayed in his role in *28 Days Later*. His character gets his name from the fact that he takes in stray dogs and has a pack of them living with him in his council house. They accompany him everywhere and he is known locally because of his eccentricity.

He takes in another stray, a girl who initially has no name and who he rescues from the sexual predation of a truck driver. She is played by Genna G and takes the name of Strumpet because this is what Strayman calls the female dogs he takes under his wing. This name can be seen to be a play on words. She likes to "strum" a guitar and "pet" can be seen either as a dialectical form of address or in regards to the fact that the dogs are pets. In this light her name becomes the instruction "Strum, pet". This request to play the guitar reflects what will occur later in the film.

After a spontaneous outburst of poetic song and dance which is recorded by Strayman's neighbour, Knockoff (played by Stephen Walters), a record company offers them a recording deal. This leads to the castration of Strumpet and Strayman's creativity in a London-based recording studio and the pressures of commercialism come into play as she is mutated into another plastic pop creation for mass consumption. However, the film ends on a high note and we witness a memorable performance by the two central characters in the BBC's *Top of the Pops* studio.

Narrative Themes

This movie has distinct echoes of *True Romance*, which was directed by Ridley Scott's brother, Tony, and written by Quentin Tarantino. In that 1993 film starring Christian Slater and Patricia Arquette, two of life's strays meet and fall for each other. They then have to escape the clutches of gangsters with a large amount of money in the hope of a bright future together. Tarantino's use of a large sum of money as a plot device in *True Romance, Reservoir Dogs, Pulp Fiction* and *Jackie Brown* creates a link with Boyle's use of such in *Shallow Grave, Trainspotting, A Life Less Ordinary, Millions* and *Slumdog Millionaire*. Both directors enjoy observing the effects these sums have on the characters, as stated in relation to Boyle in the chapter on *Shallow Grave*.

Though *Strumpet* does not include a large amount of money, it does feature two of life's strays falling for each other. In both films this attraction and connection is created simply and quickly through an obvious rapport. Essentially, *True Romance* and *Strumpet* are about people on the fringes of everyday life finding a connection and trying to better their situations together. In the former the couple try to escape the clutches of gangsters, but in the latter it is the grasp of a record company and its associated commercialism that is being fled from.

This link is seemingly cemented by the use of music that sounds identical to that used in *True Romance*. In both films this soft tune is employed as a kind of theme for the central couple. In *Strumpet* we hear it shortly after Strayman has rescued Strumpet from the clutches of a truck driver and we see her following him like one of his stray dogs. We also hear it when they are sitting on a mound of earth which has been tipped outside his home in an act of revenge conducted by the bitter driver.

In the opening scenes at his local pub we find an important theme with regard to Strayman. Rather than singing the proposed *Tie a Yellow Ribbon*, he recites Cooper Clarke's poem *Evidently Chickentown*. This poem includes lines such as "The fucking view is fucking vile, for fucking miles and fucking miles. The fucking babies fucking cry. The fucking flowers fucking die." The whole tone of the verse is one of anger towards a place without vibrancy; a depressing location where life withers rather than thrives and where happiness is absent. Its sentiment echoes that of Strayman. We see the energy and potency he instils in the words, which are clearly spoken from the heart. 'It fucking gets you fucking down,' he states with venom.

All of this positions Strayman on the periphery of society, something which becomes clearer as the film progresses. This means he occupies a place similar to the heroin addicts in *Trainspotting* or the travellers in *The Beach*. He is an observer of the everyday world from its fringe. Due to this he identifies with stray dogs and takes care of them, while at the same time allowing them their freedom in that he doesn't use leads or any obvious form of discipline. This affinity leads to his use of barking and growling, first seen after his poetic performance in the pub. He barks at the crowd, who reply in kind, implying that they know Strayman, for if they didn't they would surely be shocked by his strange behaviour.

The opening scene provides us with the presence of a clear abnormal psychology within the narrative; that of Strayman. Underscored by his barking and growling on a number of occasions, he is clearly psychologically different from most people, something not just caused by his affinity with dogs, but by his spontaneous creativity and the way in which he lives.

This Boyle thematic of abnormality is also part of Cartwright's script, in which the foundations for the character of Strayman are his creative urges, which, by definition, form a different kind of psyche from the norm. Though he is undoubtedly the least normal of all of Boyle's lead characters, he is still ordinary to a large degree, especially when compared to usual Hollywood depictions of heroes.

> It's a film about the creative instinct. Music and street poetry evolve in a spontaneous, unplanned way – and that's how *Strumpet* grew. It feels improvised, but in fact it's tightly scripted.
>
> Danny Boyle[1]

One of the director's usual thematic elements is missing from *Strumpet*, which is the only film discussed in this book not to include a dream or vision sequence. This said, flashbacks are used when Strumpet relates some details about her youth and these have the same effect of breaking up the continuity and giving us a window into the character's mind. Here we find that she grew up in a caravan with an alcoholic mother and used to make up stories while strumming a guitar, the images accompanying these revelations suitably dated in appearance.

At the beginning of one of the central narrative scenes, that of spontaneous creativity, we are presented with Strumpet walking into a virtually empty room, the walls of which are covered with Strayman's poems. The directing of this scene will be discussed later, but here it is important to draw attention to her nakedness. She is wearing nothing but a guitar. Her nudity is accentuated by the absence of distracting objects in the room, the shot concentrated on her and Strayman in the virtual emptiness. He initially approaches her and offers her a drink from his can of beer. As she takes a swig he stares at her breasts and we are also offered this sexually motivated view. To disrupt his lecherous thoughts, Strumpet throws the can upon the floor. Not only does Strayman then no longer objectify her, but the camera also draws back from such a view.

Up until this point in the film she has been a sexual object. When she is first introduced she is being given a lift by a truck driver, who states that she's "good to look at". He reveals that he never picks up "blokes", only women, and usually young ones. His gaze is one of lust and his intentions are clear when he states, 'I'll have you moaning.' This sexual motivation is his reason for giving her a lift. We can also assume that sexual activity with similarly motivated men is how she comes to have bruises, which the truck driver draws attention to. These elements of Cartwright's screenplay help to build a picture of Strumpet's life without her need to speak. The viewer understands that she has a tough existence, one in which predatory men are happy to take advantage of her vulnerability.

This element of Strumpet's past is further underlined when she gets into Strayman's bed. She expects him to get in with her, to use her like the other men she has met, but he doesn't do so. This helps strengthen the bond that is building between them because he has not taken her into his home simply to use or abuse her.

Returning to the scene that takes place in the room where poetry covers the walls, we find that at the brink of a freedom of expression and creative inspiration, her body moves from the realm of the sexual to that of innocence. The camera does not linger on her nakedness again and it thereby becomes unimportant. It is given a kind of innocent existence without sexual desire. In this light, as we see Strumpet dancing around the room while strumming the guitar, she appears not as a sexual object, but more akin to a muse, a sprite of inspiration and creativity who has come into Strayman's life and created a sense of meaning.

Another important aspect of this scene is its creation of a deep bond between the two characters, one which is formed quickly, but with greater depth than one created through mere conversation or usual dating methods. Both were lonely and isolated prior to this connection

119

and though they remain on the periphery of society, they at least have companionship. Their connection is at the heart of this film, which is filled with warmth and vitality.

The shared experience of creative spontaneity breaks down the barriers created by their life experiences and brings the characters together very effectively. This acts as a testament to Cartwright's ability to understand his characters, their primary motivations, and to create a very powerful bond through something that seems so simple at first glance.

There are a number of instances in the film where we see theft taking place. The most notable of these is concerned with the character of Knockoff. In order to make a music video for the song sung by Strayman and Strumpet, he conducts a smash-and-grab on an electrical store, only stealing what he needs, which is a camcorder. Boyle's treatment of this theft and those conducted by Strayman is not from a moralistic standpoint. He portrays such events without a judgemental perspective, which was predominantly the case in *Trainspotting* when relating scenes of drug abuse. However, because of the nature of the characters and the fact we can see they are good people who find themselves socially positioned by circumstance, we understand the needs that cause them to steal and such minor theft is forgiven in the context of the narrative entire.

Knockoff states that if the song is a hit he wants his name displayed on a mill chimney because that's something his grandfather wanted. Knockoff reveals that his real name is Richard Atkinson George Eclair. This is such a long name that he says, 'Abbreviations will do.' The abbreviation of his name spells "RAGE". This not only ties in with Strayman's delivery of Cooper Clarke's poem at the start of the film, but also to some of the lyrics of the song created by him and Strumpet. The song and Strayman's poetic rant are like rages against a lethargic and lifeless society which has pushed them into a disenfranchised position. One of the lyrics of the song is "let it out", which can be seen as either a call to let out the rage we all have within or to let out the energy and creativity that lies buried beneath the banality of everyday existence. Considering the other lyrics of the song, it appears likely that the former is the case, lines like "Mam's not there anyway, she's on Sky and Prozac, gone UK Gold and she's not coming back," being a clear critique of the state of contemporary society in Britain.

One important element in relation to this comment on contemporary life is that the song itself harks back to the 1980s and the work of such artists as Billy Bragg and The Smiths, the latter arising from the Manchester music scene, which Danny Boyle is paying homage to with this film. It is singers and bands like these who wrote songs that were social critiques, the likes of which are now rarely heard in an age of plastic, manufactured pop.

> *Strumpet* is a tribute to all the great musicians and writers who have come out of Manchester.
>
> Danny Boyle[2]

At the end of the film we see Knockoff's initials written on a mill chimney. This simple statement of "RAGE" underscores one of the themes of the film whilst also setting the stage for the rage virus, which would sweep Britain in Boyle's next film *28 Days Later*, those suffering from the virus not far removed from the image of Strayman during his opening poetic rant with spittle upon his lips and fire in his eyes.

As with a number of other Danny Boyle films, the movie is clearly positioned within a larger story which stretches beyond the limitations of the narrative. This is evident in *Shallow Grave* and *Trainspotting*, where the beginning of the narratives are relevant to events prior to the film's opening, the need to find a fourth flatmate in the former and the wish to kick the heroin habit in the latter. In *Strumpet* we enter at a point in the story after Strayman has gathered a pack of dogs and Strumpet has suffered physical abuse and been picked up by the truck driver. Due to the well-constructed screenplay, viewers do not feel as though such elements are necessary to the narrative and we are also given a distinct impression of both characters' lives up to this point.

Also, following in the footsteps of Boyle's first two feature films, *Strumpet* is largely open-ended, adding to the sense that the story is larger than the scenes we have been shown, giving us the impression that it continues beyond the closing titles. The only closure we are presented with concerns the relationship between Strumpet, whose real name is revealed as Claire near the film's close, and Strayman. We see them reunited on the stage of the UK music chart show *Top of the Pops*. However, we do not see the results of this appearance and do not find out whether or not they go on to fame and fortune. As a result of the uplifting nature of their reunion and the rediscovery of the vibrant spontaneity they exhibited earlier, this lack of closure does not leave us feeling unsatisfied. Rather, we rejoice in the fact that they are back together and sharing in the purity of their bond now that the shackles of commercialism are removed.

The record company's attempt to commercialise the song that was so spontaneously created essentially drains it of life and vitality. The wish to make money from innocent creativity has the result of corrupting it. The purity of the spontaneous moments we see in Strayman's room of poetry is sullied by the executives, who have designs on making a profit. Strayman understands this and after he leaves Strumpet in London, mainly because he realises that his presence is causing problems and may get in the way of her being a success, we see him painting over the poetry on the walls of his house.

This action reflects his disgust at what has happened to his words. He has even heard the song being metaphorically murdered at his local pub's karaoke night, all of the vitality well and truly drained from it, along with any real sense of meaning or passion. Strayman doesn't want his poems to be transformed and degraded in this way ever again and, as a reaction against the commercialism and degeneration of his work, he takes up his roller and begins to paint.

However, thanks to Strumpet taking an opportunity to escape from the music career that is being foisted on her, reminding her of the youth spent travelling from one place to the next in her mother's caravan, Knockoff takes Strayman back to London in the hope he can find her. This he does, informing her that he cannot live without her companionship, further underlining this theme of the narrative and showing the depth of the bond that has been created between them.

Knockoff calls the record company executives, who take her back to the *Top of the Pops* studio where she is due to perform. On stage before the youthful audience she goes live on air and calls out Strayman's name. He enters the studio with his pack of dogs and the couple are reunited on the stage, going on to perform a heartfelt and passionate rendition of their song, the gathered crowd caught up in the energy of the moment and the viewer overjoyed that they have renewed their friendship and rediscovered their creative vitality.

Cinematic Techniques

The use of camera angles is not as frenetic or as diverse as that seen in the director's previous film. What we see is a wonderful use of angles common to reality TV programmes such as *Big Brother*. Such shots, from the high corners of rooms, for example, also remind us of films like *The Truman Show* (Weir 1998), but located on a housing estate and with much of the colour and unrealistic gloss drained out in favour of an interplay of lighting contrast and realism. This footage makes the audience feel as though we are watching the unfolding of real events, that we are being allowed a glimpse of real lives, without those we are observing being aware of such. In this sense, the voyeuristic nature of film is heightened. We are made conscious of "spying" on the characters to a degree. This sense of realistic, covert surveillance is aided by the grainy nature of many shots. The gloss of many films is forgone in order to help create a greater realism.

> The great thing about working cheaply and quickly is that you don't spend time agonising over every decision.
>
> Danny Boyle[3]

Though the use of unusual angles is not as frequent in *Strumpet* as in "*Vacuuming*", they are still present. One of the most obvious examples is seen the first time the audience witness Strayman writing his stream-of-consciousness poetry on a wall in his house. A small camera is attached to the pen and so we are presented with a tight close-up of the nib and the words being written.

The words we see him write during the close-up are "your not even nothing". The implication, especially when the shot of his writing is immediately followed by a close-up of Strumpet waking in his bed, is that Strayman has been inspired to write by her presence in his house and his life. The incorrect use of the word "your" rather than "you're" implies a lack of education on his part, adding to his backstory.

Boyle opens this film in much the same way as *Vacuuming Completely Nude in Paradise*. We are shown an opening shot of Manchester by night, the glow of electric lights blurred in a pan to the windows of a pub, whereas in "*Vacuuming*", the windows looked into an office. This informs the audience that the setting is urban and it is after dark in a very simple and effective way. The blurred nature of this opening shot in both films also hints at the drunkenness of the people in both the pub and the office.

In the pub we are presented with a packed interior during a karaoke night. It is quite late, the patrons clearly quite inebriated. The scene begins as a performer ends his rendition and we are soon given our introductory shot of Strayman. He is sitting at the bar and despite the crowded nature of the pub, he looks alone and isolated. Boyle achieves this impression partially through Strayman's stillness. Everyone else in the establishment displays movement and conversation, whereas Strayman is motionless and silent, singling him out and allowing the audience to understand that he is of significance.

In *Strumpet* Boyle's use of light and dark is at a peak. The manipulation of contrast is visually striking, the interplay of often glaring light with grainy shadows used to great effect. Good examples of this stylistic touch are seen on two particular occasions relatively early in the narrative.

The first is when Strayman takes the spotlight at the karaoke night. As the poetic rant bursts from his spittle-covered lips, a spotlight glares behind him, at times making him virtually only a silhouette, his long coat filled with brooding darkness as his head is surrounded by an intense halo. He is like an iconic saint exhibiting righteous indignation, an image that may have arisen either consciously or subconsciously from the director's Catholic background. Here, though, his anger is not aimed at those defiling the church of God, but rather the church of life. He is the saint preaching to those who sin against the potential glory of life, those who lead a banal existence that smothers life's wonder.

The second scene highlighting the often overexposed use of light by Boyle in this movie is when Strumpet is herself naked and exposed in the bath. It is somewhat reminiscent of the use of light in the scene in *Vacuuming Completely Nude in Paradise* when Tommy looks into a large mirror, the bright light from outside obscuring his face. Strumpet is strumming a toy guitar as she reclines and the light through the window is so bright that it allows no view of the world beyond, instead flooding the left of the screen with glare. It is as if a divine light is shining upon her, linking this image with that of Strayman as a haloed saint. In this case it could be said to be the light of inspiration rather than God.

This quasi-religious undertone is again apparent in a scene which very effectively captures the vibrant energy of spontaneous creative inspiration and which has already been discussed in relation to Strumpet's nakedness and the connection made between the two main characters. Boyle's direction, coupled with Dod Mantle's cinematography and the versatile use of DV cameras, captures this scene with an energy reflecting the on-screen activity.

Its religious undertone arises through its similarity to scenes in Pentecostal and evangelical churches, when worshippers join together in enthusiastic song and praise of God. In this scene from *Strumpet* creativity takes the place of God to an extent and jubilation is exhibited through the joy of inspiration.

Strumpet enters Strayman's room of poetry, which is empty bar a few stray newspapers on the floor, this simple *mise en scène* therefore unobtrusive during the scene. As previously mentioned, she is naked and carrying a guitar and the walls are covered with Strayman's poetic scribblings. After a few moments she begins to strum and Strayman frees his words from their inky cages, setting them to the music and allowing them to soar in the vitality of the moment. We feel the excitement and joy of the characters thanks to the pace of camera-angle changes and the excellent acting. Also adding to the atmosphere is the gloom of the room, penetrated by bright light from the window and making the scene almost monotone. This, coupled with the basic *mise en scène,* means there is nothing to distract or detract from the moments of inspiration.

During this scene of spontaneity we see the use of a camera attached to Strayman, looking back at his face and upper torso. The same technique was used towards the end of *Vacuuming Completely Nude in Paradise.* Its effect is striking because the viewer is used to the subject of a shot moving while the camera remains motionless or moves independently. The movement of the subject and the camera are bound together, giving a slightly dizzy and disconcerting feel which adds to the scene.

> At one point I had a camera strapped to me and my responsibility was to shoot myself, but also get Genna in the background. It was interesting because obviously I was concerned about my own performance, but Danny and Anthony gave me another job, which was get Genna framed ... I liked that responsibility and it made me feel more involved in the whole process.
>
> Christopher Eccleston[4]

The *mise en scène* of Strayman's home gives it a dingy and rundown feel. He doesn't care for things, but for the dogs and then Strumpet. He is unconcerned with material possessions and this is clear from the decrepit state of his abode, where we see him simply emptying a tin of dog food onto the kitchen floor and then spreading it out with his foot. We also witness him having to clean dirt and dust out of his bath with a broom before Strumpet can use it. This suggests a lack of hygiene in his home, as well as his own lack of cleanliness. The general shabbiness of his living conditions is reflected in *Trainspotting* and *Vacuuming Completely Nude in Paradise*, most notably through the homes of Swanney and Leather Face.

Creating a link with Boyle's first two movies is the sight of Strumpet in the bath with a doll of a baby, squeezing it with her foot so that it makes a baby-like sound. This echoes the doll of a baby seen in *Shallow Grave* and baby Dawn in *Trainspotting*; it also implies a helplessness and innocence in relation to Strumpet's character.

The general environment in which Strayman lives is dull, is a palette of lifeless colours. The use of sunlight is rare and the skies are predominantly overcast, reflecting the location, or at least the way he views it. His appearance is unkempt, hair lank and greasy. His long coat is akin to a barrier to the world, a protective shield, its shadows concealing and adding to his characterisation.

During the narrative we witness his theft of a carton of eggs and a Cadbury's Creme Egg. The latter event is seen through one of Danny Boyle's trademark glass shots. This is the glass of the door to the shop Strayman has entered. As he purchases cigarettes and alcohol, we see him steal the egg. Most of this scene is shown through the glass, in which there is a yellow discoloration owing to a reflection, thereby distorting the usual cinematic clarity so prevalent in Hollywood movies. We also see the brief use of an unusual camera angle from within the box of Creme Eggs.

Shortly after this scene, we see another example of a shot through glass. We are given introductory shots of Strumpet, who is riding in the passenger seat of a truck, the driver having picked her up at some point prior to her introduction in the narrative. We see her through the passenger window of the vehicle's cab, the reflection of the passing world overlaying her face. This use of reflection adds movement to the shot despite the stillness of the camera and creates an additional layer of interest for the viewer.

Strumpet also presents us with a trope not seen in any other of the director's films. When the trio of disenfranchised characters meet with the record company executives in London they stay in a hotel room where we see Strayman begin to write on the wall and Strumpet joins in with the creative flow. Knockoff asks them to save their energy for the recording studio, but they take no notice of him. Rather than continuing to try to persuade them to halt their activities, Knockoff reaches for a remote control and effectively brings the scene to an end by pressing the "off" button. Boyle closes the scene in such a way that it looks like a television set turning off, the light fading to a point at the centre and then the screen going black.

This kind of self-reflexive involvement of the viewer's position is not seen in any other examples of his feature-length work. It is an unconventional touch, which makes us conscious of the fact we are watching a constructed piece of entertainment in a very direct way. This is especially jarring in *Strumpet* because of the realism present. In most Hollywood films the realism is minimal and as such, sudden breaks in our suspension of disbelief are not as striking, though they can still be used to great effect.

Boyle returns to trademark shots when we see the events at the recording studio. Here, the camera peers at Strayman and Strumpet through the large window from the control room. The recording doesn't go well, proving impossible to make because of the way in which the two characters sing the song, drifting away from the mics and dancing around the room. Strayman writes, 'Are we the creatures in the tank?' on the window, which overlays the scene and further heightens the annoyance of those trying to record the song.

The scene then changes to an office and we find Strayman looking into a fish tank containing plastic fish. Not only does this provide us with Boyle's trademark shot through the distortion of water, but it also reflects the previous studio scene. The implication is that Strayman and Strumpet are being put into an artificial environment and that in such an environment their music will be contrived and "plastic".

In the penultimate setting of the *Top of the Pops* studio we find the last element to have religious connotations. When Strayman and Strumpet are reunited on stage they sing their song, encouraging the audience and viewers at home to "let it out". Their performance can be seen as a passionate plea from a pulpit of sorts. The audience are the congregation, the worship of God having been replaced by the worship of pop idols and their church being the music show's studio.

Though this religious undertone is essentially thematic, the evidence of its existence, specifically in relation to Strayman's opening rant and the scene where Strumpet strums a toy guitar in the bath, is created by Boyle's cinematic techniques. Because his use of lighting brings this theme to the fore, it has been included in this section of the chapter, but equally belongs in the previous section.

> I always try and find stuff that you can do from the gut because I think that the things that come from the gut are the most interesting to watch.
>
> Christopher Eccleston[5]

Final Words

Strumpet, like *Vacuuming Completely Nude in Paradise*, provides the viewer with a standout performance. Christopher Eccleston is truly captivating and convincing as Strayman, giving the character a real sense of frustrated rage. His feral appearance is complemented by his behaviour, Eccleston's eyes filled with an intense wildness.

The film entire is like a parable warning us of the effects commercialism has on the creative spirit. At the same time, it shows us the beauty of spontaneity and the importance of making deep connections with others. These elements are treated with a clear passion on the part of Danny Boyle, who makes every effort to capture the moments of inspiration in the room with poetry-smothered walls. His direction complements the script, the locations and the characters, bringing the narrative alive with an identifiable panache.

[1] Smith, R. *Back from the beach* (*The Guardian*, 10 August 2001, UK)

[2] Smith, R. *Back from the beach* (*The Guardian*, 10 August 2001, UK)

[3] Smith, R. *Back from the beach* (*The Guardian*, 10 August 2001, UK)

[4] Unknown – *Strumpet – Christopher Eccleston*
(http://www.netribution.co.uk/features/interviews/2001/Eccleston_strumpet/1.html)

[5] Unknown – *Strumpet – Christopher Eccleston*
(http://www.netribution.co.uk/features/interviews/2001/Eccleston_strumpet/1.html)

28 Days Later

> I like extreme films, where you put somebody in the most
> extreme circumstance you can imagine and see what they do with
> it. So, a guy wakes up in a hospital and there's not a single fucking
> person in the whole city ... What a great starting point for a film.
>
> Danny Boyle[1]

Some of the narrative themes and cinematic techniques seen in Boyle's films up to this point readied him for this venture into the horror genre. They gave him the experience necessary to create one of his biggest hits to date. His common portrayal of abnormal psychology reaches a peak in this film and his effective use of light and dark in order to create atmosphere and narrative tension is vital.

The film was released in 2002 and had a small budget of around $8.5 million. It saw the continuation of a number of collaborations. The most notable is that with Anthony Dod Mantle, the two of them again using DV as the medium by which to capture the post-apocalyptic environments of the narrative. It also saw the return of

Andrew MacDonald as producer after not having worked with Boyle since *The Beach*.

This movie is the second example of Boyle using his directorial flare to bring Alex Garland's words to life. He had previously directed John Hodge's adaptation of Garland's novel *The Beach*, but *28 Days Later* was created from an original screenplay by the author. He took his inspiration from writers like J.G. Ballard and John Wyndham, who wrote *The Day of the Triffids*, and from films like Boris Sagal's *Omega Man* (1971), based on Richard Matheson's novel *I Am Legend*, which has recently been readapted into a film starring Will Smith and carrying the book's title. One of the elements Garland enjoys about many post-apocalyptic yarns is that they act as social commentaries and in *28 Days Later* he took his chance to include one of his and Boyle's making, the two of them sharing ideas and the script thereby being a response to their combined creativity to a degree.

Upon its release the film managed to take the top spot at the UK box office despite its 18 certificate and stiff competition from Hollywood. Part of the film's success was its release during a horror revival thanks to films like *The Blair Witch Project* (Myrick & Sanchez 1999) and *The Ring* (Verbinski 2002). Since that time a plethora of horrors have been released, quite a number of which have been British creations, such as *Shrooms* (Breathnach 2007).

Some had thought the genre virtually dead and buried thanks to parodies such as *Scream* (Craven 1996). However, true to form, it rose again like a zombie from the grave and returned with bloody vengeance, Danny Boyle riding this tide of blood with the ease of a master surfer and also producing a sequel to *28 Days Later*. This was called *28 Weeks Later* (2007) and starred Robert Carlyle, seen in *Trainspotting* and *The Beach*. Directed by Juan Carlos Fresnadillo, it was a worthy successor, taking the story of "rage" infection further, though avoiding any reference to the survivors of this film.

Basic Premise & Main Characters

Central to the plot is the rage virus, which is unwittingly released into the general populous by some well-meaning animal-liberation activists at the film's outset. Having been in a coma during the first twenty-eight days of the infection's spread due to a road traffic accident, Jim wakes to find the hospital he is in and the surrounding streets of London completely vacant of human life. He is played by Cillian Murphy, who would go on to play the lead in *Sunshine*. The choice of an unknown actor for the lead was a conscious one. Even if the budget had allowed for it, Boyle and Garland would not have used a famous actor to play Jim because they wanted him to seem like an ordinary man, something which aids in the realism of the film and underscores the portrayal of an ordinary hero.

The narrative unfolds with a well-judged pace as Jim teams up with other survivors; a woman called Selena and a father and daughter called Frank and Hannah. Selena is played by Naomie Harris, who underwent training in the handling of the machete that her hard-nosed character carries. Megan Burns plays Hannah and Brendan Gleeson plays the kindly Frank and has had prominent roles in *Braveheart* (Gibson 1995) and *Troy* (Petersen 2004).

Hearing a transmission claiming there is a place of safety from the "infected", which is the term used to describe those with the virus, the quartet of characters set off from London. The sanctuary is supposedly located at blockade 42 just north of Manchester, Boyle mentioning the city that was the location for both of his previous two films and near which he grew up.

On arrival Frank contracts the rage virus, which is blood-borne, the symbol used for the film being the internationally recognised symbol for biohazards. The remaining trio are taken to a country house, which is the base for a small group of soldiers led by Major Henry West, played with authority by Christopher Eccleston in his third and final outing in a Danny Boyle film. He and the other actors playing soldiers had to endure three days of training alongside real soldiers in order to be able to convincingly portray military men.

This safe haven is not all it seems and the three characters who have journeyed north soon find they are fighting for their lives, not just with the infected, but with others who have survived the widespread virus that has caused the UK to become a quarantined area.

> We wanted a horror/zombie film, but we also wanted it to be more emotional than horror films normally are. We wanted you to genuinely care about these people.
>
> Danny Boyle[2]

Narrative Themes

In *28 Days Later* we see Danny Boyle utilise elements seen in his first two films. The aspects of suspense, thriller and horror seen in *Shallow Grave* and *Trainspotting* are present in this movie, but to a much greater degree befitting the narrative content. We also find that the concept of rage was brought to the fore in his previous film, *Strumpet*. Even the lead character, Strayman, exhibited what could be seen as a watered-down version of the rage virus, spittle upon his lips as he growls and barks on a number of occasions in the 2001 drama. *28 Days Later* takes Strayman's rage to the extreme. The rage seen in this horror includes a mindlessness. Those with the virus are like a version of zombies, but are faster and retain a pulse. They do not die, they simply become infected and are Boyle's most prominent depiction of abnormal psychology.

The idea of using a rage virus was partially inspired by paranoia evident in British society. This related to disease and infection, not least because of a serious outbreak of foot-and-mouth disease, along with the fear of possible terrorist attacks using bio-weapons, such as anthrax. Here, it is important to mention that though the film was released after the World Trade Center attack, it was actually filmed prior to it, at a time when the idea of bio-weapons was predominant in regards to international terrorism.

The rage virus concept also reflects something that Danny Boyle feels very strongly about; consumerism's false promises of dreams coming true, of instant happiness through a new car, a different mascara, a holiday, etc., etc. The fact that these promises cannot be fulfilled, that when you drive your new car the roads aren't empty like in the adverts, that your mascara doesn't make your lashes look longer because you can't be enhanced in post production, and the tourist disco near your hotel starts up every night at nine with the song *Agga do,* builds tension within the general populous, as does the fact that people often can't afford these things.

Adverts promise a better life, magazines constantly interview those who, it is claimed, have lives we should all aspire to – the celebs and stars of this world. We are corralled into a position where our desire for all these things is brought to the boil, only to find we cannot have them as easily as is suggested. So, rather than the desire being satiated, it boils over into frustration, unrest and instances of rage. The film takes this underlying rage and accentuates it to the nth degree, allows it full control of the infected individuals, who are beyond reason.

The use of chimpanzees in the opening scenes reflects all of the aforementioned. We witness their unrest in the cages, which mark the limitations of their lives, echoing the limitations of each of our lives and the unrest this causes in the face of so much material desire.

A couple of interesting points arise in the film in relation to Jim's confrontation with a boy in a roadside store. Until this point we have not heard any infected individuals utter an intelligible word. This means it is quite surprising and haunting to hear the boy suddenly shouting, 'I hate you.' These are the only words uttered by any infected person during the entire course of the movie and are therefore striking. Linked to the points made earlier, the words reflect the venom of a child who lashes out at his parents because of their inability to satisfy his material desires, which have been inflated to unrealistic proportions by consumerism. It is also the case that this confrontation with an infected child apes a similar scene in George A. Romero's *Dawn of the Dead* (1978).

The violence conducted by both the infected and uninfected is brutal and often bloody, something shown right from the start when the released chimp attacks the female activist and she is soon possessed by the rage, vomiting thick, dark blood before turning to one of her companions with the symptomatic red eyes that mark her out as infected. The violence of *28 Days Later* is more stylistic than in Boyle's other films, which is entirely suited to the genre. The blood and gore matches many movies within the zombie horror subgenre. However, this violence is not coupled with the humour seen in films like *Braindead* (Jackson 1992) and the British *Sean of the Dead* (Wright 2004). It retains a seriousness which reflects that used in *The Shining* (Kubrick 1980) and *The Descent* (Marshall 2005).

The use of humour in relation to violence is one of the demarcation points of the horror genre. Though staying true to the generic depictions of blood-spattered violence, Boyle remains firmly in the realm of seriousness, which is consistent with other portrayals of violence in his films.

The use of two religious references is prominent near the start of the film. The first relates to a postcard Jim takes down from amidst the wall of missing persons flyers. We see him read the words scribbled on the back, ones which state, "I will prepare your grave, for you are vile." The place of origin for this sentence is clearly marked at the bottom as being Nahum 1:14. Nahum is a book in the Bible's Old Testament. In it we are told of

God's wrath against a place called Nineveh, where "carved images and cast idols" are worshipped. This directly references the underlying theme of consumerism being a source of frustration and rage, the metaphorical cause for the death and destruction seen in the film. The images and cast idols are the celebrities we are encouraged to worship and the materialistic ideals we are persuaded to aspire to. Those worshipping such images and idols are the "vile" and from the perspective of this narrative are those with the rage virus, those who have been overcome with rage because they cannot have what the adverts and media in general promise them. It is this vileness, this rage infection, which will prepare these people for the grave, for they cannot continue living for long, thanks to their much-reduced mental faculties. Some may also think this reference implies the rage virus is God's punishment for turning away from Him, but this is contradicted by the second religious reference.

Jim's first port of call after wandering the streets of London is a church. Boyle's familiar talent of intensifying a scene's impact by using a striking mix of light and shadow comes into play and gives the building's interior a feeling of threat and suspense. It is here, in this shadowy, holy place, that Jim has his first encounter with an infected person. Interestingly, this turns out to be the priest. God has not saved him from infection and neither has He saved any of the other people who have sought sanctuary there.

Early in the narrative is a religious reference when Jim enters a church and comes face-to-face with the infected for the first time.

When Jim, Selena, Frank and Hannah find their own sanctuary at some ruins in the heart of the countryside we are confronted with a burst of colour, this colour being a verdant green. Nature is visibly present, something underlined by the four horses the characters see. These unbridled horses can be viewed as a symbol of liberty and this is what the characters have found beyond the urban sprawl.

It is during their stay at the ruins that we see Boyle's use of a dream sequence. Jim dreams of being abandoned at the ruins by the others and is woken by Frank, who he refers to as "dad". This links with comments relating to "family" that Frank makes when watching the horses in the fields. Both create the impression of a growing closeness between the four characters, one resembling a family dynamic with Frank as patriarch.

> I was so impressed with how the emotionalism of the piece was carried by digital – the content was there and I didn't expect that.
>
> Brendan Gleeson[3]

In relation to other themes relevant to Boyle's direction, we find there are a number in evidence when Jim, Selena and Hannah are taken to the country house where the small group of nine soldiers has made their base. The first is a clear Scottish link. This is provided by Stuart McQuarrie, who plays Sergeant Farrell. He stands out from the other soldiers due to his quiet and thoughtful nature, one introduced into his characterisation during his first appearance in the narrative.

An interesting note in relation to Farrell being Scottish arises when he and Jim are taken into the woods to be shot. Boyle has an affinity with Scotland and Scottish characters, one at least partially created by the making of *Shallow Grave* and *Trainspotting* and his relationships with Ewan McGregor and Robert Carlyle. He also has a deep connection to Ireland because of his family's origins. In this scene we see the Scottish and Irish characters, who have tried to protect the women and exhibited a strong moral code, escorted by two English soldiers who are prepared to take advantage of the two women and kill anyone who voices protest.

Farrell's words at the banquet scene are important in the context of his character, priming the audience for his actions and words later in the movie. He states, 'If you look at the whole life of the planet, we, you know, Man, has only been around for a few blinks of an eye. So if the infection wipes us all out that is a return to normality.' These comments are greeted with ridicule by the Major, who scoffs at the sergeant's words and says, 'Have you met our New Age sergeant?' The effect of this brief interchange is to make clear the dynamic of the relationship between these two men. From their words, glances and expressions, we can see that the Major holds Farrell in contempt and that the feeling is mutual.

Farrell actually provides an important piece of dialogue while he and Jim are chained to radiators. He says, 'The rest of the world is continuing as fucking normal ... What would you do with a diseased little island? They quarantined us.' These words suddenly place the narrative in a new context, that of a global perspective. Until this point the rage virus and the struggle for survival in a much changed environment have been all encompassing. Now, with only the use of a few words, this struggle is put in a new context, one which creates the foundation for the final scenes of the film.

Further themes evident at the country house are those of sexual threat and an associated moral dilemma. Sexual predation was seen in *Strumpet*, the title character having suffered at the hands of men and being the object of a truck driver's sexual desire. Here it is the desire of the soldiers that becomes apparent when one of the men tries to force himself on Selena, Sergeant Farrell intervening on her behalf, displaying his strong values whilst also positioning himself in opposition to the other soldiers. He is trying to retain a sense of order and civility as the social values of the group begin to collapse under the pressure of the situation they find themselves in.

The Major reveals to Jim that he promised to provide women for his men, a promise made after finding one of them about to commit suicide due to the apparent hopelessness of a male-only group of survivors. It also shows his willingness to forgo values held by the society that once existed, unlike Farrell.

After trying to help Selena and Hannah escape and being knocked unconscious by the butt of a gun being rammed into his face, Jim is taken to the perimeter wall in order to be shot. The two women are left alone in the house and it is then that the sexual threat increases dramatically.

Jim returns to rescue the women, one of the most obviously heroic acts shown in relation to the ordinary heroes portrayed in any of Boyle's films, at least at first glance. In reality, he saves Selena and Hannah under the influence of his own inner rage. He becomes a thinking version of the infected, something Boyle cleverly implies by filming his motion in the same way as he does with those suffering from the rage virus, which will be discussed in greater detail later in this chapter.

The acts of violence conducted by Jim while extricating the women from the house echo the severity of violence committed by the infected. His lack of compassion and emotion also echoes the infected as he coldly leaves one helpless soldier to his death and pushes his thumbs into the skull of another.

Jim's actions and the fact he is depicted in the same way as the infected point at the underlying truth that the rage is actually within all of us and, given the right circumstances, will burst out into our lives. Examples of this are regularly seen in the news. We hear about cases of road rage, air rage, attacks on ambulance and fire crews, attacks on teachers and hospital staff; sometimes it feels as if the rage virus really has been released and is taking control not just of the British population, but the rest of the world as well.

Jim is taken by his own rage, Boyle reflecting this by making his movements similar to those infected with the rage virus.

One important element arises in relation to this concept of the rage being within each of us. It ties in with the film's reflection of the paranoia evident in British society at the time of the film's production and which is still evident. This is that paranoia looks outwards, but the real enemy is actually within us. This not only relates to inner rage, but also to the fact that it is our view of the world which moulds it. If we gossip about other people we will think others are doing the same about us. If we fear violence and abuse from teenagers we will see threat in every group of youths we come across.

It is one of the film's examples of people displaying extreme inner rage that is involved in the downfall of the soldier's compound. Private Mailer is an infected soldier who is kept chained in a yard, the Major explaining to Jim that this is done in order to "Learn something about infection." What has been learnt is that the infected have no future due to the inability to think beyond the red mist that has descended upon their minds. Major West's death is caused by Mailer, who could be said to be venting his rage on the people who held him captive.

At the close of the film Boyle creates a degree of circularity. As the black cab, containing Hannah in the driver's seat and Selena in the back with the wounded Jim, breaks through the chain-bound gates of the country house the scene freezes. We see the scene stilled as the impact of the cab smashing into the gates launches Selena and Jim from the back seat. After this still we are presented with a black screen with "28 days later ..." written in the bottom right-hand corner, just as it was after the activists released the infected chimpanzee at the narrative's outset. What follows are brief flashes of Jim in hospital surroundings, exactly the same sort of surroundings in which we saw him at the start, after the first black screen. Therefore, this short sequence echoes the film's opening and creates circularity.

The flashes of a hospital's interior occur just before he wakes in a cottage set in a rural landscape, Selena and Hannah having set up residence there. This time, as he wakes from unconsciousness, he is confronted with a location of natural beauty rather than the human-constructed urban environment of a city. The infected are seen to be dying of starvation shortly before we see that Selena and Hannah have made a sign out of bed sheets and linen, which is spread upon the ground and simply reads "hello". This is seen by a fighter passing overhead just before the end credits roll, thus leaving the film open-ended.

We do not see if the characters are successfully rescued, we simply presume this to be the case. We are also left in the dark as to Britain's general predicament, the possible spread of the virus beyond the country's shores and the continued survival of the infected, though this is hinted at with the shots of them starving to death. This clearly leaves room for a sequel, though this isn't the main reason for such a lack of closure. It is displayed in a number of other films directed by Boyle and in this, we can see that it is simply a preferred way to end a film, leaving the audience both guessing and imagining what happens beyond the narrative's conclusion.

Cinematic Techniques

The use of DV allowed this production a great amount of creative freedom, Boyle even filming some shots independently from any cast or crew, Jim's sighting of a plane flying above the trees having been shot in his backyard. It also created an aesthetic suitable for the film, creating a grittier and more direct feel that works in harmony with the post-apocalyptic narrative.

Boyle's two BBC productions prepared him for this big-screen DV outing. The energetic camerawork and rabid character of Tommy in *Vacuuming Completely Nude in Paradise* are clearly echoed here, especially in relation to those who are termed "infected".

> We storyboarded odd bits occasionally for technical reasons, but I am not a great storyboard fan ... Personally, I much prefer making things up on the day.
>
> Danny Boyle[4]

The shots of infected people and Jim during his rage-propelled rescue of the women were subject to two effects in order to make them look so disjointed and unusual, unsettling the audience and adding to the fearful nature of those displaying such an intense bloodlust. The first was related to a facility on the DV cameras, which allows high-speed filming. This, when using 35mm, would normally result in smooth, slow-motion shots, but with DV a different effect is created. Though the footage is slowed down, it also has a stutter, as if frames have been removed.

The second of these effects was created by Chris Gill during the editing process. Using a technique that compresses shot duration, he speeded up the slow, stuttering shots and made the infected move more quickly than normal humans, giving them an eerily fast approach as they run up the stairs of the tower block where Frank and Hannah live or from the trees beside blockade 42. This, coupled with the stuttering effect that is still evident after the compression, makes the movement of the infected look unnatural and gives them a disturbing sense of abnormality.

Also relating to the infected is the use of red contact lenses. The redness of their eyes is the sign of their infection, as stated. The use of this colour is symbolic on a number of levels. It is the colour of both danger and anger. It is also the colour of blood, reflecting the fact that those with such eyes have the virus within their bloodstream.

The film opens with a selection of news footage of violence, anger, unrest and general barbarity. Such footage is often filmed on DV and so the film entire retains the same feel, adding a layer of realism due to the audience's association of DV images with news reports. These images are being played to a chimpanzee which is held in place before the numerous screens. This scene echoes the use of images of "evil" shown to the character of Alex (played by Malcolm McDowell) in *A Clockwork Orange* when a new government initiative to rehabilitate violent offenders is being used on him. Kubrick's 1971 film had a big impact on Boyle when he saw it as a young man, especially the use of realistic flourishes of violence. In *28 Days Later* this segment seems to be a nod to this film, though the use of horrific and fearful images is used for the opposite purpose. In *A Clockwork Orange* the images of "evil" are used to make Alex passive. In Boyle's film they are used to make the chimp more aggressive, to make its rage more extreme.

The laboratory where the infected chimpanzees are housed gives Boyle an opportunity to indulge in his penchant for shots through glass. All the cages are made of reinforced glass (or perspex). This is unlike most cages seen in films, which are usually constructed of metal bars. The director presents us with numerous angles that capture the agitation of the animals within their confinement, the audience seeing the chimps' restlessness as they pace and bang on the walls of the enclosures. These glass walls are smeared with fingermarks and the like, and we also see the breath of one of the chimps misting the glass before its face as it pounds on the glass. The effect of these distortions upon the cage walls is to increase scene texture and create an additional layer of interest within the shot.

Jim wakes in the hospital with a stylistic flourish from Boyle. The shot is a close-up and we are only afforded a view of Jim's right eye. It is motionless, reflecting the fact he's in a coma. A few moments pass and there is a sudden, sharp intake of breath. The eye moves and Jim is returned to consciousness in a beautifully simple way, which is striking both visually and in narrative effectiveness.

After the scenes of him waking in the hospital, which are akin to the opening of *The Day of the Triffids,* we are treated to shots of London streets, which include iconic images associated with the city and Britain in general. These include the Houses of Parliament, the London Eye and a double-decker bus. This is similar to the introductory shots to London that are seen when Renton moves there in *Trainspotting,* only here there are no other people present. This last point adds a sense of eeriness to the scenes, which are removed from the usual bustle of a city. Such an effect was also used to create an unsettling feeling in *The Devil's Advocate* (Hackford 1997), starring Keanu Reeves and Al Pacino. This used the empty streets of New York, coupled with the narrative, to create an unsettling feeling of impending doom. In *28 Days Later* this feeling is also caused to stir within the audience and the silence of London is disconcerting. The absence of people can only mean one thing in this sense, especially when coupled with Boyle's use of a wall of missing persons flyers. It means that something is badly wrong and puts us on notice that something devastating has happened, is a portent of what's to come.

An important difference between the shots of London used in *Trainspotting* and those seen here is the camera angle. In *Trainspotting* the angle is low, commonly head-height, thus giving us the impression of looking around the city. In *28 Days Later* the angle is often high and quite distant. This is purposefully done so as to increase the sense of emptiness and to make Jim seem vulnerable in the unusually hushed surroundings.

The *mise en scène* of the hospital and the city streets adds to our feelings of discomfort and building tension. It also adds to the impression of what has occurred while Jim has been lying in hospital. We see money scattered on the ground, litter lying in the silent streets, a car left in the middle of a junction, a bus turned on its side, a stall of tourist gifts spilled upon the ground and the aforementioned wall of flyers displaying people's anguish. This all serves to create a distinct impression of disaster.

The elements mentioned here cause a chequered idea of what has happened to form in the minds of audience members, one constructed through familiarity with other horror films and even science-fiction movies, such as *The Day the Earth Caught Fire* (Guest 1961) and

Independence Day (Emmerich 1996). In them, we have seen the populations of cities brought to their knees and disaster strike sprawling urban landscapes. We can build a rough picture of what must have occurred, Boyle and Garland leaving our imaginations to create scenes of panic, fear and rage-infused violence. This is therefore a very effective way not only to create the impression of a backstory, but also to make us envisage events without the need of presenting them in the film, something which helps in conserving the relatively small budget.

The shooting on London's streets was aided by the use of DV. Thanks to the highly portable nature of these cameras, Boyle and his production team were able to quickly set a number of cameras along a given route and then start filming in a short space of time, editing the shots together to create a continuous and slow ramble through the streets, even though the shots were created in a rush of activity as traffic and pedestrians were temporarily kept back.

> It [London] looks deserted, but at the edge of the frame people were going nuts trying to get to work, and there were casualties from the night before hanging round. It was great because you walk around those places all the time, all those landmarks in London, and so it's strange to see them when it's not frenetic and bonkers.
>
> Cillian Murphy[5]

It is near the end of these scenes of London that Boyle uses a newspaper headline to great effect. It simply reads "Evacuation". This creates numerous mental images in our minds to reinforce those already arising due to the emptiness and *mise en scène*. We see, through this headline and the wall of flyers, that the rage virus has created a counter "dis-ease" in reaction to its existence. This is one of fear and horror in the face of the rapidly spreading violence.

During these street scenes Boyle makes fantastic use of the soundtrack as a way not only to complement that which we are seeing on screen, but to also reflect the narrative entire. The tune playing as we stare at the eerily silent streets is *East Hastings* by Godspeed You Black Emperor. It begins almost without notice and slowly builds as we watch Jim walking between the buildings. As the volume grows Boyle uses the piercing sound of a sudden car alarm to increase our tension. It finally reaches a crescendo when Jim is at the wall of missing persons flyers, reflecting the apocalyptic content of the film and the fact Jim is uncovering the terrible truth of what has happened during his coma.

Boyle also uses colour to reflect the collapsed state of British society. The clouds above London are tinted yellow in many cases, something also evident in shots after Jim and Selena have met Frank and Hannah. This yellowness is a reflection of the sickened nature of the nation, of the virus that has spread through its people.

On one of the interior walls of the church into which Jim wanders after walking London's streets are the words "the end is extremely fucking nigh". These have been daubed in large letters. This is one of the films only uses of humour and is humorous partly because of the use of a swear word in a church environment, the two elements at odds with each other in normal situations.

The use of contrasting light and darkness is evident within the church and it is also reflected beyond its confines. During daylight hours the encounters with infected individuals only occur in shadowy and darkened locations prior to the group's arrival at the blockade. Boyle creates atmospheric and somewhat claustrophobic environments in which these confrontations take place. This increases audience expectation and tension. The former is heightened because we come to expect infected people to inhabit any location that is suitably lacking in light. This brings us neatly to the scene in the supermarket before the quartet of characters finally leaves London.

In this enclosed space there is a significant use of artificial light and a noteworthy lack of shadow compared with other interior spaces we have seen. This sends the audience a subtle message when coupled with the light tone of the music which plays over the scene. Because all of the encounters with infected people have occurred in shadowy locations or at night, we are effectively being told that the supermarket is safe merely by the use of lighting and non-diegetic music. We are cleverly manipulated by the director to feel no tension as the characters wander around the establishment. This has the effect of relieving the narrative tension, allowing us to enjoy the light-hearted scenes, and creating a calm from which the dramatic tension can then be built up again.

Early in the narrative we discover that Jim's parents have killed themselves when he goes to their home. This suicide has been through the use of pills. In the lifeless hand of his mother's corpse is a picture of him as a boy. He takes it and the words which have been written on the back of the photograph are, "Son, with endless love, we left you sleeping. Now we're sleeping with you. Don't wake up."

This simple use of a prop adds greatly to the poignancy of the scene. We understand at once that the reference to "sleeping" relates to his coma. We also understand that the final words, "don't wake up" are motivated by the spread of the rage virus and the terrible chaos this has caused. In those three simple words lies a powerful hint at the gravitas of the events which occurred prior to his emergence from the hospital. The fact that his parents don't want their son to wake up shows just how dire the situation must have been in order for them to have taken their own lives and wished death on their offspring.

As we see the scene of Jim's parents lying on their bed, Boyle uses a melancholic, non-diegetic tune. A lone voice sings a song, which adds to the overall atmosphere. For those who have seen *Trainspotting*, the bodies also tug at memories of the discovery of baby Dawn's body. The stillness of their bodies, the colour and texture of their skin and their position upon the sheets of their bed are all reminiscent of the shocking scene from Boyle's second feature-length film.

We soon witness a flashback to Jim's life prior to the spread of the rage virus. This is shown within the frame of the scene to an extent, Jim watching a home movie he made of his parents. Its quality is low and the light from beyond this scene, which takes place in a kitchen, creates a glare. Its use is similar to that of flashbacks in relation to the character of Strumpet in the film of the same name. Both examples create additional background for the characters and also more emotive depth to the narratives.

Following in the footsteps of the iconic elements displayed in the scenes of Jim walking through London early in the film is the use of a black cab for the journey north. This is commonly associated with the capital not only by the British, but also people in other countries. The cab, along with the previous iconic elements, creates a distinctly British feel to the film.

As with Boyle's previous two BBC dramas, there is no pandering to the US market, the director making the choice not to include a recognisable American film star or purposeful references to American culture. This is in contrast to the work of some other British directors. Richard Curtis is a case in point, the movie *Notting Hill* (1999), featuring Julia Roberts, makes references to Hollywood and to

American cultural influences such as *Beavis and Butthead* (this particular reference seeming forced in the context of the narrative).

The director uses purposefully bleak shots of often recognisably British landscapes to help create atmosphere. We are shown urban sprawl, train tracks, motorways and the abandoned blockade 42. None of these locations displays much in the way of colour, Boyle using a muted palette to create a feeling of lifelessness.

At the country house which is the soldiers' compound, we see Boyle's use of shadows and gloom. The interior is poorly lit, both during the day and night. There is an oppressive feel despite its size. The *mise en scène* is typical of country houses, the banquet scene displaying a suitable opulence. Placing the soldiers in such a location creates a contrast to normal depictions of military compounds. Boyle and Garland subvert usual expectations and present us with a jarring juxtaposition of "common" soldiers in an upper-class environment. This serves to disturb our expectations, unsettling the audience with the unusual marriage of filmic elements, something that adds to the overall atmosphere of the film.

At this compound we see the use of a number of shots through windows. The first is seen as Jim watches the soldiers shooting infected people who are approaching across the lawn. Later, when Jim has returned to the house after his escape from execution, we see him looking through a window that is awash with rainwater. This is effectively a Boyle-esque shot through glass coupled with his trademark shot through water. The distortion caused by the rainwater creates a warped view of events beyond. This could be seen to represent Jim's own rage descending and warping his vision, the hatred and rage within affecting how he views the soldiers.

When Selena persuades the soldiers to leave her and Hannah alone so they can get changed into the more feminine clothes that they are being forced to wear, Boyle uses a mirror as part of the scene. This, as with other uses of mirrors and glass in films he has directed, creates distortion through imperfections and smears. We also see the use of a mirror when Hannah hides behind it while one of the newly infected soldiers stares at himself with confused curiosity. The mirror provides another frame within that of the camera's gaze. The audience is presented with two views instead of one. It is like a shot within a shot and in so being affords us an additional lens through which to view the scene, but one which is diegetically part of the scene.

An example of Boyle's common use of mirrors, here to give us an alternate view to a scene featuring sexual aggression on the part of the soldiers.

The final technique of note relates to a single shot. This is seen when Jim comes to after having been knocked out by one of the soldiers. When he first wakes, the shot is upside down. It is the only example of such a shot in this film, though such angles are utilised by Boyle in the finale of *Sunshine*. Here it relates to Jim's disorientation as he recovers from the crunching blow the soldier inflicted on him. It also has the effect of producing disorientation in the audience because it is both unexpected and the "wrong" way up. Thus the audience experience similar sensations to Jim, creating additional empathy between us and the character.

The creation of empathy with Jim at this point is particularly important because it is shortly before he goes on the rampage. It underlines the idea that we are all capable of succumbing to rage. It also has the effect of helping to keep us psychologically aligned with Jim, for if we didn't have a strong connection with his character his display of violence would have caused the disengagement of our bond with him and his position as an ordinary hero would have been undermined.

The virus has been growing inside people. Everyone wants everything now. There are more and more cars and less and less room. Someone who doesn't move fast enough will get beaten up … It's an instability and intolerance that we have more and more in the west.

Andrew McDonald[6]

Criticism

The scenes of the cab passing through a road tunnel when leaving the centre of London stretch the suspension of disbelief to near breaking point. Though the way is blocked by abandoned vehicles, the cab somehow manages to mount and then ride over them. Here Boyle utilises the darkness in order to hide the fact that this is actually an impossibility. It is also worth noting that an attempt to add a little realism is made by having the cab suffer a puncture when dismounting this blockage.

Immediately after these tunnel scenes we see Jim, Selena, Frank and Hannah go into a supermarket where their actions are surprisingly reserved. Rather than the expected rush of excitement, scoffing and desperate grabbing, the characters calmly walk along the aisles carefully choosing the items they desire. This seems to lack realism, something usually present in Boyle's films.

It could be argued that the characters are merely adhering to behaviour that has become ingrained after years of social conditioning. Their lack of urgency may also reflect a misplaced confidence after their escape in the road tunnel. They have successfully left the centre of London and are well and truly on their way to what they hope will be a safe haven. Therefore they are buoyed by a temporary happiness which is reflected in their return to behaviour normal to the society that had existed before the spread of the virus.

Another criticism arises in relation to the country house, which the soldiers have turned into the centre of their operations. Here we see a large garden which is heavily fortified and well lit in order to halt the approach of the infected. However, there are strands of trees to either side and no evidence that the flanks of the house are being guarded from infected individuals who approach through these trees.

This is a minor criticism and is probably related to the limited budget of the film. It could also be argued that the high wall seen when

Jim and Sergeant Farrell are to be shot stops the infected from approaching. However, we see these characters being escorted through trees which we can assume are those seen along one of the flanks of the house. The depth of this woodland means there is plenty of scope for infected individuals to enter at the bottom of the large garden, hidden in the cover of the trees rather than out in the open. Though they have extremely limited mental capacity, surely at least a few would use this means of approach, even if only by accident.

Relating to the theme of consumerism causing frustration and rage in society, something taken to the extreme in the depiction of the infected, there is a point to be made that no blame is apportioned. Those who have sold false dreams and images to the general populous are not singled out.

The fact that the public suffers from rage in this film and that this will ultimately lead to their deaths seems to symbolise the idea that it is they who are guilty and deserving of punishment. However, it could be argued that they are the innocent victims of a manipulative and unfair system which is perpetuated through a strong and all-pervasive ideology of materialism.

Awards

The film won a number of awards, judges recognising the distinct edginess created by Danny Boyle's inspired directing and use of DV. They also could not fail to notice the new take on the zombie horror film which *28 Days Later* presented, enthralling audiences worldwide.

The Academy of Science Fiction, Fantasy & Horror Films in America gave the film a Saturn Award for Best Horror in 2004. The year before it had garnered accolades at the Empire Awards in the UK, winning in the Best British Film category, and at the Neuchâtel International Fantasy Film Festival. Lastly, Anthony Dod Mantle received the award for Best Cinematographer at the European Film Awards.

Final Words

28 Days Later is essentially a horror flick with a pulse. It is not a gore fest but a tightly wound film, which echoes the importance of a build-up of tension and the use of atmospherics seen in films like *Psycho* (Hitchcock

1960) and *The Shining*, which was mentioned earlier. Special effects and sprays of blood do not overpower the narrative, but complement Garland's good judgement of pace and Boyle expertise in directing.

There is a thoughtfulness both in the script and directing, one that highlights the inherent loneliness of the human condition and the need for companionship, both of which are captured in Jim's dream sequence. There is also a thoughtful reflection as to the nature of humanity's influence and presence on the planet, one which is presented in the natural scenes shown at the ruins and at the end of the film, as well as in Sergeant Farrell's words at the banquet.

The social commentary relating to the rage within us all is an important one in an era when some schools and hospitals need to employ security guards. The film does not try to preach its message to us, but simply allows it to exist within the narrative. The inclusion of this commentary means that this movie is not only a great piece of hair-raising and darkly atmospheric entertainment, it is also a provocative statement about the state of contemporary society, one made through spittle-covered and bloodstained lips.

[1] Tallerico, B. *Danny Boyle, Director of Sunshine*
(http://www.printthis.clickability.com/pt/cpt?action=cpt&title=Danny+Boyle%2C+Sunshine)

[2] Hunter, S. *28 Days Later: An Interview with Danny Boyle*
(http://www.res.com/magazine/articles/28dayslateraninterviewwithdannyboyle_2003-0)

[3] Chaw, W. *28 Movies Later …*
(http://www.filmfreakcentral.net/notes/bgleesoninterview.htm)

[4] Hunter, S. *28 Days Later: An Interview with Danny Boyle*
(http://www.res.com/magazine/articles/28dayslateraninterviewwithdannyboyle_2003-0)

[5] Pierce, N. *Cillian Murphy: 28 Days Later*
(http://www.bbc.co.uk/films/2002/10/30/cillian_murphy_28_days_later_interview.shtml)

[6] Epstein, R. *Andrew MacDonald*
(http://www.ugo.com/channels/filmTv/features/28dayslater/andrewMacDonald.asp)

Millions

You have to go back to being a bit of a kid yourself, you know, to relate to the world through their eyes.

Danny Boyle[1]

A light-hearted family film with a young boy as the star, *Millions* saw Boyle sidestepping from one genre to another yet again. After the previous darkness and gore of *28 Days Later* the director seemed to purposefully choose to create a bright and cheery movie in order to exorcise the rabid rage virus. Due to the success of his zombie-styled horror, Boyle was offered scripts for similar movies. True to form, the director wouldn't be pigeonholed into a particular genre, enjoying his ability to surprise audiences with something new and unexpected.

The original script for *Millions* had been in existence for quite some time prior to the green light finally being given to make the movie. Written by Frank Cottrell Boyce, the final version of the screenplay only retained one of the scenes from its initial draft after a year of discussions, readings and changes by Boyce and Boyle, this scene being the train robbery.

151

Millions came to cinema screens in 2004 and is set just before Christmas. However, it was not released in the festive season, though this had originally been intended. This was because it was pushed aside by larger productions, many of which were jostling for release before 26 December, which is the deadline for release if a film is to be considered for the following year's Academy Awards. This meant that despite its festive flavour *Millions* was bumped to a March release in the US and one in June for the UK.

Distributed by Pathe and funded by BBC Films and the UK Film Council, this movie did not see the continued use of DV cameras, the film being shot on 35mm. The edge so apparent in his other films is largely absent, and for good reason. It would be virtually impossible to create a family-friendly film in such a way.

The film contains a degree of fantasy and this is complemented by the more detailed and clear appearance of the footage used. The world is a place of brightness and colour, reflecting the view of a child. It is also a place of mystery where magical events can occur, a place which has yet to be dulled and demystified by the loss of innocence. Boyle conjures this childhood world perfectly, even echoing it in a playful use of techniques, and the audience can recognise it from their own youth.

Basic Premise & Main Characters

Based at a time shortly before the fictional change from the pound to the euro and set in the Manchester area, this tale is centred on a young boy of seven, called Damian. He is played by Alex Etel, who has a wonderful look of innocence in keeping with the character. One day a holdall full of cash falls on Damian's den and he believes it is a gift from God. He is altruistic and wants to help the poor with the £227,000, but his older brother has a more materialistic approach. His name is Anthony and he is played by Lewis McGibbon.

Their mother having died, the brothers have moved onto a newly built estate with their father, Ronnie, who is played by James Nesbitt. Damian has visions of saints, often asking if they have heard of a Saint Maureen. They encourage him to do good with his money and this leads to a number of humorous situations.

Damian eventually discovers that the money is not from God, but from a train robbery. A darkly clad stranger comes looking for the cash and the climax of the film is a beautiful testimony to the innocence of childhood, Damian briefly reunited with his mother and the materialism of the other characters overwhelmed by his simple generosity.

Narrative Themes

During the introductory shots of Damian and his brother, the boys are seen riding their bikes alongside some train tracks and this prepares the audience for the location of Damian's cardboard den. We are also introduced to the building plot that will be the site of their new home, computer graphics and animation used to show the house being built around the boys as they lie on the ground inside the plot, giving us an impression of youthful imagination. It becomes apparent that their new house is called "Serendipity", which is very apt as this relates to making happy discoveries by accident.

A common element in Boyle films is the use of voice-over and in *Millions* this is used to the same effect as others we have seen; in order to identify the main character as being Damian. Here it is also used to introduce one of the main narrative themes, which is why it has been placed in this section of the chapter.

We hear Damian's words concerning money. His brother has clearly talked to him about this topic and told him to, 'Start with the money.' What Damian means is that rather than saying, 'We've moved to a new house with a green door,' people say how much the new property is worth and how much the old one sold for, as well as talking about the mortgage, interest rates and other financial information. This informs the audience that adult society is infatuated with money-related topics, that they take precedence over other things such as the design or age of the house in question.

Damian doesn't share the same feelings as the society about him, at least partially because of his youthful innocence, and so this places him on its fringe in the sense that his opinion differs from the norm. In this he surprisingly shares common ground with such people as Renton in *Trainspotting* and Strayman in *Strumpet*. All are on the fringe of society in one way or another.

Stating, 'Money is just a thing and things change,' he sets himself in opposition not only to a materially obsessed culture, but also to his brother. This dichotomous relationship brings to mind the brothers

Jamal and Salim in *Slumdog Millionaire*. Anthony and Salim are materialistic and orientated towards the accumulation of wealth, whereas Damian and Jamal are unconcerned with money and are more orientated towards people.

> The film is really about generosity and is it possible in the modern world? And I think it is and there's a lot of evidence for it.
>
> Danny Boyle[2]

Damian goes on to state, 'One minute something's there and you can cuddle up to it, the next minute it's gone.' This is a hint of what has happened to his mother. From it we can assume that his mother has died and that this death was a quick one. We can also deduce that she was caring.

The music playing over the voice-over and the scenes of Damian building his cardboard den by the train tracks is totally in keeping with this kind of family drama, which includes touches of fantasy. It has a tinkling softness and a slightly magical feel, complementing Damian's creative efforts in creating the den, which incorporates a tower and therefore has the appearance of a kind of miniature castle.

It is straight after this that we find the first religious reference in the film when we see Damian at school. The teacher asks the children to name someone they admire, all of the children naming footballers before Damian puts his hand up and gives the name Saint Roch. He is then asked to expand and tells the class that the saint was so worried about committing a verbal sin that he did not speak for twenty years. He then goes on to mention virgin martyrs, making the rest of the class moan in disgust when mentioning Saint Agatha, who ripped out her own eyes in order to escape marriage.

He continues to talk with clear enthusiasm about the topic of saints until the teacher stops him, at which point he wears an expression of disappointment and returns to sitting on the floor. This scene therefore firmly establishes not only that he has a keen interest in the saints, something shown as he was leaving the family's old home at the outset of the narrative, but that he is also very different from his classmates and the majority of other children in the country. This clarifies his position on the fringe of society. It also leads to a certain amount of empathy on the part of the audience, who realise how hard it can be for

154

children who don't fit in with the crowd. This position is certainly one of loneliness and isolation and can also be one of verbal and physical bullying. However, we also understand that his difference is an interior one and therefore he is less likely to be bullied than someone with ginger hair or pimples, for example.

The idea of Damian not fitting in is brought up by his brother immediately after the classroom scene, Anthony warning him, 'You should be careful what you talk about,' and advising him to, 'Keep off the weird stuff.' This confirms the difference between the brothers, Anthony's use of the term "weird" making it clear where he stands in regards to Damian's subject of interest.

By this point in the film, less than ten minutes into the narrative, nearly all of the themes have been introduced. These are: the family starting a new life, Damian's view of money being unimportant in a materialistic sense and his interest in Christian saints. This interest is further highlighted at a residents' meeting.

At this meeting a group of three Mormons who live nearby are pointed out. They respond by making it clear they prefer the term "Latter Day Saints". The last word catches Damian's interest, thinking they may be saints, and when it looks as though he may start talking about this subject of interest his father quickly sends him into the kitchen under the guise of getting him to help in the making of drinks for those gathered there. This not only underlines Damian's saintly interest, but also shows us that his father is well aware of his difference from most children and how others may react to this.

One of the last two themes yet to be revealed becomes apparent when Damian goes to his cardboard den and it also reflects Boyle's upbringing as a strict Catholic. The young boy sees a vision of Clare of Assisi, recognising her instantly and even being able to state her years of birth and death, these being 1194 and 1253. During the narrative he has visions of various holy Catholic figures and each subverts normal expectations in regards to such people. For example, Clare of Assisi lights up a cigarette, the act of smoking not usually attributed to saints or martyrs, and speaks in a Lancashire accent, at one point even swearing. We also saw a similar subversion in relation to the angels O'Reilly and Jackson in *A Life Less Ordinary*.

In this, the first of Damian's visions, Clare of Assisi introduces us to a different way of describing Damian's den. She states, 'I used to have a hermitage myself once.' In this light we can see the cardboard den as a place where Damian can find escape, where he can be left to his own devices without interference from the outside world. We also hear Damian ask, 'Do you ever come across a Saint Maureen?' This is not a name that we recognise, but the reason is made clear when Damian adds, 'She hasn't been there long.' From this we understand that he is referring to his mother, the audience finally given her name while at the same time finding that she is not far from Damian's thoughts.

The use of so many visions means that *Millions* displays the most dream/vision sequences out of any of Boyle's films. Here they provide us with humour and even an element of controversy. This is caused by the unholy characteristics exhibited by Clare of Assisi and Saint Peter, who swears on several occasions and even blasphemes before relating the biblical story of the Feeding of the Five Thousand (Mark 6:30–44).

In his version of the story a young boy takes a plate of sardines and bread to Jesus, who blesses the food and passes it to the next person. The people don't eat this food, having all brought their own. However, they all start to share and this was the real miracle. Saint Peter points out that it was a boy who instigated the miracle and says that Damian can have the same sort of effect on those around him.

It becomes apparent that the saintly figures have not actually been conjured by Damian's imagination because they provide him with information he didn't previously know. This makes them distinct from his mind, giving them an existence independent of the boy. This is apparent in the vision of Saint Nicholas of Myra, who speaks in a foreign language. Damian would not know this language and therefore the vision cannot have arisen from his mind. We must therefore conclude that although a number of these appearances contain comical elements, they are indeed real visions. Reinforcing this is the philosophical tone of Saint Peter's message, which Damian doesn't comprehend. This means the Saint couldn't simply be a projection deriving from his imagination.

The fact that they are genuine visions changes the context of Damian's interest in figures from Catholicism. It seems that rather than this interest causing the visions, it is the visions which have caused his interest. Therefore we can assume he has been having visions for a number of years because this interest in holy figures is already well established by the time the narrative opens. This is supported by his lack of surprise when he sees the first vision in the film. If this had been the first time he'd ever seen such a vision Damian would have been considerably more shocked by the sudden appearance of a woman in his den.

The final theme is introduced after that of visions. This is the bag of money. It lands on and destroys Damian's den as if falling from the sky. Boyle described a bag of money as being akin to a grenade in chapter two and it actually has a similar effect in this destructive scene, marking its arrival in the narrative in a dramatic way.

Damian looks out of the wreckage and in a filmic touch that implies something mysterious is at work, the zip of the holdall pulls open, revealing lots of money inside. He looks up at the sun in the blue sky, a few white clouds passing by swiftly. This shot and the music which accompanies it hints strongly that he believes God has sent the money to him. The introduction of a large sum of money is seen in both *Shallow Grave* and *Trainspotting*. In both of those films it leads to distrust and betrayal, but this is not the case in *Millions*, reflecting the times in which it was made.

After releasing lots of pigeons in an innocently magical scene, Francis of Assisi appears to Damian and suggests that he helps the poor. What follows is one of the film's most memorable, humorous occasions, one instigated by Damian's childish naivety when it comes to the concept of helping those less fortunate.

Approaching a young woman selling *The Big Issue* on a city street, he buys a copy and asks if she'd like to join him for a meal at Pizza Hut. He and Anthony end up dining there with a gathering of homeless people who are only too happy to take advantage of his generosity.

The use of humour counterbalances the serious elements within the narrative, such as the stranger, the threat of burglary during the Christmas period and the recent death of the boy's mother. Along with the aforementioned scene where homeless people have a meal bought for them by Damian, there are many other good examples of this film's humour. These include Anthony's retinue of shade-wearing friends as he plays on the fact he has money. He is treated as a celebrity, clearly revelling in the attention. There is also a humorous scene that helps to add to the overall perception of Damian's innocence. This is set in his brother's bedroom and we see Anthony showing Damian pictures of women in bras on his computer, something which provides the audience with a minor example of Boyle's use of TV and computer screens. Anthony comments,

'Look, you can see it protruding,' after enlarging one of the images. It is clear from the continuing dialogue that Damian did not know women have nipples prior to this point, which shows a sexual innocence.

The release of the pigeons and the ensuing efforts to help the poor, along with such things as Damian thinking the Mormons are saints, show he is an innocent child. This innocence is shown to extend to his knowledge of society's darker side. After calling his bother away from the stranger, who has recently arrived on the waste ground where the den is located, Anthony asks, 'Did he do anything to you?' Damian replies, 'What sort of things?' Anthony does not expand, but most audience members know what is being referred to. The fact that Damian is completely ignorant of what is being implied underlines his innocence, which is a kind of purity. This puts him in the position of young saint, especially considering his attempts to help others.

Ultimately, Damian's innocence is summed up by his belief that God had sent him the money as a gift by which to do good. He is upset when this belief is destroyed by a re-enactment of the train robbery, which is organised by Anthony in order that his brother should learn the truth about where the money really came from. In relation to Damian's belief, it is also worth mentioning that the money that Damian pushed into the Mormons' postbox is seen by them as a gift from God, the three of them echoing the boy's innocence.

It is soon after this that the audience is informed of the imminent changeover from pound sterling to the euro when we are shown a TV infomercial. The countdown to E-day is taking place and all pounds must be changed into euros before that day, which is shortly before Christmas.

Dorothy, a fundraiser who has visited Damian's school, cooks a meal for the family in return for Damian's father having mended her remote-control bin. We see all four characters upon the settee watching *Who Wants to be a Millionaire*. Not only does this tie in with the title and thematic of this movie, but it also acts as a clear link to *Slumdog Millionaire*, which uses the game show as a useful trope by which to tell the main character's backstory. It is also the case that this creates a link with *Shallow Grave*, which featured Chris Tarrant, the UK host of "*Millionaire*", presenting a forerunner to that show called *Lose A Million*.

During the performance of the nativity which takes place at the school we find that the vision of Joseph takes Damian's role in the play and speaks one of his lines. This is the only occasion in the film when one of the Catholic icons interacts with anyone other than Damian.

Somewhat surprisingly, we discover that Damian's father doesn't believe in God. Mr Cunningham goes to see his son as Damian lies in bed after voicing disagreement as to the proposed spending and changing of the money, its presence discovered when Damian returned to the family's old home and his father went looking for him. At one point in the dialogue, Damian states, 'Don't you want to go to heaven?' His father responds by saying, 'Look around you, Damian. We're on our own. No one is smiling down on us.' He goes on to firmly state that Damian's mother is dead and that he'll never see her again, something which understandably upsets the boy, but is ultimately proved wrong.

This brief scene therefore heightens the contrast between Damian and the other family members. It also seems to hint at the fact that Damian's religious beliefs were not arrived at through his parents, but through his visions.

The next day is the last in which British pounds can be spent, deposited or exchanged. We find this out through a public information film like two others which have previously featured in the movie. These infomercials provide a countdown and a frame of reference for the audience, as they indicate the narrative's timescale. They feature Leslie Phillips in a sleigh with a busty blonde, along with the voice of Channel 4 newsreader Krishnan Guru-Murthy.

Later that day, as Mr Cunningham and Dorothy (Daisy Donovan) drunkenly decorate a room with the British currency they didn't manage to exchange, Anthony launches a venomous attack on his younger brother. He is angry that Damian has brought Dorothy into their lives, believing that she'll leave when the money runs dry and feeling disgust at the thought of her potentially staying with their father. We also discover that he is aware of Damian's visions. Near the end of his rant he states, 'The truth is, you're a loony,' and Damian is clearly upset by his brother's cutting words.

Near the end of the film Damian sets the money alight on the train tracks near the location of his den. A train rushes by and his mother is revealed sitting nearby. She is the last of six visions he sees during the narrative and he sits beside her. Damian asks if she could talk to his father, but she informs him that he cannot see her. When he enquires as to the reason, part of her response is to say, 'The money makes it harder to see what's what.' In the context of the conversation, this relates to the bag of money and the concerns of everyday life, these concerns apparently blinding people to deeper truths, such as the visions he experiences. She also reveals that she is a saint, the criteria being the performance of a miracle, Damian being her miracle.

They hold each other close, the vision gaining a solidity not previously seen, though hinted at a little earlier in the narrative when we witness Joseph walking the model of the donkey towards the door in the Cunningham's house, the fake donkey curiously sporting a halo. Anthony appears on the railway embankment and looks down at Damian and their mother embracing.

After a train passes she has vanished, but it is revealed that Anthony saw her. So here, with the final vision, it is made clear that the appearances of saints and martyrs have not simply been projections of Damian's imagination. They have been real and he sees them because of his innocence, especially concerning money and materialism.

> When you look at babies, there's something in their eyes sometimes. They look over your shoulder sometimes, and they're looking at something. And you look back, but you've lost it. And you think, "What are they looking at?".
>
> Danny Boyle[3]

The next day, Dorothy, Mr Cunningham and Anthony reveal they have each kept some of the money. We find out what each of them wanted to spend their cash on, Anthony having a huge wish list, which reflects his materially obsessed character, this list adding to the popular culture references within the narrative with its inclusion of items such as a PlayStation 3 and an iPod.

The use of popular culture referencing is far more apparent here than in Boyle's other films. *Millions* is packed with such references, just as the sweet counter containing such things as Aeros and Yorkies is packed with temptation for the children queuing beside it. Other examples of pop-culture which are mentioned include the ex-Manchester United footballers Roy Keane and Van Nistelrooy, the then Manchester City footballer Robbie Fowler, and the north London club, Arsenal. The first two footballers mentioned reference the largest clubs of the area in which the film is set, which is not too distant from where Boyle grew up.

Manchester is also the location for *Vacuuming Completely Nude in Paradise* and *Strumpet* and is also seen burning on the horizon in *28 Days Later*.

Even more popular references arise through Damian and Anthony playing Jenga with bundles of cash and the Nike tick on the side of the black holdall containing the money. Pizza Hut, *The Big Issue*, toy trains and cars, Newcastle United, mobile phones, *Who Wants to be a Millionaire*, Maltesers ... the list could go on, but what it shows is Boyle's clear identification with the elements of contemporary society that interest children. He has included so many references because children will identify with them, thereby creating greater interest.

At the end of the film, after the others have revealed their small piles of money, Damian states, 'That's how Anthony would want this story to end, with big piles of stuff, but it's not his story, it's mine.' Therefore we can see that the others didn't get to spend the money in the way they had hoped.

What we see is the four of them getting into Damian's cardboard den. A train goes by and the structure shakes. The central unit of the den takes off like a rocket, a trail of smoke behind it. Then, lowered safely to the ground by parachutes, we see the four characters exit into the desert where it has landed. This is located in Africa and the closing scene features local villagers using a new water pump that we can safely assume was bought with the money. The four characters join in with the celebrations of having clean water, splashing each other in a scene of colour and vitality. The scene ends in a still of Damian's happy, smiling face. We see the water trickling down an irrigation gutter and the film ends, using the same title shot seen at the start, one using a black screen with numerous copies of the word "*millions*" fading until only one remains.

This ending makes it clear that this film is about generosity, something which ties in with the fact it is set in the run-up to Christmas. *Millions* is like the positive to *Shallow Grave* and *Trainspotting*'s negative, showing an individual who is not stricken by greed and material desire and whose wish to help others is granted, as it should be in the festive season. The film reflects a change in British society from the Thatcherite selfishness and individuality, to a more caring and socially responsible outlook.

Cinematic Techniques

Millions is set in a newly built part of suburbia. The move made by the family to this suburban setting is the first of many changes to come, setting the scene for a narrative that starts with the disruption of equilibrium right at the start. This is slightly subversive as many family films begin by showing an equilibrium, which then gets disrupted during the course of the narrative *The Wizard of Oz* (Fleming 1939) being an example.

We can also see that the opening sequences are very much in line with most of the other films that Boyle has directed in that they give the audience the impression of entering a wider story. The family are moving house, but we do not know why. There is also no evidence of the boy's mother and so we are left in the dark as to what has happened to her. This adds depth to the narrative by placing it in the context of a wider story.

The opening scene also introduces us to the tone of the film through the use of colour. The boys are initially shown cycling through a field of oilseed rape. This is green and bright yellow, creating a bright and cheery atmosphere from the start, one which will dominate the film, as is common to family films.

The title of the film is made to reflect both itself and the amount of money that Damian will find. "*Millions*" is written numerous times in small, white lettering upon a black screen. The repeats of the word fade until only one remains on screen, also echoing the fact that the money will be spent.

When the family are moving house at the start of the film Boyle uses a pause on the part of Mr Cunningham in order to show his feelings. As he goes to leave the house for the last time, he stands in the front hall and takes a melancholic look back, pausing only a moment, but for enough time so that the audience can see his sadness and regret. This is very effective in letting us know that the house has been important in their lives and makes us wonder as to their reason for leaving. We also see a pause as Damian enters later in the film, reflecting his father's action and showing that the house is more than just a building, but a place of memories.

After the classroom scene, when Damian begins talking about saints, we see children creating the words "Welcome to our school, Damian Cunningham" with brightly coloured magnetic letters and in high speed. Not only does Boyle let us know that this is Damian's first day at

162

school through this message, but he also adds to the general brightness of the film. Using the sound of a school bell, the director then moves the film along to break time, cleverly using a non-diegetic effect to make the letters look as if they are being wiped from a blackboard, something very in keeping with the school location.

The school children provide us with one of Boyle's familiar shots through glass. They are in the local store and we see them jostling for position through the glass of the confectionery section, rows of chocolate bars before them. We also see the use of a glass cupboard door to frame part of a scene shortly afterwards.

There is a meeting of residents in one of the local homes and the community police officer is comically speaking to them about the possibility of being burgled, which is apparently high, and through his dialogue we learn that it is coming up to Christmas. Damian and Anthony go through to the kitchen under the pretence of giving Terry, the resident, a hand in getting the drinks ready. They stand near the entrance to the room on the right whilst Terry stands to the left of the scene. The audience are only afforded a view of Terry's head, which is framed by the door frame of a glass cupboard. This gives us two distinct images within the scene.

We see further shots through glass when there are only three days to E-day and the brothers go to a bank in the hope of depositing their money. In the glass of the bank teller's position the interior of the bank is vaguely reflected, creating an additional layer of texture to the images. The same is also true of the teller positions seen when the characters later go to exchange as much of the money as possible.

Another shot through glass arises when Damian leaves the nativity and goes to his old home. He leaves the model of the donkey outside the front door and it is then shown in silhouette through the frosted glass. This glass creates the impression of cold and ice, something in keeping with the fact it is approaching Christmas.

The fact Christmas is approaching is shown in a number of ways. The first is the "Twelve Days of Christmas" style countdown to E-day. There is also the use of Christmas lights in the *mise en scène* of the new estate, the local PC's mention of Christmas, the Christian nature of the visions, Damian seeing the star akin to that which reportedly guided the Magi and also the performance of the nativity. All of these underline that this is a seasonal film.

It is shortly after the bank scene involving Damian and Anthony that we are presented with Boyle's love of screen-within-screen shots. The brothers, after failing to put the money in the bank, have purchased new video-messaging mobile phones. We see a shot from just above Damian's head, in which he is holding his phone and his brother is pictured on its screen, talking to him with the sky behind. This creates the juxtaposition of a primary shot towards the ground with an upwards shot towards the sky contained within it. Therefore, using the screen-within-a-screen effect, Boyle contrasts these two angles.

Also in this sequence involving the mobile phones is a red line representing the phone signal. The boys are sitting on a hill and this line ascends from Anthony to vanish off screen and then descends to Damian. The sound of a mobile phone ringing when this line reaches the second phone is a key element when coupled with the visual depiction of the phone signal, for it confirms this to the audience.

> Alex auditioned and he was really interesting. He wasn't very good, and that put off a lot of people. And a lot of people wanted this other guy who was a much better actor. But you don't want an actor – you want a presence who's actually going to live in this world.
>
> Danny Boyle[4]

When Damian wanders around the new home in red pyjamas looking to be comforted, first by his brother and then his father, we see a wonderful continuous shot from a high position just above ceiling height. The shot begins motionless, showing Damian having trouble sleeping in his bed. He gets up and walks across his room to the door, the camera gently moving back and following his movements. He goes into the hall and into his brother's room. As Anthony tells him to go away the camera movement continues. Damian shuts his brother's bedroom door and the camera passes above a number of walls to then give us a view of his father's room as the boy enters. He stands by the bed and states, 'I don't like having my own room.' His father pulls back the covers and Damian climbs in beside him, the camera still moving to the right. Then, once both father and son have settled into stillness, the camera finally comes to a stop and there is a brief pause before the scene changes.

This entire sequence is beautifully directed. The camera's languid movement reflects the hush within the house and the sleepiness of Damian. The fact it passes over the walls and we can clearly see the tops of them is quite unexpected, thus subverting audience expectations.

Just before the audience witnesses Damian's first saintly vision we see Boyle's use of contrast coming into play. Damian is sitting in his den. There is bright, slightly glaring light coming in through the entrance and also through one of the windows he has cut into the cardboard. The light from the window falls on his happy expression as a train passes on the nearby tracks, casting regular shadows upon his face. The rest of the scene, other than the entrance to the den, is in darkness. Damian's happiness is therefore central to the scene, Boyle using the strobing light from the window to highlight the fact that he is a cheerful child.

It is also worth mentioning that this strobing effect gives this scene the feel of a zoetrope, something which many older audience members will remember from their childhood and which were from a time of greater innocence. This innocence is of the kind that Damian displays, for the idea of building dens is from yesteryear (though some children still do so). It is also the case that unlike many children in contemporary society, Damian is not seen playing computer games or watching lots of television. We do see his brother at a computer and this fits in with his more normal persona.

Anthony is a child of the modern world, his innocence lost. Damian is akin to a child from decades past, his association with saints helping to confirm this due to the fact they are historical. It is also the case that this sense of an innocence belonging to another era is added to by the fact Boyle shows Damian with a copy of the book *Six O'Clock Saints* early in the film, a book which was popular in the 1950s.

Following this use of dark and light is a shot that is not seen in any other films Boyle has directed. Over a shot of the train passing by Damian's den a number of "postcard" shots are placed. Each shows a different view from inside the den and includes Clare of Assisi, who we are just about to see in full. As with Boyle's use of TV and computer screens, this gives us a view into another location, while at the same time we can still see the original scene. However, here there are numerous views and each is different, creating a collage on screen, which connects with the theme of childhood. A number of halos "fall" into the pictures and one settles on Clare of Assisi's head, taking us into the next scene inside the den.

Another effect that fits with the childhood theme, and which the director has not used in any of his other films, is the block construction of one shot over another. The initial shot is of a woman wearing a bra, which Damian is gazing at on his brother's computer. Then, Boyle builds the image of the school's exterior over this shot with a series of zigzagging blocks, which are akin to children's building blocks. Both this and the previous effect subvert usual expectations because they are not commonly used in films. They are also ingeniously playful, like examples of a child having fun with the medium of film.

When we are introduced to Clare of Assisi Boyle's use of lighting is of note. Daylight shines down on the vision of Clare like divine light shining down from heaven, adding to her holy credentials. Also adding to them is the halo that hovers from side to side over the rear of her head. Such haloes can be seen in most of Damian's visions and they are something many children will instantly recognise from depictions of saints.

> I prefer to use flights of the imagination and often that can be spiritual as well. There's a strong bond with the spiritual side of life. I don't mean in a religious sense, I mean in a general sense in that we all have that kind of spiritual side to ourselves.
>
> Danny Boyle[5]

When Anthony and Damian first carry the holdall containing the money into the latter's bedroom, Boyle provides us with an unusual shot that concentrates our attention upon the bag. The camera is placed under Damian's bed, its height allowing us a perfectly framed view of the holdall and little else. This highlights how important it is to the film. After a sequence of quick shots and scenes set to upbeat dance music that reflect the boy's excitement at having found the money, including a reverse shot of a tower of cash rebuilding itself, we are left with a lingering shot of the bag under the bed, resting where the camera was placed when the holdall was first brought into the room. In the darkness beneath the bed the black bag is all but invisible, only the highly recognisable Nike tick showing clearly.

Another example of quick shots and camera-angle changes comes when one of the boys at the school relates the events of the recent train robbery. Coupled with rock music, we see rapidly changing images that reflect the story being told.

The arrival of a stranger (played with great menace by Christopher Fulford) is handled brilliantly by Boyle. The music accompanying his appearance near the wasteland is eerie, creating a sense of danger. His clothes are dark and he is unshaven. These elements, along with the fact he is initially simply standing watching Damian, create the impression that he is the "bad" guy. This is aided by the use of shots of him in silhouette walking away, turning once to look over his shoulder. It is also the case that when we see him again Boyle employs the dirty habit of spitting to increase this man's unsavoury characterisation.

Boyle uses non-diegetic writing to inform us that the nativity play is about to start. The words written on screen are "All Saints School presents The Nativity Story". Here it is important to draw attention to the name of the school, which reflects the visions Damian has.

When Damian returns to his old home with the nativity donkey we see him pull down the step ladder to the attic and then place the bags of money in the roof space. This is reminiscent of David putting the suitcase full of money in the attic of the flat in *Shallow Grave*. The fact that Damian then has to hide in the loft echoes David dwelling in the darkness in Boyle's first film.

An excellent example of the director's skills can be seen during these scenes in the family's previous residence. The softly lit and shadowy house has an eerie feel to it, the emptiness adding to this feeling. The sound of the doorbell pierces the hush suddenly, making the audience alert and tense. When a hand reaches through the letterbox its movement is quick, its appearance sudden, both elements clashing with the calm that had been in evidence only moments earlier.

The hand reaches for the key and unlocks the door. Boyle cleverly uses the same deep-toned sound used in previous scenes featuring the stranger, making the audience link the arm and the entrance of a figure to the unsettling man. We also hear a sound akin to a heartbeat in the soundscape used for this sequence, something that increases the suspense and echoes Damian's fear as he hides in the loft.

The dark figure of a man is shown ascending the stairs and Boyle purposefully allows us no view of his head so that identification is not possible. Adding to the tension is the fact that the man ascends slowly, such considered and quiet movement used in many horror films to heighten suspense and prolong the inevitable confrontation. It is also the case that the figure is silent.

We see Damian in the dark loft, the light from an unseen source illuminating his face, highlighting both his fear and the darkness about him. This shot is in stark contrast with one mentioned earlier, when his happy face is highlighted with light as a train passes his den.

His mobile phone rings as he hides in the loft, giving away his hiding place. The intruder pulls down the ladder to the loft and climbs up, the audience provided with an initial shot of the back of his head once it appears above the edge of the hatch, further prolonging the reveal. A drum beat has slowly been building in power and volume, reaching a crescendo just before the figure turns. Then we discover it is Damian's father.

All the elements of this scene combine to produce tension and suspense in a very effective way. Boyle utilises the shadows and darkness, indistinct silhouettes, sudden motion contrasted with stillness, careful and quiet approach, sudden sounds and non-diegetic sounds to heighten audience feelings and make them think the stranger is about to come face-to-face with the boy. The effect is a manipulation, which is then gladly revealed as false.

When Damian, Anthony and their father leave their home after the aforementioned scenes, we are provided with another shot through glass in which we see them getting into the car from a window, the camera gently pulling back as they pull away.

Soon after this shot through glass the family enter and look around the living room of their new home after the burglary. We see most of this scene in a mirror upon the wall which bears the cracks of being hit by some unknown object. The *mise en scène* shows the devastation of what has happened. Dorothy comes down from upstairs and informs the others that she has contacted the police. We then see shots distorted by the crack in the mirror, echoing the distortion of emotion and the normality of the house caused by the break-in.

During the scenes when the main characters attempt to change the money, not only do we see the use of numerous shots through glass in relation to the bank cashiers, but we also see further use of mirrors. This occurs when Damian and Dorothy go to the department store where his mother used to work. Here a number of mirrors are used to provide us with secondary angles of views within the primary angle of the camera's gaze. The health-and-beauty section of the store is bathed in light, somewhat reminiscent of the images of heaven at the beginning of *A Life Less Ordinary*. This is also the result of the extensive use of white.

A little later in the narrative we are presented with an unusual shot looking down upon Damian's bedroom as his father talks to him. We are only afforded a slim and sloped view of the scene and it is not until the stranger makes his presence known that we realise this was a point-of-view shot as he looked out of the loft hatch.

When we watch the stranger exit the loft the camera travels along the ceiling to bring the shot in tight and close to the hatch. With a loud sound to contrast with the hush that had been dominant, we see each of his hands grasp the edge in turn and then he swings down into the room. The quick movement of the camera and the loud sounds, coupled with the sudden appearance of the stranger's hands, creates tension, especially when juxtaposed with the quiet slowness of what had taken place previously. We also see the use of the stranger's silhouette against the barred light spilling in through the bedroom window as the man prepares to leave. This scene echoes those witnessed when Damian had returned to the family's old house and also highlights the fact that Boyle has created a visual theme that runs through the movie, which consists of bars of light and shadow caused by window blinds.

The use of voice-over at the start of the movie is echoed at the end of the film, as is the title shot teaming with the word "millions" on a black background. We are therefore presented with another small example of circularity, Boyle creating such in six of his films.

Criticism

There are two particular criticisms that arise towards the end of the film. The first relates to the crowd of people who have gathered outside the Cunningham's home. No explanation is given as to how they found out about the money. Also, surely those arriving first would have rung the doorbell without waiting for a mass of others to arrive.

The second concerns Damian's act of burning the money. Considering his initial desire to use it to help people and then his inclination to hand it in to the police, his act seems out of character. This is made even more apparent when, rather than burning the money that his father, Anthony and Dorothy have kept for themselves, he uses it to help others.

Awards

Frank Cottrell Boyce received the only honour for this film. He won a British Independent Film Award for Best Screenplay. However, the film received nominations for a few other awards, including three for Alex Etel, whose performance was perfectly matched to the innocence of Damian's character.

Final Words

Ultimately, this is a family feel-good film with a light fantasy touch. It is a contemporary fairy tale and a great Christmas film. Its magical nature is underscored perfectly by the soundtrack, which predominantly features gentle music and always complements the on-screen action.

Boyle counterbalances the light content with an increased use of particular shots, which add texture and underline his directing style. He creates a gentle, dreamlike tone with a mix of bright colours, bands of light and shadow, and with visions containing humour and poignancy. He also adds touches of darkness that interrupt the dream with well-constructed suspense, making this film a spellbinding tale of innocence and generosity.

---

[1] Murray, R. *Director Danny Boyle Talks About His Family-Friendly Film, "Millions"*
(http://movies.about.com/od/millions/a/millions030105.htm)

[2] Unknown – *Danny Boyle Interview*
(http://www.bbc.co.uk/manchester/content/articles/2005/05/19/danny_boyle_interview_170505_feature.shtml)

[3] Overstreet, J. *Movies with Morals*
(http://www.christianitytoday.com/movies/interviews/2005/dannyboyle.html)

[4] Overstreet, J. *Movies with Morals*
(http://www.christianitytoday.com/movies/interviews/2005/dannyboyle.html)

[5] Murray, R. *Director Danny Boyle Talks About His Family-Friendly Film, "Millions"*
(http://movies.about.com/od/millions/a/millions030105.htm)

Sunshine

What a great starting point: eight astronauts strapped to the back
of this massive bomb, behind a shield, flying towards the sun.
Fantastic! I'd go and watch that.

Danny Boyle[1]

With this film Danny Boyle ventured into the depths of space, while at
the same time he created a studio-based movie for the first time,
creating a dichotomy between the on-screen and off-screen
environments. There are elements of thriller and horror present, ones
which are underpinned by dark atmospherics and high tension. This
film therefore echoes other sci-fi horrors like *Alien* (Scott 1979) and
Event Horizon (Anderson 1997), rather than movies such as *Star Wars*
(Lucas 1977) and *Independence Day* (Emmerich 1996).

It was first shown in cinemas in 2007, three years after *Millions*. The
budget, though small, was bigger than most that Boyle had previously
experienced, being £20 million. This money had been raised by the
company formed by Andrew MacDonald called DNA Films. Because

funding hadn't been acquired from a major film studio Boyle could retain full control of the movie while MacDonald had control of its finances.

Boyle had previously turned down the chance of directing the fourth film in the *Alien* franchise because at the time he did not feel ready to take the helm of an effects-laden sci-fi film. Now that he had more experience behind him, he took the captain's chair and piloted the film with his usual flair.

Moving away from the energetic style of *Trainspotting*, his two BBC TV dramas and *28 Days Later*, Boyle used an approach more like that seen in classic science-fiction cinema. The first portion of the film has a classical slowness that reflects the pace of the journey. This then builds as the narrative gains in tension and activity, reaching a crescendo at the end.

Danny Boyle likes to prepare his actors for their roles and *Sunshine* was no exception. To help create the siege mentality of eight astronauts contained in the fragile claustrophobia of a ship in the cold depths of space the actors lived together in a student dorm in East London. This echoes the fact that the three main characters of *Shallow Grave* had to live together prior to filming.

To give the cast a sense of being removed from everyday reality, of being plunged into an environment far removed from normal conditions of human life, Boyle sent them scuba-diving. To give them background scientific information and to get them into the right mentality for this kind of classic science-fiction movie there were also lectures, film screenings and a group of quantum physicists were present on set for a day.

He also had them use a flight simulator, which they all crashed, and fly in a stunt plane, which produced moments of zero G. These two experiences helped give the actors a grounding for their performances as the crew of a space craft. All the elements mentioned combined to produce fine performances from the international cast, who predominantly spoke with American accents in order to give greater appeal to a US audience.

Boyle brought in science adviser Dr Brian Cox from the particle physics laboratory in Geneva called CERN. Cox, who had a number one chart hit in the UK while a member of the band D:Ream with a song called *Things Can Only Get Better,* not only advised on the scientific

172

elements of the story, but also spent time with Cillian Murphy, who adopted some of his body language in the creation of Capa's character.

Another actor who benefited from an experience directly related to their character was Michelle Yeoh, who plays the botanist Corazon. She was sent to the Eden Project in Cornwall, England in order to have a crash course in botany. Yeoh was Miss Malaysia in 2003 and she had previously starred in a number of films, including Ang Lee's highly acclaimed *Crouching Tiger, Hidden Dragon* (2003) and *Memoirs of a Geisha* (Marshall 2005). She was the first actor to be cast and was offered any part she wished.

It wasn't just the cast that had to go on excursions. Production designer Mark Tildesley and cinematographer Alwin Kuchler went with Boyle to visit a nuclear submarine to get a feel for enclosed and claustrophobic atmospheres that cannot easily be escaped. Boyle also watched the film *Das Boot* (Petersen 1981), which portrays a stifling claustrophobia, and he spoke to NASA about the fictional mission taking place in the film. They told him that they would never send astronauts on a long journey in such a confined space because the crew would go mad. So, to add to the realism, Boyle included the oxygen garden, thereby creating a relatively large space containing organic material.

This still shows not only the claustrophobic nature of the interior of Icarus II, but also Boyle's use of unusual angles.

The screenplay was written by Alex Garland with input from Boyle and Cox. This was Boyle's third occasion working with Garland, whose girlfriend played the part of the woman with children seen on Earth at the end of the film.

There were a number of influences on this film, including the classic science-fiction films *2001: A Space Odyssey* (Kubrick 1968), *Alien*, and *Solyaris* (Tarkovsky 1972), the former two by British directors. *2001* and *Alien* both break down into three constituent parts, just as *Sunshine* does. These are: a ship, a crew and a signal that changes everything.

One of the most unexpected influences is the US animated series *South Park*. The design for the helmets of the distinctive gold spacesuits used in the film were partly based on the funnel shape of Kenny's hood, this character virtually never surviving an episode and thereby being a perfect reference considering events in the movie.

Basic Premise & Main Characters

Set fifty years in the future, we discover that Earth is in the grip of a solar winter thanks to a dimming of the sun's brightness. Flying to the star are eight astronauts with a huge bomb the size of Manhattan, known as the "payload", attached to the front of their ship, which is called Icarus II. Their mission is to launch the payload into the sun in the hope that it will cause it to burn brightly once again. They have already been travelling for sixteen months by the time the narrative opens and they are nearing their destination.

The eight crew members are the main characters, along with the captain of a previous mission that went missing called Icarus I. The crew's names are Captain Kaneda, Capa, Cassie, Mace, Corazon, Trey and Harvey. The performances that all the actors give are perfectly suited to the environment their characters find themselves in, something no doubt aided by the programme of events created by Boyle to help them prepare for their roles. The cast members are: Hiroyuki Sanada, who can be seen in *The Last Samurai* (Zwick 2003); Cillian Murphy from *28 Days Later* and *Batman Begins* (Nolan 2005); Rose Byrne from *28 Weeks Later* and *Troy* (Petersen 2004); Chris Evans, who starred as Johnny Storm in *Fantastic Four* (Story 2005); Michelle Yeoh, who has already been mentioned; Benedict Wong, who has appeared in a number of films and also as DS David Chiu in the UK's long-running police drama *The Bill*; and lastly Troy Garity, who has made over twenty film and TV appearances. All of these actors combine to make a convincing crew.

The final main character is Captain Pinbacker from Icarus I. He is played by Mark Strong, who gives a wonderfully threatening and psychotic performance. Strong has starred in a great many films, including *Stardust* (Vaughn 2007), *The Young Victoria* (Vallée 2009), and interestingly also appeared in István Szabó's 1999 film about a family of Hungarian Jews, which happened to be called *Sunshine*.

> Just for once there's a film where the physicist looks like Cillian Murphy rather than some old man. That's a good thing.
>
> Dr Brian Cox[2]

As Icarus II nears the sun and the end of its mission the distress signal of Icarus I is picked up. Deciding to rendezvous with the other ship, the mission begins to slowly unravel from the point of Captain Kaneda's death after he and Capa conduct necessary repairs to the heat shield.

Finding charred remains in the observation room of Icarus I, the crew of Icarus II presume the crew to be dead. However, Captain Pinbacker is still alive and boards Icarus II intent upon bringing the mission to an unsuccessful end. In a finale filled with breathless action, imagery and directing, the payload plummets into the sun as Capa and Cassie come face-to-face with Pinbacker.

Narrative Themes

As with most of Boyle's films, the narrative is clearly positioned within a larger story. This is apparent from the start of *Sunshine* as the mission has already been under way for sixteen months. However, unlike other science-fiction films of a similar ilk, like *Armageddon* (Dunn 1999), Boyle resists including scenes from Earth to highlight the danger to our planet and underscore what is at stake. This makes the narrative more defined, the story of events on Earth left to the audience's imagination, like the story of the spread of infection in *28 Days Later*, for example.

As with his venture into horror, *Sunshine* is post-apocalyptic, but in a much more gentle way than in *28 Days Later*, which concentrated on the problem and not the solution, whereas *Sunshine* is the opposite. It is also the case that this post-apocalyptic vision was deliberately chosen by Boyle because it didn't portray an Earth in the throes of global warming, but rather in a global freeze.

At the start of the film the audience is primed in regards to the existence of a previous mission to the sun. We are informed that a ship called Icarus I was initially sent to complete the same mission, but that it vanished without a trace. This creates natural audience expectations in relation to this previous mission. We fully expect it to be of some importance in the plot, though how is obviously not clear.

As with the film *Alien*, the ship's computer has a name and a voice by which it communicates to the crew. In the former it was Mother and here it is Icarus. In *Alien* the symbolism was related to gender issues and the emergence of a strong and independent female hero after the death of the male hero figure. In *Sunshine*, the symbolism of the ship's name relates to the myth of Icarus from Greek mythology. He created wings with wax and bird feathers in order to fly. His father warned him not to pass too close to the sun because the wax would melt and he also warned him not to fly too close to the sea because the feathers would become wet. Due to the powerful feelings he felt when successfully taking flight, Icarus flew too close to the sun, the wax melting and Icarus tumbling into the sea. This echoes humanity's use of science to raise it from its primitive roots and implies this will eventually be our downfall. Those who know that story will therefore find themselves expecting some kind of disaster to occur as the craft flies close to the sun.

The naming of the ship's computer creates a further link with a classic sci-fi film. The computerised voice of Icarus is akin to a female version of HAL 9000's voice in *2001: A Space Odyssey*, Kubrick's seminal adaptation of Arthur C. Clarke's novel of the same name. In Kubrick's film HAL 9000 seems to malfunction and this not only causes the death of crew members in suspended animation, but also threatens the lives of the rest of the crew. Because of this factor, people familiar with this movie expect the Icarus computer to have a significant role in the plot line, probably one with a negative impact on the astronauts, who, it is important to mention, may have a higher degree of education and training than most, but are still ordinary people.

This expectation is confirmed when, during a space walk conducted by Capa and Captain Kaneda in order to repair segments of the heat shield, the computer takes control of the ship in order to manoeuvre it, thereby threatening the lives of both crew members because they will be subjected to the direct heat of the sun. Cassie issues the command, 'Negative, Icarus. Manual control,' to which the ship responds, 'Negative, Cassie. Computer control,' in a very blunt and dismissive tone.

The computer is changing the position of the ship because the mission is in jeopardy, but at first it seems that she is malfunctioning, as is the case with regard to HAL 9000. In the case of Icarus, we find that it unintentionally causes the death of Kaneda, who does not have time to get to safety after repairing the final damaged segment of the heat shield.

From the event of Kenada's death the narrative tension begins to rise more quickly and the mission begins to unravel. This is aided by the trope of a lack of oxygen. Due to a fire in the garden there is not enough oxygen to complete the mission unless the crew could be reduced from seven to four. This is an interesting plot device employed by Garland and from it arises the question of how the three extraneous members will be chosen and how they will be disposed of. The audience are pulled into the narrative further, intrigue blending with Boyle's atmospherics.

We find that *Alien* is again reflected in the fact that Captain Kaneda is the only male with a beard. This may seem insignificant, but it actually singles him out as commander and potential male hero. Beards are a sign of maturity and wisdom and therefore the fact he has one places him in the position of leader and, to a degree, patriarch. Like the captain in *Alien*, named Dallas and played by Tom Skerritt, Kaneda is removed relatively early in the narrative, thus leaving no clear leader. This disrupts usual cinematic expectations because we are used to seeing a leader taking charge of the other characters during such films, see *Armageddon*, *Starship Troopers* (Verhoeven 1997), *Predator* (McTiernan 1987), etc. No clear leader then takes his place, the continuation of the mission becoming more of a group effort under general consensus.

In *Alien* the dispatching of the captain and male hero allows the emergence of a female hero, one who finally kills the alien without the need of a man's help and after strikingly revealing her femininity when taking off her uniform. In *Sunshine* Boyle and Garland do not depict the emergence of a female hero, but rather the emergence of three males exhibiting heroic qualities. These are Searle, Mace and then Capa.

Searle is the ship's psyche officer and we first see him in the observation room looking at the sun at only 2 per cent and 3.1 per cent brightness. He is then at the round table where the crew gathers in a way reminiscent of similar scenes in *Alien*. He talks with an element of religious zeal about the effect of being enveloped in light. He contrasts it with being in the darkness of a flotation tank, where he felt that he and the darkness were separate. In the case of being immersed in light, Searle says that he and the light merge rather than being separate and distinct.

This is the first hint of a theme relating to the psychological effect of approaching the sun's vastness. It gives us a glimpse of the abnormal psychology which will be very apparent at the film's climax. The act of being completely immersed in the sun's glare is presented as a religious experience of sorts, the brightness being the light of God and the human being insignificant in comparison. Bathing in the light and feeling at one with it is akin to feeling at one with God.

In the moments before Kaneda's death, Searle, rather than trying to persuade him to head for safety, asks him, 'What can you see?' He is more concerned with the sights as Kaneda is bathed in sunlight, consumed by it in an echo of Searle's words at the table. The fact that Kaneda turns to face the sun, rather than trying to escape, also adds to this element of strange fascination with the immense light of our star.

This scene and Searle's words from near the start of the film create a foundation on which Pinbacker's madness stands. The audience can also see that had Kaneda or Searle remained aboard Icarus II they may have also lost their minds in the glare of the sun's brightness towards the end of the film.

Further priming the audience in regards the abnormal psychology that becomes very evident late in the narrative is Captain Kaneda's viewing of footage made by Captain Pinbacker. In this footage he is talking about a "minor asteroid storm" that caused nineteen punctures to the ship. Despite the fact the storm created a risk to the ship, its crew and the very important mission, Pinbacker is grinning and is clearly overawed by the beauty of the sight of the asteroids approaching the ship through space. His expression shows that he is not concentrated on the mission, but is distracted by other thoughts. Of great significance is his viewing of the asteroids because he was in the observation room at the time. This adds background and believability to the deformed, irradiated form of Pinbacker that we later see in the film.

Capa is made central to the narrative when the distress beacon of the Icarus I mission is picked up. The decision of whether or not to make a rendezvous with the other ship is left to him. It is made clear that the payload Icarus II carries will be the last that humanity can send in the hope of brightening the sun, because there is no more fissile material left on Earth with which to create another bomb. Therefore, the chance to utilise the payload carried by Icarus I is presented as a means to get a second bomb, just in case the first fails. Because Capa is the scientist in charge of the payload and understands the mathematics and operation of the bomb, he is the one who must make the decision based on his specialised knowledge.

During his evaluation of the given situation, Capa talks to the ship's computer, which is simulating the dropping of the payload Icarus II is carrying. During the simulation, as the bomb enters the sun, the computer states that the variables are infinite. Capa then turns to Kaneda and states, '... the velocity of the payload will be so great space and time will become smeared together. Everything will distort, everything will be unquantifiable.' This, as with the video message he records for his family (to be discussed later in this chapter), and Searle's comments concerning bathing in the sun's light, adds to the elements which prepare the audience for the events that occur in the film's finale.

There is also a dream sequence that adds to the priming, and this is had by Capa. He dreams of falling into the sun and wakes to find Cassie watching him. She guesses at his dream and it becomes apparent they share the same subconscious vision. It is a vision that is tied to the end of the film, almost a premonition of what will happen.

This is further cemented shortly after Kaneda's death. 'We're going to die out here, like the other crew. I know it. So do you,' states Cassie to Capa. This links not only to the dreams of falling into the sun that both characters have had, but also to audience expectations in regard Icarus I.

> Working with Danny has always been a big fantasy of mine, in the wish list of directors that I've wanted to meet or whatever. So, to me it was like one of the best experiences I've had as an actress.
>
> Rose Byrne[3]

Cassie's certainty that the crew of Icarus I are dead is confirmed when the hushed ship is explored. 'They had an epiphany. They saw the light,' states Searle upon discovering the ashen remains of the crew in the observation room of Icarus I, his words continuing the religious connotations relating to the glare of the sun. These crew members have been reduced to ashes by viewing the sun without the use of a filter.

The opening words to this scene are, 'I have something to say.' This line, its tone, style of delivery and the pause which follows, bring to mind a small segment of dialogue from another science fiction film, this being *Highlander* (Mulcahy 1986). In this film the "evil" character, called the Kurgan, states, 'I have something to say … It's better to burn out than to fade away.' This sentiment is very apt in relation to the burnt corpses that have been found and to the ending of *Sunshine*. This dialogue from *Highlander* also has relevance because it is said in a church. Searle says the line of dialogue in the observation room of Icarus I, which is like a church where the crew members have gathered to worship in the light of the sun, of God. Further to this, the sentiment of the Kurgan's words is echoed in the character of Pinbacker, both of these characters also being regarded as "evil". Though this reference may not be intentional, it is certainly relevant.

In the film's climax we hear Pinbacker state, 'For seven years I spoke with God. He told me to take us all to heaven.' It is clear that he intends to halt the mission and end all hope of humanity's survival. His religious zeal, his born-again fanaticism, is going to bring death to billions. In this we can see a clear parallel with terrorist activities on Earth. These are driven by fanaticism, which can often be interpreted as insanity from the viewpoint of those witnessing things such as the World Trade Center attack. It is this attack that is echoed in Pinbacker's wish to take over the flight and thereby cause death and destruction on Earth. He is symbolic of terrorists who, in truth, lose their religion as soon as they commit to a path of murder, for no major religion condones the killing of innocent people.

Of primary importance is the fact that Pinbacker's zeal is a response to an emotional and psychological need to come to terms with not only the enormity of the mission's importance, but also with the enormity of the sun and of space. In the vast expanses and confronted with the violent beauty of the star, it is easy to be overcome by a feeling of insignificance to the point of nihilism. An alternative to this feeling is to take up a belief in something beyond the life he knows, beyond the science and the mission, something to end the loneliness and insignificance. Pinbacker therefore throws himself into religious belief, his single-minded fanaticism counterbalancing the almost overwhelming feelings of vulnerability and meaninglessness. In the face of the vastness and the intense beauty and violence, it is not surprising that his only way of coping is to adopt a maniacal fanaticism. However, it is his choice to put his faith in God rather than science that is of note. In his eyes only God can fill the void, even contain it within His sphere of existence and therefore diminish its psychological impact.

Through Pinbacker we find there is a theme of science verses religion. Pinbacker is firmly on the side of God and Capa's allegiance is with science. The outward expression of God is the sun and in relation to science it is the payload. Due to Pinbacker's fanaticism, he attempts to kill the man of science and thereby stop the expression of science, the bomb. He and his religious beliefs are unsuccessful and the mission is completed. Ultimately, science wins over religion in the film's narrative. Pinbacker, the symbol of zealous religion, is devoured by the very source of his divine light, one that science then has an influence over when the bomb is successful in making the sun burn brighter.

It is through Pinbacker's character that we come to understand that the sun is essentially a character in the film, something we saw in relation to the apartment in *Shallow Grave*. This is why the film *Solyaris* was used as a reference. It is about an alien consciousness that cannot be understood by humans and is far removed from what we recognise as life. The idea of consciousness existing in things other than obvious life-forms is transposed to the sun to a degree. Boyle gives it a strong presence and links it with an idea of God, not just through Pinbacker, but also through Searle, and it gains in significance because of its effects on the characters.

The use of a solitary shoot of growth in the oxygen garden towards the end of the film acts as a symbol of hope. Boyle effectively contrasts the green of its fragile leaves against the darkness of the charred remains, accentuating the shoot's presence and its meaning. Life will survive; the Earth will be freed from the grip of solar winter after the characters have sacrificed their lives in the fire of the sun.

The idea of sacrifice leads on to the fact that there are five suicides in the narrative. This subject is something Boyle had previously portrayed in relation to the character of Daffy in *The Beach* and Jim's parents in *28 Days Later*, Major West also revealing in a segment of dialogue that he had found one of his men about to shoot himself. The first suicide is Captain Kaneda's. He decides not to make an attempt to reach safety after fixing the heat shield, but instead opts for death, turning to face the sun. Searle also chooses suicide, not by simply staying aboard Icarus I with no chance of escaping its silent confines, but by going to the observation room and sitting, waiting for the full brunt of the sun's light to devour his life.

Trey's bloody and more traditional suicide takes place in the simulation room, where environments and scenes from Earth can be played and experienced. At the time of the discovery of Trey's body a flock of birds is being simulated, flying about the room. Birds are a symbol of liberty and here they can be seen to symbolise not only Trey's liberation from life, but from the guilt he felt in relation to the mission. When making his calculations concerning a change of course in order to intercept Icarus I he forgot to change the angle of the shields, thereby causing the damage that Capa and Kaneda had to fix.

It is through Trey that a moral dilemma arises in the narrative. Once Harvey and Searle are removed from the crew of Icarus II the remaining members nearly have enough oxygen to complete the mission. They still need the death of one more crew member in order to drop the payload and it is decided that Trey must be killed, his life being traded for that of all humanity. Cassie is unable to agree to this despite the logic of the argument for such a course of action. Her values will not enable her to vote for a fellow human's death, despite the fact the mission will fail if Trey's life isn't taken.

The fourth suicide is that of Mace. Finding that Pinbacker has disabled the mainframe computer by raising its four circuit towers from pools of coolant, he chooses to give his life in order to save the others by entering the coolant and manually dropping the towers back into place one at a time. His choice to give his life for the mission provides us with one of Boyle's trademarks; an underwater shot of a character.

The fifth and final suicide is that of Capa. He boards the payload and sets off the reaction that will cause it to explode, thereby causing his own death and those of Pinbacker and Cassie.

> There are some great deaths available in space because it's so hostile. You can kind of kill people in interesting ways as well.
>
> Danny Boyle[4]

We can now clearly see that the story is that of a suicide mission. This is especially the case after the garden is destroyed and oxygen supplies are depleted, the crew realising they cannot make it home. They all knew the risks associated with such a task and so we can assume that all the characters were prepared to sacrifice their lives in order to save humanity. This possible need to sacrifice themselves creates a positive link with the audience, for we admire people who are prepared to give their lives for others.

This admiration is especially present in regards to Kaneda, Searle, Mace and Capa. This is because these four characters consciously lay down their lives in order to ensure the success of the mission. It is interesting to note that three of them die in a similar way; consumed by the light of the sun.

Cinematic Techniques

This is by far the most special effects-laden film that Boyle has directed. With computer-generated images of space, the sun and the two craft central to the narrative, we are treated to some fantastic shots that would be perfectly home in a big-budget Hollywood blockbuster. There are smooth fly-bys made by the "camera" in relation to the ships and Boyle utilises a large heat shield at the front of each payload to create some truly stunning effects shots. This is no surprise as these shields are essentially giant, multifaceted mirrors and we have seen Boyle's employment of mirrors in his directing of a number of other films, including *28 Days Later*. In *Sunshine* the shield of mirrors is predominantly used by Boyle to reflect the bright oranges and yellows of the sun, the multifaceted element creating a cascading effect a little like water running over a smooth surface while capturing the sun's reflection or like a swarm of brightly coloured butterflies flexing their wings.

In relation to the computer-generated exterior of the ships, we find a very apparent example of Boyle's use of contrasting light conditions. The front of each ship is bathed in bright light from the sun, whereas the rear is deep in shadow, creating a strikingly visual contrast.

Though the film is reliant upon special effects, Boyle created real sets where the actors then performed, in part because he believes CGI to still be inferior to the use of models and real sets. This meant they had actual points of reference rather than imagined or implied ones. The acting therefore didn't suffer and most of the scenes have a genuine solidity, unlike many seen in Lucas' *Star Wars* prequels, which relied far too heavily on insubstantial CG locations and blue-screen filming techniques.

By using real sets not only does Boyle aid the actors in creating great performances, but he doesn't detract from the narrative by breaking our suspension of disbelief. The inclusion of visual effects can cause audience members to make comments such as: how did they do that? This pulls the audience out of the viewing experience, lessening the impact of the film and degrading the cinematic experience of being transported beyond our own lives.

> I've never done a film that's this effects heavy, but the performance is always the primary thing and the most important thing. There was never a case of any of us having to act to a dot or anything like that.
>
> Cillian Murphy[5]

The claustrophobia of the ship is placed in juxtaposition with the sun's gargantuan enormity, making the ship and the crew trying to survive in its purposefully drab confines seem all the more vulnerable. The existence of the ship and crew is extremely fragile in the face of the sun's monstrous power, one that is coupled with its beauty in a heady mix of threat and appeal.

As with his first four films, Boyle employs the use of voice-over at the start of the film. This at once identifies the main character to be Capa. It also provides the audience with the backstory for the narrative, informing us that he is on a journey with seven crew-mates to drop a huge bomb into the sun in order that it should return to full brightness, the earth suffering from a solar winter.

Boyle's use of somewhat androgynous uniforms echoes Ridley Scott's use of such in *Alien*. The effect is to blur the boundaries of gender, bringing a greater degree of equality to the characters in the way we observe them, reducing the existence of any sexually orientated gaze on our part.

The effect of such androgyny is to create an atmosphere that is beyond gender distinctions to a degree, but also different from everyday life in a way that creates audience uncertainty in relation to reading the film. Such reading is based on past experience of watching movies and when we are confronted with something unfamiliar our reading is disrupted. This has the effect of unsettling the audience, in that we have little or no frame of reference. The fact that Boyle has

184

been seen to subvert our expectations on a regular basis during his career shows that he realises the impact such subversion can have, an impact he uses to great effect.

An interesting point arises in relation to the scene when Capa is recording a message for his family. He is sitting facing the audience, looking directly at the camera. The diegetic words "record", "send", "delete", and "review" are written in reverse at the bottom of the screen and this helps in cementing the idea that he is recording a message to be beamed back to Earth.

Because he is addressing the audience in a way we recognise from things such as news reports and because this is the only example of looking straight at the camera throughout the entire movie, his words are given greater significance and stand out more than they would had they simply been part of a conversation in the narrative. Thus, his instruction to, 'Look out for a little extra brightness,' and his comment, 'If you wake up one morning and it's a particularly beautiful day you'll know we made it,' are made to stand out because they are directed at us. Here Garland's script and Boyle's directing combine to create an impression upon the viewer that lasts until the film's close and which ties in with the final scenes.

The soundtrack Boyle uses complements the imagery perfectly. As usual, the director marries the soundscapes to the scenes he has created in a way that brings out emotion and atmosphere. The film often features simple sounds that echo those used in other science-fiction movies. We hear a faint moaning, like solar winds or the distant howl of the emptiness beyond the ship, something also heard in *Alien*. There are noises like the gentle bleeping of satellites and we hear the groans of the ship's hull. There is occasional music and the sound of the distress beacon of Icarus I. This is detected shortly after we see a stunning computer-generated shot of the planet Mercury passing before the vastness of the sun. The proximity of Mercury helps to enable an important plot line to develop, one which the audience were primed for in the opening voice-over by Capa when he mentioned the previous mission. Due to Mercury, Icarus II is able to pick up the distress signal despite the fact they have entered a transmissions dead zone.

Before arriving at Icarus I, Capa and Kaneda are forced to make a space walk to repair the heat shield, as previously mentioned. In the sequences relating to this event Boyle uses camera angles from within the space suits as the two crew members are getting into them and when they have left the ship's safety to make the repairs. These tightly framed shots add to the overall impression of claustrophobia in the movie, something which has been in evidence in a number of other films he has directed, including *Trainspotting* and *Strumpet.*

In *Sunshine* these angles create a distinct impression of confinement and limitation, allowing the audience to see the conditions within the suits and understand their lack of manoeuvrability. We also feel the claustrophobia with an increased intensity when Capa and Kaneda are cocooned and isolated in space. This is achieved with shots from cameras placed inside their helmets, the audience able to see their faces and the extremely limited view afforded by a slim visor slit. This slit accentuates a feeling of imprisonment, but also provides us with a framed view within that of the camera. This additional view looks beyond the realm we are being presented with by the camera, as if we are looking firstly into one dimension and from that dimension into another. These are effectively examples of Boyle's trademark shots through glass.

We clearly see the claustrophobia within the spacesuits and are provided with one of Boyle's trademark shots through glass, here acting in a similar way to his screen-in-screen shots in that the audience are afforded an alternative scene within that of the helmet view, creating a multi-layered shot.

We see other shots through glass when the oxygen garden is on fire and Corazon is outside the door. She is the crew member in charge of tending the plants and pummels on the glass as the fire viciously devours all of her hard work. This glass captures the dancing, lively reflection of the fire. The view through the glass is further distorted by flowing water as sprinklers operate within the garden. This therefore supplies a shot through glass and water, using the latter's rippling distortion to add additional texture to the shot.

Another significant use of reflection is seen when Capa, Mace and Harvey attempt to get back to Icarus II from Icarus I after the connection between the two ships has failed. The latter two crew members have scant protection against the sub-zero conditions of space, are merely wrapped in lengths of insulation torn from the walls of Icarus I. Capa and Mace manage to return to Icarus II, but Harvey ends up drifting in space beyond Capa's ability to affect a rescue. This is where Boyle then uses an interesting, yet horrific reflection. Harvey sees his own reflection as he freezes to death, gets to witness the last moments of his life in the cold and dark of space. Such a terrible, self-witnessing demise can be seen in a number of other films, most notably in the French science-fiction film *The City of Lost Children* (Caro & Jeunet 1995), and always adds to the dark atmospherics of a movie.

When four crew members from Icarus II enter Icarus I and explore the ship prior to the escape sequence mentioned above, Boyle utilises a number of techniques by which to increase audience suspense. The first is non-diegetic silence, there being initially no soundtrack. All we can hear are the faint groans of Icarus I, which adds to the sense of tension. This hush is very effectively disturbed when one of the crew causes a container to fall, creating a loud and sudden banging, which causes audience members to jump, unsettling us.

The dialogue is also used to create suspense. There is dust in the air and it is revealed through the characters' conversation that dust mainly consists of human skin. This puts the audience on notice that there are bodies on board. This is highlighted by Boyle's clever use of image flashes. There are six of these sudden flashes, each from a colour photograph and each featuring a member of Icarus I's crew. They act in the same way as the sudden sounds of the falling container in that they unsettle and surprise us, their shock value increased by the contrast between their colourfulness and the near monotone qualities of the interior of Icarus I. These images add weight to our thoughts of bodies within the ship.

Also mentioned in the dialogue are aliens when Mace jokingly states, 'Might get picked off one at a time by aliens.' Though this is not a serious comment, it causes the audience to think about this subject. The idea of being "picked off one at a time" is also suggestive, bringing to mind *Alien* and horror films in which the characters often meet their demise in such a way.

The trope of splitting up the four crew members is used to reinforce the possibility held in Mace's jovial words. Together they may have had a chance of fighting off a sudden attack from the gloom, but individually they are more vulnerable and the words "picked off one at a time" gain in significance.

The last element of this scene that creates tension is Boyle's use of darkness and light. The interior of Icarus I is without light; a murky, dusty hollowness with the potential to harbour hidden danger. Torch beams pierce this darkness with obvious inadequacy, leaving us wondering what could be lurking in the deep shadows that remain.

> Eight astronauts going up to save the world, we've heard that so many times before. You have to see it. It's got an edge.
>
> Michelle Yeoh[6]

Once Pinbacker's existence on Icarus II is discovered Boyle's directing plays on what could be termed as Jungian archetypes. Psychoanalyst Carl Jung proposed the "collective unconscious", within which are certain archetypal impressions shared by the whole of humanity. These images are associated with things such as good and evil, the sex drive and fear. The quick shots of Pinbacker, the blurred and unclear nature of his form, the use of darkness and of glaring light in which he becomes nothing more than an indistinct figure of malice, all combine to create an image of menacing evil that we all recognise. He is not a man, but a monster lurking in the ship and in our subconscious. His voice adds to the impression of evil, his words revealing his madness. Though not as apparent as the abnormal psychology in *28 Days Later*, Pinbacker is still an unforgettable example of such.

Interestingly, and thanks to Boyle's expert direction, the voice of the Icarus II computer displays a change in volume level at one point late in the film's narrative. This change is crucial to audience suspense and occurs when Capa is inside the payload checking the operating systems. As he conducts his checks he chats with the computer and discovers that there isn't enough oxygen for the completion of the mission. In sixteen hours all those aboard will be dead, but to complete the mission would take nineteen hours. Capa questions this, stating that, 'Corazon was certain,' referring to her calculations in regards to there being enough oxygen for four crew members. The computer responds, 'Affirmative. Four crew could potentially survive on current reserves.' When Capa states, 'There are only four crew members,' the computer responds by stating, 'Negative.' It goes on to inform Capa that there are five crew members and the fifth is unknown and located in the observation room.

During this entire exchange the computer talks in a whisper rather than at normal volume. This seemingly minor touch is actually one of the key elements to the scene. It reflects the disturbing discovery and creates additional tension very effectively. Whispering is often what people do when in danger or when fearful. This aspect of the scene therefore makes the audience more tense and fearful, while also raising anticipation of a horrific encounter.

Boyle also uses flashes of images to accompany the words in the latter stages of this conversation, as he did to accompany the sequence when the crew from Icarus II entered Icarus I. Here, the images are of an indistinct figure surrounded by a bright yellow glow. The figure is menacing when considering the conversation Capa has just had with the ship's computer. They are also part of the use of archetypal imagery, a shadowy figure being commonly associated with evil.

It is shortly after this that we see one of the most notable uses of light glare in any of Danny Boyle's films. Such glare is used in his other films, particularly *Strumpet*, but in *Sunshine* this is taken to an extreme level due to the proximity of the sun and the existence of observation rooms on both Icarus ships. Though by this point in the film the director has already created scenes in the observation rooms, the one in which Capa meets Pinbacker is the most memorable.

Capa goes into the room after the computer has informed him that the unknown crew member is there. The glare from the sun is immense, the character vainly trying to shield his eyes. In the midst of the exceptionally bright room is a figure. There is little definition to his form, the audience only seeing silhouettes and indistinct glimpses of the man who used to be the captain of Icarus I, but who is now mentally deranged and waiting for God, asking Capa if he is an angel come to fetch him and wishing to be the last man alive as he greets the Almighty.

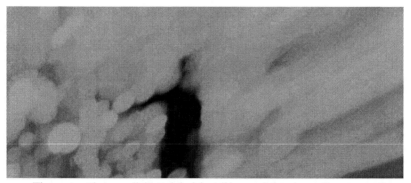

The contrast between light and dark is striking, and the observation rooms of
both ships provide us with the most obvious example of Boyle's use of glaring
brightness, here providing us with a vague image of Pinbacker.

This use of light glare is followed by shots through a small window in
one of the ship's doors. Capa is on one side and Pinbacker on the other.
The audience are presented with shots from either side, the window's
edge used by Boyle to frame each character's eyes. Pinbacker's are
presented with a double-vision style blur as he looks insanely through at
Capa. In shots of Pinbacker he is usually blurred, as if the glare of the
sun has so much power that it has loosened his very essence, making it
radiate from his body and his body in turn losing definition.

Not long after these scenes we find voice-over used for the second
time when the payload has been released from the ship, Capa in a
space suit attempting to reach the bomb before the thrusters fire. We
hear Cassie's voice referring to the dream she and Capa have shared
about falling into the sun, also seeing a flash of Capa's version of this
vision. This actually serves to strengthen our perception of the bond
between Cassie and Capa, for at a time of great stress and heightened
emotion he is hearing her words. It also serves to remind us that she is
still alive and it is interesting to note that in the first drafts of the script
there was actually a love scene between these two characters.

Cassie's was the more emotional character in the film, obviously.
I mean, she's kind of the moral conscience of the story. You know,
the emotional barometer for the audience in a lot of ways.

190

Rose Byrne[7]

The closing scenes of the mission offer the audience not only the peak of on-screen action, but also a peak of camera-angle change, shot alteration and editing. The film becomes frenetic in both a narrative and directorial sense, just as *28 Days Later* did at its finale. We see that Boyle is an expert at judging his pace to complement the screenplay, something which increases the impact of what the audience witnesses on screen. His calm shots and relatively normal angles during the majority of the film makes the increase of shot and angle change a stark contrast to what has come before. This contrast creates more tension and unsettles the audience.

As the payload hurtles into the sun with Capa, Cassie and Pinbacker aboard, we see trembling shots, stills, distorted shots, upside-down images, skewed angles and turning shots. The film cuts from one shot to another in quick succession, the audience bombarded with imagery. This rapidity of shot alteration reflects the velocity of travel. This rapid angle change coupled with image distortion also reflects the blending of space and time predicted by Capa when discussing the mission's chance of success with Kaneda earlier in the film. Through quick cuts and unusual shots Boyle manages to translate such a strange phenomenon into the language of cinematic technique.

In order to show us what is happening in the narrative the rapidity of angle change and the distortion has to necessarily become calmer. This allows the audience to see Capa setting off the reaction that will cause the bomb to go off. We then witness this reaction and its results, the scene echoing the comment made by the character of Dr Dave Bowman in *2001: A Space Odyssey*, when he states, 'My God, it's full of stars.' This statement is made when he is observing the black monolith near Jupiter. In *Sunshine*, the appearance of stars arises through the chain reaction of the bomb.

The sparks of energy that mark the reaction within the payload are related to the sparks of energy seen in the monolith, as both are connected with life. The former will cause the bomb to explode and the sun to burn brighter, thereby allowing life to continue on Earth. The latter causes Jupiter to become a new sun in order that life can continue on one of its moons, called Europa, which is also in the grip of ice. Though this occurs in the sequel, *2010: The Year We Make Contact* (Hyams 1984), the similarities are clear.

Following the reaction of bright sparks is the fireball explosion. In the place where space and time blend, in the realm of the unquantifiable, this fireball surges before Capa while the sparks of the initial reaction still blaze behind him. In this moment beyond normal reality, he reaches out with a smile, knowing the mission has been a success.

During this sequence the soundtrack provides us with a suitable, dreamlike tune that then plays over the scenes on Earth that follow, providing the audience with a chronological link between the two scenes. This use of the same track over scenes separated by great distance very effectively informs us that the shots of Earth follow immediately after those of the explosion.

The film closes with the anticipated beautiful day upon Earth. As described by Capa near the start of the film, the sunlight suddenly increases as we see a wintry scene. The iconic Sydney Opera House can be seen in the distance and this is shown in order to highlight how cold Earth has become as most people associate Sydney with sunshine and warm weather. There is a closing voice-over, the third use of this technique evident in the movie: Capa's recorded transmission repeating some of his words from the scene when he created the message, thereby creating a degree of circularity at the film's close.

> *Sunshine* might perform a useful task, as well as being a good film, because it does show what might be necessary. It shows that we live in a dangerous universe, which I think is really important.
>
> Dr Brian Cox[8]

Criticism

Though there has been some criticism relating to elements of the science involved in the film such as the unrealistic portrayal of the sun's gravitational effect, this is of no interest here. Such concerns are simply pedantic nit-picking, leaving no room for creative freedom, which is vital in science fiction. There are few, if any, films in this genre that strictly adhere to all the science. Creative licence is employed, as can be seen with any explosion seen in space which involves noise or flames without the presence of oxygen.

Criticism arises because *Sunshine* could be seen as a missed opportunity on the parts of Garland and Boyle. There are clearly links with the film *Alien* and this makes this opportunity more apparent. They could have created the first mainstream sci-fi film since that classic 1979 movie to portray a truly independent and strong heroine.

It may come as quite a shock that no other depiction of such a heroine has been created in over thirty years, but it is true. In the following films of the *Alien* quartet the strong, independent and very competent depiction of Ripley in the first film is undermined in stages. In *Alien*s (Cameron 1986) she needs the help of men. In *Alien* 3 (Fincher 1992) she needs the help of men and gives birth to a monster. In the fourth film she is no longer even human, something which is symbolic of independent women being unnatural. In the *Terminator* films, Sarah Connor needs the help of a man and goes on to be portrayed as insane, needing her son and the cyborg to take charge in bringing an end to the possibility of apocalypse. In *Total Recall* (Verhoeven 1990) the independent woman portrayed by Sharon Stone is manipulative and shot by the woman who is dependent upon a man, demonstrating a clear ideological standpoint. In *Jurassic Park* (Spielberg 1993) the independent woman is shown to need a man in the end and one of the final shots of the film is of her with the male hero and two children, visually portraying a traditional family unit. In *The Fifth Element* (Besson 1997) the universe's perfect being may be female, but she needs a man's love in order to reach her potential. Wherever you look it is clear that *Alien* remains the only contemporary sci-fi film with a truly independent heroine (though there are plenty of examples of independent male heroes).

Though the character of Ripley was originally intended to be male, the final result is a standout film within the genre. Boyle and Garland had the opportunity to create another depiction of an independent heroine and thereby subvert expectations to a greater degree, especially as physicists are traditionally thought of as male.

In defence of the director and writer it is important to point out that before the casting process, the characters had not been assigned any specific gender. Michelle Yeoh was the first actor cast and was able to choose which character she played, as mentioned at the beginning of this chapter. Boyle and Garland didn't define which characters were male or female, but allowed the actors a choice of role. Therefore they are not entirely responsible for this missed opportunity to portray a strong heroine, though they could have insisted Capa were played by a female.

There is also another point worth mentioning in relation to these gender issues. Cillian Murphy is by no means a rugged or macho man. He has a clear femininity, something evident in his thoughtfulness, gentleness and the way he carries himself. When coupled with his lack of machismo, this means that his character, though being male, is not blatantly so.

Another opportunity to subvert and interrupt the normal reading of films would have been to have Captain Kaneda perform the opening voice-over. This would have created an expectation that he was the main character, one which would have then been overturned upon his death. It would have also been undermined by the concentration of the narrative on Capa and audiences would have enjoyed the uncertainty and disruption brought to the reading of the film.

Awards

Though the film is visually impressive, displays gripping performances from the cast and travels to a place where no other modern sci-fi has gone, it only received one award. This was a British Independent Film Award for Mark Tildesley's production design.

Final Words

Sunshine is a bold journey into space which reflects Danny Boyle's use of extremes in a very obvious way. Not only is the situation itself extreme in contrast to everyday life, but the portrayal of dark and light, science and religion, small and large, beauty and violence are all extreme in this film.

This impressive film was Boyle's first studio-based movie and let's hope it wasn't his last, for it contains thrilling visuals, brilliant performances and a narrative that keeps us gripped till the very end. Unlike many contemporary sci-fi movies the characters were primary and the effects only there so that the story could be effectively told. Partly because of this, *Sunshine* truly belongs in the pantheon of science-fiction greats.

[1] Barkham, P. *The sun is the star (The Guardian,* 23 March 2007, UK)

[2] Rea, D. *Dr Brian Cox* (http://www.sci-fi-online.com/2006_Interviews/07-08-27_brian-cox.htm)

[3] Layne Wilson, S. *Rose Byrne Interview* (http://www.horror.com/php/article-1653-1.html)

[4] Murray, R. *Director Danny Boyle Discusses the Sci-Fi Thriller: Sunshine* (http://movies.about.com/od/sunshine/a/sunshine070407.htm)

[5] Unknown – *Sunshine – Cillian Murphy interview* (http://www.indielondon.co.uk/Film-Review/sunshine-cillian-murphy-interview)

[6] Unknown – *Michelle Yeoh talks Danny Boyle and "Sunshine"* (http://twitchfilm.net/archives/004264.html)

[7] Layne Wilson, S. *Rose Byrne Interview* (http://www.horror.com/php/article-1653-1.html)

[8] Rea, D. Dr Brian Cox (http://www.sci-fi-online.com/2006_Interviews/07-08-27_brian-cox.htm)

Slumdog Millionaire

'The film is beautiful. The plot is riveting. The child actors are breathtaking.'

Vikas Swarup, author of Q&A from which the film was adapted[1]

Set in India, this film is different from Danny Boyle's previous movies, though it still retains many of the themes and tropes that are common to his work. However, this difference is only to be expected in light of the director's other big-screen outings, for Boyle has never been one to stick to a particular genre or location. Here he explores new territory with his usual style and flair. He has lovingly directed the movie, reflecting his feelings for the people and places he came across while filming.

The performances Boyle gets from the actors are as good as any that have been seen in his previous films, something that speaks volumes about his people-management skills. This is especially the case when considering the children portraying the main characters in the early part of their lives were from the slums, not from acting school.

Boyle's assistant director Loveleen Tandan must take a great deal of credit, especially when it comes to these slum children. Her understanding of Indian culture and sensibilities was invaluable to Danny, as was her ability to communicate with the children in their mother tongue: Hindi.

The film was produced with funding from Pathé and FilmFour, Boyle having a good and ongoing relationship with both. Also involved were Celador, the production company behind *Who Wants to be a Millionaire*. After Warner Independent was closed down and could no longer distribute the film in the US, they screened it for Fox Searchlight, who jumped at the opportunity to take the film on, a decision they must be very pleased with now that it has proved so popular on a global scale. Had this not been the case the film was all set for a straight-to-DVD release.

The tag line of "feel-good movie of the decade" didn't sit well with Boyle and the reason is obvious. What people expect when they see a feel-good film is something along the lines of *Mamma Mia!* (Lloyd 2008). They certainly don't expect violence, torture, mutilation and a struggle for survival. These elements are clearly present in this film from the outset, though the first three are kept to a minimum. However, the film does end on a positive and uplifting note, one tempered with a touch of darkness.

The film is gritty and its realism is aided by Boyle's insistence that the slum scenes were shot in an actual slum. This location is the ramshackle Dharavi slum in Mumbai. It has a population of 2 million, making it the biggest in Asia. Further realism was created by casting children from Dharavi in lead roles, as mentioned.

Rather than the slum images making the audience feel sad or upset they actually encourage a faith in humanity. They contain a sense of community and closeness, not of despair and suffering. Rahman's score also helps to give us the feel of a vibrant existence and keeps pace nicely with the on-screen action.

Slumdog Millionaire's closest relation in terms of Boyle's other films is *Trainspotting*, partially due to the gritty realism evident in the cinematography and narrative. Though these two films have much in common stylistically, *Slumdog Millionaire* deviates in its use of colour. In *Trainspotting* the landscape in which the narrative takes place is often dull and dismal, using a limited palette. *Slumdog Millionaire* is alive with colour, something that reflects the culture and the vibrancy of the slum which, despite being a tough place to live and survive, is filled with activity and even glimpses of happiness, such as the early scenes of the children playing on the runway.

> They [the people of the Dharavi slum] are happy like that. It's their home. How dare you come and say about it, "That's not good enough." They're very proud and very industrious people … You know, very wonderful people really. I just tried to tell it from their perspective.
>
> Danny Boyle[2]

In comparison with some of Boyle's other films, *Slumdog Millionaire* tends not to be subversive when it comes to audience expectations, but this is probably a good thing. We are watching a film set in locations that most will find unfamiliar and this is enough to keep audiences engaged without the need to subvert in any way.

Despite the environment being a world apart from that which the majority of Western audiences are used to, we are drawn into the narrative because it is centred on elements we can all identify with, such as love. We can also recognise aspects such as religious hatred. We have seen the results of this ideologically driven hatred in many news reports, not least in relation to fanatical terrorism.

Though this story is set in India and was predominantly filmed in Mumbai, it could have been told using any cultural background. This is because its themes apply to all humans and the events portrayed have their equivalents in every country in the world.

The film *Millions* was a good counterbalance to making *28 Days Later* and *Slumdog Millionaire* acted in a similar way after making *Sunshine*. Boyle's gripping science fiction was set in the vast emptiness of space and the interior of the spacecraft where most of the narrative takes place was intentionally dull. It featured only nine people on-screen for the majority of the film and its predominantly gentle pace was well measured. *Slumdog Millionaire* features a striking use of colour and a mass of human existence. Its pace is fast and there is a sense of vitality that permeates the entire film, making the audience feel energised and uplifted by the time the end credits roll.

Basic Premise & Main Characters

Jamal Malik is being detained at a police station in Mumbai (formally Bombay). He has been accused of cheating after appearing on the show *Who Wants to be a Millionaire* and answering all but the final question which, if he is released, will be asked in the next instalment of the game show. Jamal is played by British actor Dev Patel, who had only starred in a UK television series called *Skins* prior to *Slumdog Millionaire*.

Playing a recording of Jamal's appearance on the show, the police inspector pauses it after each question and asks Jamal how he came to know the answer. In response we are shown biographical sequences, during which we discover how he came by the answers.

In the earliest of these sequences we see Jamal as a boy, played by Ayush Mahesh Khedekar. We are also introduced to his brother Salim, played by Azharuddin Mohammed Ismail at this point. After their mother's murder, they meet Latika, who joins them after having also lost her parents. The youngest Latika is played by Rubiana Ali. The acting of the children portraying the characters in their early years stands up well alongside experienced artisans from Indian cinema and is actually far better than those seen in films such as *The Chronicles of Narnia: The Lion, the Witch and the Wardrobe* (Adamson 2005).

The brothers become separated from Latika, but Jamal cannot forget her. He and Salim eventually head back to the city in order to find her and succeed in this purpose. At this stage the characters of Jamal, Salim and Latika are played by Tanay Chheda, Ashutosh Lobo Gajiwala and Tanvi Ganesh Lonkar.

Soon after this Jamal loses contact with both Salim and Latika, and the next time we see them they are played by different actors once again, these being Madhur Mittal and Mumbai-based actress Freida Pinto.

After being released with no charge from the police station, Jamal goes back on the game show for his chance to answer the final question and win 20 million rupees. At the end of the film Jamal answers the final question correctly as his brother shoots the crime lord and is then shot himself. Jamal and Latika are finally reunited and we close on a lover's kiss.

> He [Boyle] has passion for what he does. He just engages you when he talks to you.
>
> Dev Patel[3]

Narrative Themes

The brothers Jamal and Salim Malik show us the results of following different routes when confronted with a moral dilemma. Such dilemmas are common to Boyle's work, but, unlike the others we have come across during the course of this book, the brothers create the ability to play out the results of both choices available to them. The dilemma is whether to put money and power above people. Jamal, the younger of the two, chooses the path of love and trust, is motivated by his love for Latika and his brother. Salim is happy to slip into a life of crime as he follows the the path of greed. In this way the brothers have a dichotomous relationship, showing the positive and negative alternatives open to children growing up in such conditions. The final scenes give the results of their decisions, Jamal finding happiness and his brother only death. *Slumdog Millionaire* is therefore about human nature, showing both its good and bad sides.

It is pertinent to note that the alternatives of choice given are not merely connected with their upbringing in the Mumbai slums, for they are not limited by nationality or culture. We are all faced with such choices. We can all choose to follow lives which enrich those around us and society as a whole or to pursue lives that wound those around us emotionally or physically and only serve as a poison to society.

The choices are connected to the central narrative themes of the film, these being love, brotherhood and friendship. Tying all of these together is a theme of loyalty. The idea of brotherhood extends beyond Jamal and Salim to those who live in the slums. This can be seen in the early scenes of the slum children being chased from a runway and their efforts to outrun the security guards. Brotherhood can also be seen in the encampment to which Jamal, Salim and Latika are taken, one which at first seems like a haven, but which is revealed as basically a child labour camp where they are prepared for lives as street urchins begging for money in order to line the pockets of their master.

The use of Alexandre Dumas' novel *The Three Musketeers* fits in with the theme of brotherhood. The title characters of that classic text share a close bond and overcome sometimes great odds. The novel is also an adventure, just like *Slumdog Millionaire,* and so its use in the narrative befits the content of the movie. Because the majority of references to this book occur early in the film they help to underpin the relevant themes with which it is connected.

The story of Jamal's youth is cleverly told in response to police enquiries as to how he knew the answers that allowed him to reach and correctly answer the penultimate question on *Who Wants to be a Millionaire*, which has won him 10 million rupees. He is suspected of cheating; after all, how could a boy from the slums possibly know the answers to questions such as "whose head is depicted on a $100 dollar bill?" In order to get him to talk he is initially tortured, these scenes coming at the start of the film.

The use of a game show that is internationally recognised is a brilliant trope, allowing the film to be understood by audiences the world over, the format having been used in over 100 countries. It also provides an anchor of identification within the narrative. Even though many of the locations and situations are beyond those experienced by Western audiences, the *"Millionaire"* format, which is at the centre of the narrative and is shown at regular intervals, is something which is familiar to most.

This show and the often harsh reality of Jamal's life create an interesting juxtaposition. The former is artificial and relatively safe, accentuating the "reality" of what Jamal has had to go through in order to survive. Its artificial nature, along with its order and cleanliness, are in direct contrast to the biographical flashbacks, something that serves to heighten the reality.

Despite the removal of the game show from reality, this reality still leeches into its environment when the host, Prem Kumar, pretends to give Jamal the answer to a question. Thankfully Jamal realises that he is being misled, but this deception and unkindness reflects what we have already come to expect from the reality beyond the studio where the show is filmed.

Using a video of the show, the police inspector, brilliantly and convincingly played by Bollywood star Irrfan Khan, shows each question in turn and then pauses the recording in order for Jamal to explain how he knew the answer. It is then that we are given the story of Jamal's life. They are told as flashbacks and we understand that the inspector is being told about the events that we witness on screen. These biographical segments are filled with energy and vibrancy, hardship and suffering, crime, humour, friendship and love.

Poverty is a very changeable expression ... [There] is a poverty of bricks and mortar, and there's a poverty of the soul.

Danny Boyle[4]

Early in the story of Jamal's life we are presented with a toilet scene that allows us to see an antagonism between the young Jamal and Salim. The former is using the toilet, which is no more than a shack on stilts, while Salim takes money from a customer who wishes to use the basic facilities. Because the toilet remains in use by Jamal, the customer leaves and takes his money back from Salim. Jamal is then trapped inside the shack by Salim despite the fact he knows his younger brother is a fan of Bollywood film star Amitabh, whose helicopter has flown overhead and is landing on the nearby airstrip that was introduced at the start of the film. This shows that Salim is motivated by money and prepared to make his brother suffer if he gets in the way of making a profit.

The difference between the brothers, along with the antagonism, is then clearly shown in a scene that follows. After stealing the autographed photo, Salim sells it for a "good price". Salim's actions in both scenes show that he is guided by self-interest. He is prepared to knowingly upset his younger brother in order to gain monetary profit and this gives us a glimpse of what is to come. The young Salim's greed is like a seed with the potential to grow into something much more virulent during the course of the movie.

The crime at the outset of Jamal and Malik's life is petty and as with *Trainspotting*, we are shown its motivations. In *Trainspotting*, this is an addiction to heroin, but in *Slumdog Millionaire* it is a necessity in order to survive. This is especially the case due to the fact they are left without parents, their mother being murdered in a religious confrontation as Hindus attack Muslims in the Mumbai slum, creating one of the film's religious references.

It is as a result of this attack that Latika ends up joining the brothers. Though not stated in dialogue, we presume both of her parents are dead, Jamal asking about her mother and father and Latika's response being a shake of her head. The three children are soon taken to an encampment, which at first seems like a haven for street urchins. We see numerous children playing and laughing, some of them physically disabled, and we are led to think that this is a place of happiness, possibly a charitable establishment existing in order to help the less fortunate. In a clever twist, this view is turned on its head as the film progresses and it becomes clear the children are living in a holding camp where they are moulded into effective beggars who are sent onto the streets in order to earn money for the camp's owner Maman.

It is during Jamal and Salim's stay at the camp that the difference between the brothers becomes much more apparent. Salim gladly takes charge of the children when they are sent onto the city streets and seems quite taken with his perceived authority amongst his peers. He also appears to be party to Maman's plans for some of the children, knowing what fate lies in store for Latika.

The petty crime that we see the brothers engaging in after their escape from the camp is excused by their lives. We can identify with their desire to survive, one of the most basic of human instincts, and we can also admire their often ingenious ways of doing so. This creates a link with *Trainspotting*, for we also understand the drug addicts' need to commit crime in order to feed their habit.

The Mumbai children, unlike the addicts, are vulnerable, something which is mainly concerned with their youth. The childhood innocence of the brothers is shattered by the death of their mother and they are forced to fend for themselves, leaving the life they have known behind and forgoing an education beyond their early years.

The portrayal of the brothers and Latika is done using three different actors for each, used to show three different ages during the course of the film. In the scenes from the early part of their lives their dialogue is in Hindi, but this changes as they grow older.

It is during the course of the middle-age bracket that the brothers begin to drift apart and come to symbolise the two paths open to them. Jamal leaves the life of crime behind and finds a job. He no longer needs to continue with theft to survive and so begins to lead a lawful life. His brother has tasted the power of wielding a gun and even commits a murder using the weapon. He then descends steadily into a world of serious crime motivated by greed and power. They become a dichotomy, showing us the results of choosing each particular path.

It is soon after this that Salim goes in search of crime lord Javed Khan and becomes one of his goons, doing Javed's dirty work and, we presume, killing other people in the process. Filled with a new-found sense of personal power afforded by his gun-toting, Salim then sleeps with Latika despite his brother's vocal protestations. It is at this point that Jamal loses contact with the other two characters and we then jump to scenes set in the early stages of adulthood.

This element of sexual encounter is akin to others witnessed in Boyle's films, as it is sexually aggressive. This kind of aggression is seen or hinted at in *A Life Less Ordinary, Strumpet, 28 Days Later* and *The Beach* to a lesser degree. Here Salim essentially forces himself on Latika, showing his lack of concern when it comes to others' feeling or wishes. Such selfishness is also apparent in all the other examples seen in Boyle's work.

Amongst the themes and tropes used in this film that correspond to Boyle's other work is an amusing Scottish reference. Here we see Jamal temporarily taking over a fellow employee's "Friends & Family" station in the busy call centre where he works as a tea boy. A Mrs Mackintosh rings through and he pretends he is Scottish and claims he lives near a loch called Big Ben and that Sean Connery is his neighbour, something Mrs Mackintosh clearly knows is untrue. This plays on many people's perceptions of call centres, but allows us a more human angle, one in which we actually get to see the conditions in which the employees work.

Shortly after the Cambridge Circus question is presented to Jamal on *Who Wants to be a Millionaire*, the characterisation of the show's presenter, Prem Kumar, can be seen vividly when he comments, 'It's getting hot in here,' and Jamal replies, 'Are you nervous?' Prem's reaction, especially in light of the laughter which erupts from the audience in response to Jamal's witty response, is to snap, 'What!' at the young man. His expression instantly darkens and he looks at Jamal and states, 'Am I nervous? It's you who's in the hot-seat, friend,' the final word spoken with a condescending and slightly unkind tone.

This fits perfectly with the way Prem has treated Jamal during his entire time on the show. We have seen that he is conceited and arrogant and we have also witnessed him being unkind to Jamal under the thin veil of humour, referring to him as "chai-wallah", which is basically a term for a serving boy and is derogatory in this context.

Here it is pertinent to note a point of relevance to the idea of "it is written" which permeates the film. This is played on when Prem tries to mislead Jamal. The two of them are in the Gents' washroom and Jamal admits he does not know the answer to the 10-million-rupee question. Prem claims to feel that Jamal will win and states, 'Maybe it is written, my friend.' Not only does this refer to the fourth possible answer at the start of the film, but it also refers to the fact that he has "written" the answer "B" in the condensation on the mirror of the washroom. The link with an idea of destiny is also added to just before the show is due to go back on air, when Prem says, 'From rags to Rajah, it's your destiny.' However, Jamal finally answers "D", which the presenter finds galling, his surprise and aggravation clearly apparent.

Interestingly, there are two questions Jamal cannot answer during the course of the film and both relate to his cultural heritage. The first is his second question on *"Millionaire"*, which asks: "A picture of three lions is seen in the National emblem of India. What is written underneath it?" The answer is "A – the truth alone triumphs", but Jamal has to ask the audience in order to obtain it.

The second of these questions is posed by the police inspector. After watching the *"Millionaire"* question relating to which American president is depicted on a $100 bill, the inspector asks Jamal who is depicted on a 1,000-rupee note. Jamal doesn't know and is informed that it is Gandhi.

There is also another significant scene in relation to Jamal's lack of cultural knowledge. When the brothers come across the Taj Mahal, India's iconographic mausoleum, Jamal asks, 'What is it, some hotel?' Not only is his reaction somewhat comical, but it is also surprising considering the fame of the building. He clearly has no idea what it is and neither does he know its history.

These scenes leave us with the impression that Jamal's knowledge of his own culture is somewhat lacking. This could be because he belongs to a disaffected part of society, has had an existence at its fringe. It could also be due to the fact that Western society has leeched into that of India's, at least partly through such things as call centres.

This latter point does not hold water in the context of the film entire. There are only two other examples of Western culture being present and both are non-evasive. These are through tourism and American dollars. So it would seem that it is existence at the fringe of society which has caused his lack of knowledge in relation to his own culture. It is not so much that he has ignored Indian culture, for that is impossible because he is embedded in it. It is more that Indian culture, in part at least, has ignored him. He is a mere "slumdog", not a constructive part of society, but a member of a mass of humanity existing in crowded slums.

Returning to the game show, we find that Prem calls the police, claiming that he thinks Jamal is cheating. The show comes to the end of its allotted time slot before the final question can be asked and Jamal is passed over to the police by the presenter, who tells one of the show's staff that, 'He's a cheat.' He says that he provided Jamal with a wrong answer and he still got the question right, therefore he must have been cheating. Then, revealing the true reason behind his anger and distaste, he states, 'It's my show. It's my fucking show.' This highlights his dislike of Jamal's popularity with the Indian public and his success on the show.

> Danny is a very encouraging man. He lets you do what you want. He has no rules for a particular scene. He lets you emote the way you want. He would tell us where we would go wrong and motivate us to do better.
>
> Freida Pinto[5]

The film has a distinctly Dickensian feel. This is not to take away from the Indian culture, but, for the Western audience, it adds a kind of vague recognition to the situations in which the children find themselves. Characters like Maman would be equally at home in *Oliver Twist*, preparing the children for begging on the streets of old London.

It must be stressed that this in no way implies that India is backwards for, as with corruption amongst police and officials, this kind of behaviour is evident in all societies. We can, for example, point to the illegal gang masters bringing workers into the UK who are treated like slaves and live in terrible, impoverished and crowded conditions or British Members of Parliament being paid money by interested parties in order to amend legislation. Cruelty and corruption is present in the West and so in no way is this chapter or the film giving a condescending view of India, its culture or its people.

The corruption mentioned in the previous paragraph is evident in a number of aspects of the narrative, though this is corruption in its broadest sense. The first clear example of corruption occurs right at the start of the film when Jamal is tortured in the police station, something that even the inspector comments would be a human-rights issue if it were discovered. Another element of corruption seen in the film is the lack of action on the part of the police when the attack takes place on the Muslim slum dwellers. Jamal and Salim approach a truck full of officers, but are told to go away even though a man who has been set alight is running down the street.

We also see a hint of corruption in the existence of Maman's encampment, which surely the authorities must know about. Another arises through Salim informing Jamal that Javed, a known criminal, is behind the building of the tower blocks.

Another notable element of corruption concerns the game show and the potential of Jamal winning the top prize of 20 million rupees. Prem shows he is corrupt as a person when he tries to lure Jamal into giving the wrong answer for the final question. This also leads to the possibility he has done so with previous contestants and so the show may well be corrupt.

The most important depiction of corruption in the film is via the character of Salim. We see how money and power corrupt him; something made all the more prominent when juxtaposed with his brother.

When Jamal follows Salim and discovers Latika is living with crime boss Javed Khan we see that she has the fading remains of a bruise around her left eye. When Javed returns to the house it is clear he treats her with aggressive disdain, like a servant there to please him and do as he says. This scene is not only important in order for us to see Jamal and Latika meet once again and the direction her life has taken, but also, critically, to see that she is a fan of *Who Wants to be a Millionaire*. It is playing on the TV in the kitchen and when he asks her why she watches it Latika states, 'It's a chance to escape,' thereby underlining her unhappiness. This then gives credence to Jamal's assertion later in the film that he is not on the show for money, but for love.

We discover this fact towards the end of the film. Jamal knows that Latika watches the programme and hopes that she will see him and somehow get in contact now that she is in an unknown location with crime lord Javed Khan and his henchmen, including Salim. This underlines just how different he is from his brother: that the two are motivated by very different things, one by friendship and love, the other by greed.

In a tradition very much of Hollywood films, the "bad" brother, the brother who has committed murder and who is mostly driven by lust for material things and power over others, eventually receives his punishment, meeting his death at the hands of those with whom he had chosen to associate. Jamal being the "good" brother means he also receives his relevant reward; winning 20 million rupees on *Who Wants to be a Millionaire* and reuniting with Latika.

Shortly before the closing scenes, we witness another notable religious reference. Salim's last words before dying are, 'God is great.' Before being killed he has heard that Latika and his brother have renewed their contact and that his brother has won 20 million rupees by opting for a lucky guess on the final question, despite not knowing the answer. In these elements and in aiding Latika to find freedom from Javed, he finds his final redemption, something underlined by his words to her after he has given her his mobile phone and car keys so that she may escape; 'And for what I've done, please forgive me.' In his last actions and their results he is redeemed for what he has done.

The final scene, along with another earlier in the film when Latika unsuccessfully tries to meet Jamal at the train station and escape from Javed, was shot at the Chhatrapati Shivaji Railway Terminus. The final scene opens with Jamal sitting on the floor of the station beside a statue. Though what follows is relatively useless information in relation to the film, it has been included because you never know when it might come in useful; maybe one day you'll need to answer a game show question about it. The statue is of English architectural engineer Frederick William Stevens. He designed the terminus, which was then called the Victoria Terminus, and it is possibly the second most highly photographed building in India after the Taj Mahal. After designing other buildings in Mumbai he died there in 1900 of malaria.

The end of the film shows Jamal and Latika reunited upon a train platform in the terminus building. The final words of the film not only tie in with the theme of destiny, but also love. They hold each other close and Jamal says, 'This is our destiny,' to which Latika responds, 'Kiss me.'

Jamal is like the heroes in all of Boyle's films; he is an ordinary person. In none of his movies are we presented with a traditional, alpha-male hero. What Boyle presents us with in his films are ordinary people and because of this we can identify with his characters more readily. This portrayal of ordinary heroes also adds to the humanity of the stories told. We are drawn in because we recognise these people from everyday life, see that they are reflections of ourselves to an extent. This is the case with *Slumdog Millionaire* despite the cultural differences and this shows the strength of Boyle's ability to convey real human situations and get the best from his actors in portraying the thoughts and emotions of their characters.

The overcoming of adversity also helps us to identify with Jamal, for most of us have had to do so at some point in our lives. The film is concerned with what it is to be human, to overcome obstacles in one's life, to form friendships, to fall in love, to have family ties and to make choices which effect the directions our lives take.

All the narrative themes are very effectively carried by acting of a high standard throughout the film. The cast includes some impressive talent from Indian cinema. Irrfan Khan, who plays the police inspector, has already been mentioned. Another is Anil Kapoor, who plays Prem Kumar, the game-show presenter. He was partially persuaded to take the role by his children, who knew of Boyle's work, and he donated his earnings to Plan India, a child development organisation. There is also Mahesh Manjrekar, who plays the crime lord Javed Khan. Not limited to acting alone, he is also a writer and has directed critically acclaimed films such as *Astitva* (2000) and *Vaastav: The Reality* (1999). Playing Sergeant Srinivas is Saurabh Shukla, who has not only appeared in Indian films, but has also written a number of screenplays. In fact, Boyle used one of Shukla's films called *Satya* (1998) as a reference, because it is about the Mumbai underworld.

> Thanks to Danny Boyle, Indian talent is getting noticed in international forums. The point that it would not have been such a huge success if it was made by an Indian director is debatable. The fact remains that it is a Danny Boyle film, and that makes all the difference. All thanks to him, we are hoping things will change now and Indian films will win recognition.
>
> Mahesh Manjrekar[6]

Cinematic Techniques

As the film opens we are informed of the location and date. This is done non-diegetically with the words "Mumbai 2006" shown on the screen. We are then introduced to the *Who Wants to be a Millionaire* format with which we are familiar and which is used as an ingenious device by which to tell the story of Jamal's life.

The set of this show is familiar to many nationalities. It is predominantly blue and is often at least partially hidden in shadow. This is contrasted against the scenes from Jamal's life, which are often filled with colour and light. Boyle cleverly uses unfamiliar shots of the set, such as from behind the show's cameras, mingled with those we recognise from seeing the programme. This creates audience interest, because we are not simply seeing the show as it would appear on TV.

The audience is given four alternative ways by which Jamal Malik has managed to be only one question away from winning 20 million rupees. These choices, like the identification of location and date, are presented non-diegetically, thereby involving us in the game show format to a degree, allowing us to "play along". The options given are: (A) He cheated; (B) He's lucky; (C) He's a genius; or (D) It is written. The story then begins to unfold and we are left with an unspoken promise that the answer will be given by the time the end credits roll.

"It is written" has a clever double meaning. At first glance we understand that it is referring to destiny, but if we take a second glance we can also see it is literally written, that this is a screenplay, a story that has been penned by a writer.

Also shown at the start of the film are hands sprinkling lots of money. Boyle uses these images to lend weight to the concept of winning a large sum of money, to give it a visual reality, to create thoughts of greed and temptation. They also imply that Jamal is on the show for the money. It is not until the final scenes of the movie that we come to realise these are actually Salim's hands, the director thereby creating a small sense of circularity.

During Jamal's torture we see a shot of his face from beneath water as his head is thrust into a bucket, and the same kind of shot can be seen in *Shallow Grave* when the two criminals are seeking Hugo's whereabouts. Such underwater shots appear in the majority of Boyle's films and display his use of elements that distort usual filmic images. In the room where he's being tortured we also see the use of yellow as a predominant colour. It is commonly associated with sickness and ill health, here reflecting the nauseating use of torture.

At the start of the biographical flashbacks relating to Jamal's life there is a chase scene that effectively acts as a clever way by which to introduce the audience to the slums and their ramshackle nature. This chase was created using DV cameras and the combined talents of Boyle and Dod Mantle. The grainier nature of DV adds to the realism. It is also the case that it would have been impossible to shoot this sequence with 35mm cameras. As soon as film cameras are seen in the slums crowds always gather, partly because they hope to witness the filming of a Bollywood scene. To avoid such crowds and the inevitable glancing into the camera that some slum occupants would do, Boyle opted for the versatile DV option so that the chase could be filmed quickly and efficiently without attracting too much attention.

This chase is a nod to an Indian film directed by Anurag Kashyap, called *Black Friday*. Made in 2004, it was about the 1993 bombings in Bombay. In it there is a police chase which lasts twelve minutes and Boyle took his inspiration from this.

It is shortly after the chase through the slum in *Slumdog Millionaire* that we see the aforementioned toilet scene, one reminiscent to that depicted in *Trainspotting*. In fact, Boyle was a little hesitant to include it because of the similarity. In both scenes the lead character enters a toilet. The result in *Slumdog Millionaire* is considerably messier and leads to the young Jamal being able to make his way through a crowd of film-star admirers due to his stench and coating of sewage. In both scenes the main character's hand is the first thing to reappear from the toilet. Renton is holding suppository drugs in *Trainspotting* and in *Slumdog Millionaire* Jamal is holding a picture of his idol, Bollywood star Amitabh Bachchan. Jamal, after his emergence from the pit of sewage, manages to get Amitabh's autograph in what is a delightfully comical scene.

During the shocking and disturbing attack on the Muslims we see people set alight and a child dressed as the God Rama, which is the reason why Jamal knows the answer to the question concerning what Rama holds in his right hand. Boyle uses a quick pace of camera-angle change to reflect the on-screen action, but pauses the shot perfectly on the boy dressed as Rama.

During these scenes the camera angle stays low, echoing the head height of the boys and therefore allowing us to see from their perspective. This makes the warren of passageways seem oppressive and creates suspense as we wait to see what's around each corner. The cutaway sight of a man being set on fire, along with a rush of other images, adds to a feeling of confusion, creating a gripping scene which captures the audience's attention fully.

When the film reaches a climactic point in the brothers' stay at Maman's camp we see a touch from Boyle that reflects *Shallow Grave* and *28 Days Later*. This is because he employs darkness and a slowing of action to create a build-up of tension. Salim witnesses one of the other boys, Arvind, being purposefully blinded by Maman and his henchmen. This blinding is conducted purely because Arvind will then become a more successful beggar, earning Maman more money. It is greed-motivated and thus we see greed clearly linked with abuse, mutilation and child labour.

Salim is then told to go and fetch his brother in order that he, too, can be blinded. The inner conflict caused by his loyalty to Maman and that to Jamal is clear to see through his lingering passage to the house and his facial expression. He collects Jamal and takes him to the place where the blinding is to take place, but at the last moment rescues his brother and they take flight. This echoes the end of the narrative and gives it more realism. We can see that, ultimately, Salim will choose his brother above all else, not just because he is family, but also because of their friendship. This is his redemption and in these scenes he is redeemed of his role as organiser of the children. It is also at this point that the boys become separated from Latika, who is not so lucky and fails to find liberty from Maman.

Boyle purposefully sets these scenes at night because this echoes the darkness of the situation. It also creates a contrast with many of the other biographical scenes we have witnessed, singling this segment out, identifying it as threatening. Because of this darkness faces are in shadow, the blackness closes in on all sides and feels oppressive, these elements having the effect of putting the audience on edge.

The *mise en scène* Boyle uses complements these narrative events perfectly. The location for Arvind's blinding is amidst a ruin. This symbolises and reflects not only the ruining of the child's eyesight, but the ruinous nature of Maman's abuse and use of children in order to make money. It complements the action and the intent with a shadowed subtlety that doesn't intrude on the events taking place.

> I don't know if it's true that there are beggar masters who blind children to make them more effective when they beg on the streets. It may be an urban myth, but it's useful to the story.
>
> Vikas Swarup[7]

Maman is murdered by Salim after Jamal has caused the brothers to return to Mumbai. Jamal is seeking Latika, has never forgotten her and feels it is their destiny to be together. Tracing her whereabouts, he and

Salim then find her dancing in a room with an instructor. Maman appears shortly after with two henchmen in tow. He states, 'I never forget a face … especially one that I own,' which clearly shows his opinion that the children are his property. Salim pulls a gun, much to the surprise of his brother. In order to ensure that Maman doesn't pursue them and his claim of ownership is ended, Salim shoots him and the three youths make their escape.

Boyle's use of walled confinement in this scene creates a feeling of Salim almost being forced into drastic action. It is the lack of an escape route that causes him to draw the gun. The minimum use of set decoration means that there is little to distract the audience from the action as the director uses tighter shots of the characters to highlight their reactions to the situation. This effectively allows us to see Jamal's shock, Salim's determination and Maman's attempt at sincerely promising not to pursue the children. These close shots also help to build tension, increasing the sense of entrapment within the room.

When Jamal is shown working in a call centre we find that it is littered with British street names and pictures of iconic landmarks, such as Big Ben. Using some shots close to the ceiling of the workplace, Boyle allows a better view of these elements of the *mise en scène,* without making it obvious that he is drawing attention to them. Thanks to this scattering of names and pictures, Jamal is able to arrive at a logical answer for the 5-million-rupee question on *Who Wants to be a Millionaire.* The question is "Cambridge Circus is in which UK city?" It is a question that many people in the UK would probably struggle to answer correctly, but Jamal does so, also demonstrating some of his other knowledge relating to the subject in that he knows of Oxford Circus in London and that Oxford and Cambridge have a boat race.

One of Boyle's trademarks is shown in the call centre during and after the call from Mrs Mackintosh. This is the use of a TV or computer screen by which to create another frame within that of the camera. Here Jamal uses the workstation he is seated at in order to search for a telephone number for Latika. Finding numerous people listed and having no idea of her surname, he then types in his brother's full name and after two calls to men he doesn't know he is third time lucky, finally ending up talking to Salim.

We find screens used widely in this movie, from the police station where a recording of Jamal's appearance on the game show is being shown, to Latika watching *Who Wants to be a Millionaire* in Javed's mansion and the final scenes of people gathered around television screens to see if he will win the grand prize of 20 million rupees. All create a frame within a frame, which is mentioned above. Many also provide us with a view of a different location to that where the primary scene is taking pace. For example, the police station is the primary scene and the game show is the secondary. We are able to see both and this adds an additional dimension to the shot. In the case of the police station, it also allows Boyle to close in on the screen at one point and move through it in order to take us into the studio environment.

Another Boyle trademark is seen when Jamal follows his brother after Salim has received a call from his "employee" Javed Khan. It becomes apparent that Latika is Javed's woman and Jamal gains entry to the crime lord's luxurious, gated mansion by pretending to be a staff member sent by an employment agency. As he walks towards the kitchen where Latika waits for his arrival he can see her distorted image through a wall made of glass blocks. This shot through glass is a common Boyle touch, but here the distortion created by its use is far more extreme than examples in his other films. The figure we can see is only a vague suggestion, looking almost as if distorted by ripples in water.

The penultimate question after which Jamal is arrested and taken away for questioning is the point when the artificial nature of the game show is intruded upon by the harshness of real life. As previously mentioned, the host of the show tries to mislead Jamal and pretends to give him the answer to the 10-million-rupee question. This deception provides the audience with yet another identifiable Boyle touch; the use of a mirror. As with the use of a mirror in *Vacuuming Completely Nude in Paradise*, the one shown in *Slumdog Millionaire* is distorted. This is as a result of condensation on its surface, something vital in order for Prem to write the false answer.

The emotions of the main characters as they journey through life are fittingly captured with camera shots that linger on their expressions. In the early stages of Jamal's life story the camera focuses on all three children, capturing their confusion, joy, fear – the array of emotions that Boyle and Tandan managed to get them to display so believably. We find moments of happiness mingled with those of heartache and each is made more apparent by being abutted against the other. The death of the boy's mother is a case in point. Shortly before the attack Jamal and Salim are playing in water, an act filled with carefree fun. Only moments later they witness the murder of their mother and are taking flight in order to stay alive.

Such juxtapositions help to raise the intensity of the viewing experience. Every moment of lightness is balanced with shadow and vice versa. Placed so closely together, they can't help but accentuate each other, making the film come alive in such a way that it reaches out and takes the audience in its grasp, carrying them along for the ride.

The lingering camerawork is concentrated on Jamal and Latika in the latter stages of Jamal's life story. In this way Boyle brings into focus their feelings for each other and their sense of frustration and helplessness relating to the situations they find themselves in. The careful pauses created by these lingering shots are like gentle, melancholic sighs amidst the more lively scenes which surround them. An example of one of these calm moments occurs when the characters come face-to-face at Javed's house. The camera moves closer, becomes more intimate in its portrayal of their feelings, so expertly acted and displayed in their expressions.

> Danny and Dev should be given Indian passports because they have embraced the culture so beautifully and it's not a very difficult culture to embrace because it's warm and generous by nature.
>
> Freida Pinto[8]

From Book to Film

The film is adapted from the best-selling novel *Q&A* and is the third adaptation Boyle has directed. The original novel was written by Indian diplomat Vikas Swarup in just two months and has been translated into numerous languages, receiving awards all around the world. Anyone expecting to see it faithfully portrayed on the big screen will be disappointed. Under the skilled guidance of screenwriter Simon Beaufoy, who wrote *The Full Monty* (1997), the book has undergone numerous significant changes, the title being the most obvious.

Other notable changes include the use of two brothers as central to the narrative of the film, whereas in the book they were merely friends. This increases the bond they share and makes it more believable that

Salim will give his life so Jamal has a greater chance of happiness. In the book the main character's name is Ram Mohammed Thomas, which was intended to reflect the main religions of India, these being Hinduism, Islam and Christianity.

The book has the main character getting arrested on suspicion of cheating after answering the final question. Boyle preferred the idea of the arrest taking place after the penultimate question and in the movie this trope works very well. It creates additional suspense relating to whether or not he will be released and allowed to continue as a contestant on the game show. It also allows for the final scenes of him answering the last question and winning 20 million rupees to be shown in real time rather than in flashback.

Swarup was kept informed of changes made by Beaufoy and seems to have virtually no qualms about the considerable tinkering which took place. The only worry he had related to the attack on Muslims carried out by Hindus, thinking that it may upset members of Indian cinema audiences. This is the only concern he has voiced, but considering his job it is clear that he knows the art of diplomacy.

The seed which grew into the idea for the novel was the conviction of Major Charles Ingram, who cheated his way to winning the UK version of *Who Wants to be a Millionaire*. It was clear that a boy from the Mumbai slums would certainly be accused of cheating if successfully answering questions rooted in areas of knowledge well beyond that expected of a "slumdog".

Swarup's own background was far removed from his main character's existence. He was born and raised in a city in the north of India called Allahabad. His parents were lawyers and he loved to read the leather-bound books in his grandfather's library. He belonged to a middle-class Indian family, far removed from the Dharavi slums, which he had never visited at the time of writing the book.

> The novel strikes a chord with ordinary people because it's about endless possibilities of life – anything is possible. The themes the novel explores, like love, friendship and fate, are universal.
>
> Vikas Swarup[9]

Criticism

The use of children from the slum to play the three main characters in their early years has caused a certain amount of controversy. There have been allegations concerning the exploitation of the children and these centred on the fact that they had been paid relatively low amounts for their work. However, this was countered by a statement released by Boyle and producer Christian Colson. In it they pointed out that the children were enrolled in school after the film was made and that funds had been set up to ensure their education, living costs and health care were taken care of throughout the duration of their schooling. Not only this, but the children would receive a lump sum if they remained in school until the age of eighteen. This information silenced the critics by and large.

Bollywood star Amitabh Bachchan, who is the idol of the young Jamal in the film, has also criticised the movie. He seems to have taken it almost as an attack on India in that its portrayal of the country is biased by a Western view. He also comments that it is this kind of film and not Bollywood blockbusters of escapist fantasy that receive acclaim in Western award ceremonies.

It seems to be a case of sour grapes that has drawn this attack, which was written on his Internet blog. Not only have his films not won any notable accolades in the West, but he was the original host of the Indian version of *Who Wants to be a Millionaire*, called *Kaun Banega Crorepati*. The fact that the role of host in the movie is played by a Bollywood rival, Anil Kapoor, could have easily irked Amitabh, especially considering the great performance given by Kapoor.

It is also worth mentioning that other Indians have defended the film on the star's blog. This shows that Amitabh in no way speaks for the people of India. Though his words are understandable in light of that mentioned earlier, it is rather disappointing that such a big and influential star cannot see that *Slumdog Millionaire* could lead the way to greater interest in Indian cinema, including his great many films. Not only that, but it could have a positive effect on tourism and thus the economy.

Further to this, it is the case that the film only shows a particular element of Indian society and culture. It would have been impossible to show all of it in one movie and as this story is centred around children from the slums it is clear that the film will, on the whole, portray the lower echelons of Indian society and their struggle to survive. If this had been a film about affluent Indians removed from the slums it seems likely there would have been claims that Boyle ignored the slums and those living in hardship. In this light there was no way to avoid such criticism, however ill-judged and unwarranted.

It has also been suggested that Boyle portrays the whole of India as a kind of underbelly of the world. This is akin to stating that *Trainspotting* portrays the Scottish as a bunch of heroin addicts and is clearly ridiculous.

There are also two minor criticisms of the narrative that can be forgiven in light of the film entire. The first is that most of the questions asked on *Who Wants to be a Millionaire* result in conveniently chronological events in Jamal's life, fitting into a neat timeline. The second is that it is rather obvious that one of the questions will concern the identity of the third Musketeer from Alexandre Dumas' novel after it is referenced a number of times in the early part of the movie.

Awards

Despite the criticism from some quarters concerning the portrayal of India the film has won an astounding seventy-two awards. The most prestigious of these were a total of eight Oscars. The most notable of these Academy Awards were for Beaufoy's screenplay, Rahman's original score, Dicken's editing, Dod Mantle's cinematography, Best Motion Picture of the Year and, not forgetting, Best Achievement in Directing for Danny Boyle.

When Boyle gave his acceptance speech he jumped up and down, revealing that he'd promised to accept the award in the spirit of Tigger from the *Winnie the Pooh* stories. He thanked his assistant directors and gave a special mention to Gail Stevens. Boyle also mentioned the St Mary's Social Club in Bury, England, a place that his family frequent, and on his return to the UK took his Oscar to the club, where he received a rapturous reception worthy of an ordinary hero.

Other important awards included seven BAFTAs, including Best Film and Best Director. The film won three British Independent Film Awards for Best Film, Best Director and a brilliant Most Promising Newcomer for Dev Patel, who also received the Best Actor of the Year Award at the London Critics' Circle Film Awards. There were four Golden Globes for Best Screenplay, Best Original Score, Best Motion Picture and Best Director. The Screen Actors Guild Awards gave the film an award for Outstanding Performance by a Cast in a Motion Picture and the Directors Guild of America awarded Boyle for Outstanding Directorial Achievement in Motion Pictures.

Plenty more awards were picked up by the film, underlining the quality of every aspect of the production, from acting to editing, sound to score, cinematography to directing. During the 2008–09 awards season there really was only one film on everyone's lips, and that was *Slumdog Millionaire*.

Final Words

As a whole this film is akin to a fairy tale in the oldest and truest sense, with gruesomeness, violence and human weakness all thrown into the cauldron. These, along with the possibility that the lead character will overcome adversity, hold you spellbound as the plot unfolds and we discover that life is an excellent university.

The film itself is part of the university of life for all who watch it and has an important lesson to teach. *Slumdog Millionaire* speaks of an important truth and it speaks through the warmth and vivacity of a people often wrongly thought of in terms of squalor and misery. Its lesson is clarified in the final scene on the station platform when Jamal and Latika are reunited: Being rich has nothing to do with money, it is concerned with brotherhood, friendship and, ultimately, love.

[1] Jeffries, S. *"Slumdog Millionaire is not a social critique"* (http://www.dawn.com/2009/01/18/int7.htm)

[2] Kelly, K. *Danny Boyle Interview, Slumdog Millionaire, Toronto 2008* (http://blog.spout.com/2008/09/13/danny-boyle-interview-slumdog-millionaire-toronto-2008/)

[3] Rohit, P.M. *Dev Patel Interview* (http://www.buzzine.com/2008/11/dev-patel-interview/)

[4] Kelly, K. *Danny Boyle Interview, Slumdog Millionaire, Toronto 2008* (http://blog.spout.com/2008/09/13/danny-boyle-interview-slumdog-millionaire-toronto-2008/)

[5] Ramani, N. *"It's natural to want to become an actress after living in Mumbai"* (http://specials.rediff.com/movies/2008/jun/16slid1.htm)

[6] Unknown – *Mahesh Manjrekar* (http://www.bigoye.com/web/guest/interviews/Mahesh-Manjrekar/42321)

[7] Jeffries, S. *"Slumdog Millionaire is not a social critique"*
(http://www.dawn.com/2009/01/18/int7.htm)

[8] Elfman, M. *Exclusive Interview: Freida Pinto Co-Star of Slumdog Millionaire*
(http://screencrave.com/2008-11-18/exclusive-interview-freida-patel-co-star-of-slumdog-
millionaire/)

[9] IANS – *Slumdog is a success for the India story: Vikas Swarup*
(http://www.thaindian.com/newsportal/uncategorized/slumdog-is-a-success-for-the-india-
story-vikas-swarup-interviewrepeating-for-all-needing_100142045.html)

Boyle in the Bag

> I try to make all the films the same way – I try to make dazzling
> and vibrant entertainment.
>
> Danny Boyle[1]

It doesn't matter which of Danny Boyle's films is being discussed, all of them display flourishes of brilliance on the part of the director. They are stimulating in both a narrative and cinematic sense. They may jump from one genre to another, but this is purposeful and part of what identifies his work.

Boyle doesn't want to be given a generic straitjacket and finds that his enthusiasm for each film is elevated by changing genre. He also likes to surprise audiences with each film and part of this element of surprise is the generic change, which can be quite severe, as with the jump from zombie horror to family movie, seen when he made *Millions* after *28 Days Later*. Unlike other auteur directors like Scorsese, Boyle would prefer not to be identified in a generic sense, but in a stylistic and thematic one.

As for future plans, it has been suggested that Boyle revisit both *The Beach* and *28 Days Later* in order to create director's cuts. However, he is non-committal and unsure whether or not to proceed with these projects.

Since the success of *Trainspotting*, Irvine Welsh has published a sequel entitled *Porno*. In this novel, the characters are considerably older and changed by the intervening years. Despite the fact that Danny Boyle would like to turn *Porno* into a film, Ewan McGregor has dismissed the idea partly because he doesn't think Welsh's follow-up is as good as the original novel. This said, it is possible that at some point in the future McGregor will change his mind and agree to the much anticipated return of Renton to the big screen.

One Boyle film which is in the production process is *Johannesburg*, which is due for release in 2011. Set in South Africa at the end of apartheid, it tells the story of a young woman who moves to the Ponte Tower in Johannesburg, which had once been a symbol of white affluence. Once there, she falls under the influence of a drug lord, the building plagued by a gang culture.

Another film that Boyle is involved in is the adaptation of the nursery rhyme *Solomon Grundy*, about a man who grows old in a week. This was also due for release in 2011, but has unfortunately been put on hold due to the similarity of *The Curious Case of Benjamin Button* (Fincher 2008) starring Brad Pitt.

Whatever Danny Boyle chooses to do next it's sure to bear his distinctive style. With the immense success of *Slumdog Millionaire*, both critically and in the eyes of audiences around the globe, the world is his oyster. Boyle can dictate his own terms to those who are sure to come knocking at his door, the awards this film has garnered adding a distinctly golden sheen to his already glowing CV.

Ultimately, it doesn't matter what his next project is, there's one thing we can be sure of – there may not be an ordinary hero on screen, but there'll definitely be one in the director's chair.

[1] Unknown – Danny Boyle Interview
(http://www.bbc.co.uk/manchester/content/articles/2005/05/19/danny_boyle_interview_170505_feature.shtml)

Bibliography

Aames, E. Interview: Tilda Swinton & Skandar Keynes on *"The Chronicles of Narnia"* (http://www.cinecon.com/news.php?id=0512072)

Asner, J. *Ewan McGregor Revealed with Jules Asner Interview* (http://www.geocities.com/a_perfectgrace/ewanasner.html)

Baggs, M. *Shallow Grave* – degenerating relationships (http://mosaicmovieconnectgroup.blogspot.com/2008/12/shallow-grave-degenerating.html)

Barkham, P. *The sun is the star* (*The Guardian*, 23 March 2007, UK)

Barry, P. *Beginning Theory* (Manchester University Press, 1995, UK)

Burns, A. *Train Conductor: Interview with Danny Boyle* (http://zakka.dk/euroscreenwriters/interviews/danny_boyle_515.htm)

Cannon, D. *Shallow Grave* (1994) (http://www.film.unet.com/Movies/Reviews/Shallow_Grave.html)

Carnevale, R. *Sunshine* – *Cillian Murphy interview* (http://www.indielondon.co.uk/Film-Review/sunshine-cillian-murphy-interview)

Chambers, B. *Strumpet*
(http://www.filmfreakcentral.net/tiff/fest2001capsules.htm)

Chambers, B. *Virginie Speaks* (sorta)
(http://www.filmfreakcentral.net/tiff/vledoyeninterview.htm)

Chaw, W. *28 Movies Later ...*
(http://www.filmfreakcentral.net/notes/bgleesoninterview.htm)

Child, B. *Slumdog Millionaire makers deny allegations of child exploitation*
(*The Guardian*, 30 January 2009, UK)

Christopher, J. *Slumdog Millionaire* (The Times, 8 January 2009, UK)

Djurica, R. *Probe: Kerry Fox*
(http://www.wildviolet.net/birthday_blue/fox2.html)

Dobson, A. *Trainspotting: Addicted to Denial*
(http://metaphilm.com/index.php/detail/trainspotting-denial/)

Ebert, R. *Trainspotting* (1996)
(http://rogerebert.suntimes.com/apps/pbcs.dll/article?AID=/200001
01/CRITICALDEBATE/40308077)

Elfman, M. *Exclusive Interview: Freida Pinto Co-Star of Slumdog Millionaire*
(http://screencrave.com/2008-11-18/exclusive-interview-freida-patel-
co-star-of-slumdog-millionaire/)

Epstein, D. R. *Andrew MacDonald*
(http://www.ugo.com/channels/filmTv/features/28dayslater/andrew
MacDonald.asp)

Fischer, P. *Diaz, Cameron: A Life Less Ordinary*
(http://www.urbancinefile.com.au/home/view.asp?a=594&s=interviews)

Fischer, P. *McGregor, Ewan: A Life Less Ordinary*
(http://www.urbancinefile.com.au/home/view.asp?a=593&s=Interviews)

Gane, M. *Baudrillard: Critical and Fatal Theory* (Routledge, 1991, UK)

Garland, A. *The Beach* (Penguin Books, 1997, UK)

Grady, P. *All of Spall*
(http://www.reel.com/reel.asp?node=features/interviews/S/spall/2)

Grant, F. *Wankerdom: Trainspotting As a Rejection of the Postcolonial?*
(http://muse.jhu.edu/login?uri=/journals/south_atlantic_quarterly/v
103/103.1farred.html)

Haflidason, A. *Trainspotting* (1996)
(http://www.bbc.co.uk/films/2001/01/19/trainspotting_1996_review.shtml)

Hattenstone, S. *Sink or swim*
(http://www.guardian.co.uk/film/2000/jan/28/1)

Hunt, M. *Boyle, Danny* (1956–)
(http://www.screenonline.org.uk/people/id/470997/)

IANS – *Slumdog is a success for the India story: Vikas Swarup (Interview) (Repeating for all needing)*
(http://www.thaindian.com/newsportal/uncategorized/slumdog-is-a-success-for-the-india-story-vikas-swarup-interviewrepeating-for-all-needing_100142045.html) www.imdb.com

Jeffries, S. *"Slumdog Millionaire is not a social critique"*
(http://www.dawn.com/2009/01/18/int7.htm)

Kelly, K. *Danny Boyle Interview, Slumdog Millionaire, Toronto 2008*
(http://blog.spout.com/2008/09/13/danny-boyle-interview-slumdog-millionaire-toronto-2008/)

Kermode, M. *Aliens come to Wales* (The Guardian, 15 February 2008, UK)

Law, L. *The Beach, the gaze and film tourism*(http://tou.sagepub.com/cgi/content/abstract/7/2/141)

Lee, P. *In Alex Garland's 28 Days Later, old-school horror is all the rage*
(http://www.scifi.com/sfw/issue323/interview.html)

LIFS – *Mahesh Manjrekar's Crusade*
(http://www.bigoye.com/web/guest/interviews/Mahesh Manjrekar/42321)

LJS – *The Sprocket Trainspotting Interview*
(http://www.bradcolbourne.com/iwsprocket.txt)

MacDevette, B. *Danny Boyle*
(http://www.independentfilmquarterly.com/ifq/interviews/dannyboyle.htm)

MacGregor, F. *Robert Carlyle interview: He's made a name for himself playing troubled characters. It might not be glamorous, but it's the type of role he enjoys best* (http://news.scotsman.com/entertainment/Robert-Carlyle-interview–He39s.4759594.jp)

Mack. *Danny Boyle okays Chinese Shallow Grave remake*
(http://twitchfilm.net/archives/002147.html)

Martinson, J. *Bringing a ray of sunshine to British films*
(http://www.guardian.co.uk/business/2007/apr/06/film)

Maurer, M. *Trainspotters*
(http://www.richmondreview.co.uk/features/maurer01.html)

McKay, A. *To be and to pretend (The Guardian,* 13 August 2005, UK)

Murray, R. *Director Danny Boyle Discusses the Sci-Fi Thriller: Sunshine* (http://movies.about.com/od/sunshine/a/sunshine070407.htm)

Murray, R. *Director Danny Boyle Talks About His Family-Friendly Film, "Millions"* (http://movies.about.com/od/millions/a/millions030105.htm)

Nelmes, J. ed. *An Introduction to Film Studies* (Routledge, 1999, UK)

O'Connell, D. *Naomie that girl …* (*The Observer,* 20 October 2002, UK)

Otto, J. IGN *Interviews Danny Boyle* (http://uk.movies.ign.com/articles/594/594459p1.html)

Overstreet, J. *Movies with Morals* (http://www.christianitytoday.com/movies/interviews/2005/dannyboyle.html)

Parry, G. *Sex on The Beach: What 80s Bikini Comedies Tell Us About Gender and Class* (http://www.alternet.org/movies/100168/sex_on_the_beach:_what_80s_bikini_comedies_tell_us_about_gender_and_class/)

Pereira, P. K. *Anil Kapoor reveals how 'Slumdog Millionaire' fell into his lap* (http://www.screenindia.com/news/anil-kapoor-reveals-how-slumdog-millionaire-fell-into-his-lap/399115/)

Pidd, H. *Profile: Danny Boyle* (*The Guardian,* 9 January 2009, UK)

Pierce, N. *Cillian Murphy: 28 Days Later* (http://www.bbc.co.uk/films/2002/10/30/cillian_murphy_28_days_later_interview.shtml) www.play.com

Potts, R. *A Spy on "The Beach"* (http://archive.salon.com/travel/diary/pott/1999/05/04/beach/index.html)

Potts, R. *Backstage on "The Beach"* (http://archive.salon.com/wlust/feature/1999/02/10feature.html)

Potts, R. *Live from the trans-global Beach Nation* (http://archive.salon.com/travel/diary/pott/2000/02/11/transglobal/index.html)

Ramani, N. *"It's natural to want to become an actress after living in Mumbai"* (http://specials.rediff.com/movies/2008/jun/16slid1.htm)

Ramesh, R. *Bollywood icon Amitabh Bachchan rubbishes Slumdog Millionaire* (http://www.guardian.co.uk/film/2009/jan/14/amitabh-bachchan-rubbishes-slumdog-millionaire)

Rawlinson, N. *Alex Garland: The Beach: Backpacker Blues* (http://www.spikemagazine.com/0599alexgarland.php)

Rea, D. *Dr. Brian Cox* (http://www.sci-fi-online.com/2006_Interviews/07-08-27_brian-cox.htm)

Reich, J.S. *Lord of The Beach* (http://www.reel.com/reel.asp?node=features/interviews/boyle)

Rich, K. *Interview: Slumdog Millionaire Star Dev Patel* (http://www.cinemablend.com/new/Interview-Slumdog-Millionaire-Star-Dev-Patel-10821.html)

Rohit, P. M. *Danny Boyle Interview* (http://www.buzzine.com/2008/11/danny-boyle-interview/)

Rohit, P.M. *Dev Patel Interview* (http://www.buzzine.com/2008/11/dev-patel-interview/)

Romney, J. and Morrison, J. *Ewan McGregor waves goodbye to 'Trainspotting' cast reunion* (http://www.independent.co.uk/news/media/ewan-mcgregor-waves-goodbye-to-trainspotting-cast-reunion-539032.html)

Routledge, C. *Ewan McGregor* (http://www.filmreference.com/Actors-and-Actresses-Ma-Mo/McGregor-Ewan.html)

Sacks, E. *'Sunshine' star Michelle Yeoh hits the heights* (http://www.popmatters.com/pm/article/sunshine-star-michelle-yeoh-hits-the-heights)

Sandhu, S. *Slumdog Millionaire, review* (http://www.telegraph.co.uk/culture/film/filmreviews/4176184/Slumdog-Millionaire-review.html)

Smith, N. *Shallow Grave* (1994) (http://www.bbc.co.uk/films/2001/01/24/shallow_grave_1994_review.shtml)

Smith, R. *Back from The Beach* (*The Guardian*, 10 August 2001, UK)

Solomons, J. *'The leading man? They all were'* (*The Observer*, 2 November 2008, UK)

Swarup, V. *Slumdog Millionaire* (Black Swan, 2009, UK)

Synnot, S. *Danny Boyle interview: Always on the Boyle* (http://scotlandonsunday.scotsman.com/14072/Danny-Boyle-interview-Always-on.4824574.jp)

229

Travers, P. *Slumdog Millionaire*
(http://www.rollingstone.com/reviews/movie/20192670/review/2401
3911/slumdog_millionaire)

Unknown – *28 Days Later claims UK box office*
(http://www.guardian.co.uk/film/2002/nov/05/news1)

Unknown – *Danny Boyle Biography*
(http://www.britmovie.co.uk/directors/d_boyle/biog.html)

Unknown – *Danny Boyle interview*
(http://www.bbc.co.uk/manchester/content/articles/2005/05/19/danny_
boyle_interview_170505_feature.shtml)

Unknown – *Danny Boyle: It was a good day. Man U beat Chelsea and I won four Golden Globes*
(http://www.themalaysianinsider.com/index.php/showbiz/15924-
danny-boyle-it-was-a-good-day-man-u-beat-chelsea-and-i-won-four-
golden-globes)

Unknown – HCC *Interview – Vikas Swarup*
(http://savvyreader.typepad.com/my_weblog/2008/12/hcc-interview-
vikas-swarup.html)

Unknown – *Interview: Danny Boyle*
(http://video.barnesandnoble.com/search/interview.asp?CTR=717275)

Unknown – *MMKF Trainspotting interview*
(http://www.jonnyleemiller.co.uk/trainspotting/trainspotting.html)

Unknown – *Slumdog Millionaire Film Critique*
(http://simplycinema.blogspot.com/2008/12/slumdog-millionaire-
film-critique.html)

Unknown – *Strumpet All Movie Guide Review*
(http://www.artistdirect.com/nad/store/movies/reviews/0,,2335379,0
0.html)

Unknown – *Strumpet: Christopher Eccleston*
(http://www.netribution.co.uk/features/interviews/2001/Eccleston_st
rumpet/1.html)

Unknown – *Strumpet Review*
(http://www.channel4.com/film/reviews/film.jsp?id=108826&section
=review)

Unknown – *The Beach*
(http://www.shell.linux.se/treggy88/Leo/beach/beacharticles.html)

Unknown – *The Beach made a man out of Leo*
(http://www.guardian.co.uk/film/2000/jan/12/2)

Unknown – *The Danny Boyle interview: You feel guilty about money ...*
(http://www.theherald.co.uk/features/features/display.var.2481973.0.
The_Danny_Boyle_interview_You_feel_guilty_about_money.php)

Unknown – *UK film production triumvirate*
(http://everything2.com/e2node/Figment%2520Films)

Unknown – *Vacuuming Completely Nude in Paradise Review*
(http://www.channel4.com/film/reviews/film.jsp?id=109804&section
=review&page=all#reviewnav)

Various – *Danny Boyle Webchat: The Transcript*
(http://www.empireonline.com/interviews/interview.asp?IID=824)

Various – *Holy Bible: New International Version* (Hodder & Stoughton,
1987, UK)

Wagner, R. *Shallow Grave dissects murder plot with humor and wit*
(http://tech.mit.edu/V115/N6/shallowgrave.06a.html)

Walker, T. *All you need to know about Slumdog Millionaire*
(http://www.independent.co.uk/arts

entertainment/films/features/all-you-need-to-know-about-slumdog-
millionaire-1452119.html)

Welsh, I. *Trainspotting* (Minerva, 1996, UK)

www.wikipedia.org/

Wilkinson, A. *Sunshine Superman*
(http://www.eyeforfilm.co.uk/feature.php?id=346)

Wilson, S. L. *Rose Byrne Interview* (http://www.horror.com/php/article-
1653-1.html)

Wootton, A. *Ewan McGregor*
(http://www.guardian.co.uk/film/2002/oct/23/features)

Zacharek, S. *The Beach*
(http://archive.salon.com/ent/movies/review/2000/02/11/beach/in
dex.html)

Zacharek, S. *Tough Love*
(http://www.salon.com/ent/movies/1997/10/24ordinary.html)